YOU'VE HEARD THESE HANDS

YOU'VE HEARD THESE HANDS

From the Wall of Sound to the Wrecking Crew and Other Incredible Stories

DON RANDI with
KAREN "NISH" NISHIMURA

Hal Leonard Books
An Imprint of Hal Leonard Corporation

Published in 2015 by Hal Leonard Books
An Imprint of Hal Leonard Corporation
7777 West Bluemound Road
Milwaukee, WI 53213

Trade Book Division Editorial Offices
33 Plymouth St., Montclair, NJ 07042

Printed in the United States of America

Book design by Michael Kellner

Library of Congress Cataloging-in-Publication Data

Randi, Don, author.
You've heard these hands : from the Wall of Sound to the Wrecking Crew and other incredible stories / Don Randi with Karen "Nish" Nishimura.
    pages cm
Includes index.
ISBN 978-1-4950-0882-5
1. Randi, Don. 2. Keyboard players–United States–Biography. 3. Jazz musicians–United States–Biography. I. Nishimura, Karen, author. II. Title.
ML417.R26A3 2015
786'.164092–dc23
[B]

2015024276

CONTENTS

FOREWORD

Growing up in the '60s and '70s in the home of a Los Angeles Studio musician, there were certain names you heard all the time. As a child, I may not have known these musicians by face but I knew their names. Don Randi was one of those names. I was too young to understand why there was so much respect when Don's name was spoken. Not until many years later, when I started working on my documentary and labor of love, *The Wrecking Crew*, did I understand why this was the case.

When I approached Don eighteen years ago to be a part of this film, I never foresaw a friendship that would become very special to me. His kindness and giving heart have been there for me in the best of times and the worst. He has become not only a friend but a surrogate father after the loss of my dad. I knew I could count on someone to talk to when I just needed someone to listen.

I can't imagine what music of today would be like if it wasn't for Don Randi. Yes, he is a brilliant piano player and session musician, but think of all the great musicians he helped by having a club that gave them a start when he let them play at The Baked Potato. One of the few clubs in Los Angeles where musicians come to hear other musicians, The Baked Potato allowed so many musicians to show their fantastic talents, and many of them became legends themselves. Including my father, Tommy Tedesco, who in 1976 played his first live gig there in twenty years. Thank you, Don, for everything.

Denny Tedesco
Lunch Box Entertainment
The Wrecking Crew

NOTES FROM . . .

Don Randi is a beloved and world-renowned musician. But to me as a young boy growing up in Los Angeles, he was my grandpa, my hero, my best friend, and one of the biggest inspirations in my life.

As a child, I would hang out with my grandpa a couple of times each week. We'd watch movies, go miniature golfing, go to Dodgers and Raiders games, or stuff our faces with food from restaurants all over Los Angeles. My grandpa treated me like I was his best friend, which is why we are still best friends today.

We go to lunch as often as possible. During these lunches, my grandpa will regale me with tales of his life as a child as well as how he became the musician he is today. Many people see my grandpa for the talented musician he is, but I will always see him as the caring and loving grandfather that helped raise me.

Along with my mother, my grandpa helped teach me the meaning of loyalty, hard work, determination, and how to make people laugh. Still to this day, my grandpa will tell me jokes every time we hang out. That's the essence of my grandpa: hardworking but always willing to put a smile on someone's face.

As most people around here know, you can't mention Don Randi without bringing up The Baked Potato. At one time or another most of our family has worked at The Potato, contributing to its great success. My grandpa created a club where people could relax, enjoy wonderful-tasting potatoes, and listen to some of the best jazz in the world. My grandpa has kept this a family business and knows we're all here to ensure its continued success.

I think the greatest compliment I ever received was the day my grandpa told me, "I love hearing about your work and how you create movie poster art. It always makes me happy inside to know how much of a success you have become. I am so proud of you, and I know your mother is, too." The fact that I've made my lifelong hero proud inspires me daily. Finally, I'll never forget my favorite joke my grandpa would tell me as a child . . .

Don: "What did the monkey say when he got his tail cut off?"

Me: "I don't know, what?"

Don: "It won't be long now."

That was my grandpa, always looking on the brighter side of life.

Donald Schwartz
Creative Director
BLT Communication, LLC
Hollywood, California

Growing up with my dad was a rich experience that is incomparable. The star-studded Hollywood Hills where we lived made an amazing backdrop for an unforgettable youth in the 1970s and 1980s. I rode my bike in our neighborhood where, among other famous music artists, Frank Zappa was one of our neighbors and Ringo Starr lived down the street.

I was about eight years old when I realized who my dad really was in the world of music. It was at The Baked Potato while watching my dad play with his band, Quest, and his hands were flying at lightning speed up and down the piano keys. I stood there stunned, in awe of his talent.

I also loved watching my dad chart music at our dining room table. I began to learn the circle of fifths and time signatures, and from that point on, I would take every opportunity to sing with my dad as he played, or just watch him play. Through him, I learned how to play in a band setting, listen carefully to the other musicians, and play with dynamics.

My dad also gave me the gift of relating to others on a deeper level: having a rapport and connecting with people no matter who they are, without prejudice. That is something my dad does so effortlessly. Because of him, I also learned to play music with anyone, no matter what, harmoniously. If someone asked if I could play a certain genre of music, I would say yes, and quickly go home, chart the music, then show up at my gig ready to play. I am truly blessed by what has been musically passed on to me from my dad, Don Randi.

Leah Randi

ACKNOWLEDGMENTS

We want to express our thanks and appreciation to the very special people who helped us and generously gave their support to make this book a reality.

Russ Wapensky

Gary Gardner

Camille Alcasid

Sandra Jimenez

Paul Chesney

David Libman

Denny Tedesco

Donald Schwartz

Iris Bass

Jessica Burr

John Cerullo

Mary Vandenberg

Brad Smith

Wes Seeley

Bill Moynahan

INTRODUCTION

I'm Don Randi and you've heard my hands. Before you picked up this book, the songs my hands have played, arranged, and composed were some of the songs you grew up listening to and love because they are connected with significant and important stories in your life. The music you love is also connected to events and important stories in my life and spans a wide range of genres that include rock 'n' roll, folk music, R&B, country and western, and jazz.

Back then I could do as many as twenty-six recording dates in a week with various record producers and artists. It was not uncommon for me to turn on the radio and everywhere I tuned, I heard a song I had played on. I can still turn on the radio today and hear the music I've recorded.

I've been a member of Phil Spector's Wall of Sound band, a.k.a. the Wrecking Crew, and played on the countless number of hit songs produced by Phil Spector.

Brian Wilson is one of the many talented producers and artists that are part of my story. I worked with him on many of the Beach Boys songs and most notably the album *Pet Sounds*.

My first recording date with Nancy Sinatra was "These Boots Are Made for Walkin'," and that date led to years of working with her on nearly all of her recordings as well as concert tours all over the world, some of which included her father, Frank.

I have scored and was the music director for a number of television shows and movies that have featured Sonny and Cher, Raquel Welch, Bob Hope,

Tom Jones, James Garner, Paul Newman, Bobbie Gentry, Glenn Ford, Larry Hagman, Cliff Robertson, John Wayne, and more.

In 1970 I opened a jazz club in Studio City, California, called The Baked Potato, which is still going strong and features live music seven nights a week. Many top recording artists you know have played and still play there, and I play there with my current band, Quest, at least once a month.

Retirement? No way! I still love doing recording sessions and working on new projects all the time. Recently I did a session with Hal Blaine on drums, Joe Osborn on bass, and my good friend Glen Campbell on guitar. The song we recorded is part of Glen's documentary film *I'll Be Me*, about his farewell tour and battle with Alzheimer's disease. The song was written by Glen Campbell and Julian Raymond for the film and was awarded a Grammy for Best Country Song of 2014.

I released a new jazz album in 2013 of original compositions I wrote with John DePatie. *Acoustimania* is an all-acoustic instrumental duet album with John on acoustic guitar and me on piano. This is my twentieth jazz album release.

For years now, I have been telling my stories to music fans that come to The Baked Potato, or to friends and aspiring musicians and in various interviews I've done for radio, TV, film, magazines, and live events. A reaction I often get is, "Don, you need to write a book of your memoirs." People have told me they are astonished that all these years they've been a fan of mine and didn't know it, because they never knew I played on so many songs they love. For this reason I titled this book *You've Heard These Hands*. Never in my wildest dreams would I have imagined the career, experiences, opportunities, and music history I'm a part of and the incredible life journey I have been on. It blows my mind, and as I tell you my stories, I think it will blow yours, too.

YOU'VE HEARD THESE HANDS

CHAPTER 1

The Wall of Sound and the Wrecking Crew

The most influential time in popular music came in the 1960s with producer Phil Spector and his famous "Wall of Sound" production method. The number of artists and hits he produced in the '60s was huge and his success went on throughout the years, producing major artists with top-selling hits. The studio musicians he engaged for his sessions became known in the industry as the Wall of Sound band. The "Wrecking Crew" tag started many years later and was not created by Phil. I became a member of the studio band in 1962 when sax player Steve Douglas asked me to play piano for an upcoming recording session with Phil Spector. Steve was not only a band member, but he was the contractor and would call in and contract the musicians for Phil Spector sessions. When Steve went on tour with Duane Eddy, Phil asked me to fill in for Steve as contractor to call and contract the musicians for recording dates.

That first session I did with Phil was the recording of "He's a Rebel" by the Crystals (Darlene Love) at Gold Star Studios in Hollywood. You have to imagine the studio building as a small, unimpressive storefront you'd miss if you blinked driving by. This did not detract from the "Gold" that came outta there! Gold Star Studios, owned by David Gold and Stan Ross, had more hits recorded there from the '50s to the '70s than most of the big, impressive studios in LA or New York. Located on Santa Monica Boulevard near Vine Street, Gold Star Studios closed in 1984.

I had met and was already friends with Phil Spector a few years earlier, but this was my first time recording with him on a major session. My impression of Phil at work in the studio was this guy is a real genius. The way he directed the musicians and what he was having them do was mind blowing! He had several guitar players there and they all played the same thing, but differently. Phil would have the guitarists (four or more) playing the same chord but in different positions on the neck. Phil has a great knowledge of the guitar and was in fact a great guitarist himself. He knew how to get the sounds he wanted and would be very vocal about it, but the guys respected that approach. Imagine Phil telling guitar pros like Tommy Tedesco, Barney Kessel, Howard Roberts, Bill Pitman, and Russ Titelman what to do and how to play!

When I arrived, there were four or five different pianos (brands and sounds) set up in the studio. Al De Lory, Mike Rubini, Mike Spencer, and I played in unison, hitting the same notes. It was amazing. The whole thing was designed to get the biggest sound you could possibly get when played on a car radio or hi-fi speaker. In 1962 records were in mono, so you can imagine the impact this method had on pop music in those days.

We had very limited multitrack recording (three tracks) in those days. Recording live with multiple musicians playing many of the same instruments at once and overdubbing is how Phil created the "Wall of Sound."

After the song "He's a Rebel" went to number one in December 1962, I played on many more hits by various artists with the same group of musicians in the Wall of Sound band. The word was out about Phil and all the hits he was producing with a particular group of musicians. As other producers started wanting a piece of that pie, calls started pouring in for recording dates for all of us. Pretty soon I was working for other producers, too, like Lee Hazlewood, Brian Wilson, Nik Venet, Jimmy Bowen, Ray Ruff, Dick Glasser, John Boylan, Richard Perry, Joe Wissert, and many more. Just like the "Wall of Sound" effect, the recording business just started exploding! Some sessions I did with other producers were also done at Gold Star Studios.

The name "Wrecking Crew" came about to describe how we could destroy a date (recording session). What that meant was, we'd start joking around and God help you if you were on the other end of the joke! For example, Hal

Blaine had picked up a prop telephone from a movie set at MGM (now Sony Studios) where we were recording the day before. While we were in the middle of a session you could hear a muffled phone ringing and ringing. Drove Phil NUTS! At one point Phil screamed, "Where is that fucking ringing coming from!" A few seconds later the phone rang again and Hal opened up his drum case, picked up the phone, and said, "Phil, it's for YOU." We did crazy, hilarious things like that to have fun and disrupt the date for laughs. Many years later, once it became public knowledge that the same studio musicians played on hundreds of hit songs, the iconic name "Wrecking Crew" was created by the producers and engineers who had to put up with our bullshit for many years, and Hal Blaine used the term in his book.

Steve Douglas, Hal Blaine, and Jack Nitzsche were among my close friends during those years, and we were earning good money making hit records. Living the "Hollywood" lifestyle when all we ever really intended was to play jazz and make a decent living was truly "the American dream" gone wild! We had a hell of a great time together in and out of the studio, but honestly, we worked so much that we didn't have time to get into too much trouble. We also didn't have anything to prove; we were already pros. But as members of the Wall of Sound band, we were anonymous to the public who were buying the hits we played on. Little did we know back then that many of these recordings would become the enduring and celebrated songs of all time.

Most of us were a little older and much more musically experienced than most of the artists we recorded for. In addition, almost all of us came from jazz and classical music backgrounds, so we are able to sight-read music. But unlike so many schooled musicians, we had natural "ears" and were musically versatile. In other words, Wrecking Crew players knew how to ROCK! Even though rock 'n' roll is a simpler style of music compared with other styles, a true Wall of Sound/Wrecking Crew player had to possess the musical "soul" that brought out the heart in songs like "Be My Baby" and "You've Lost That Lovin' Feelin'." There was something unique and magical the Wrecking Crew had as a group of musicians that hasn't been duplicated since the '60s and '70s.

The full roster of musicians working all these sessions was BIG and we were considered the "first call" group that producers wanted for their sessions. Keyboards: Larry Knechtel, Leon Russell, Mike Rubini, Mac Rebennack (Dr. John), Mike Spencer, Mike Melvoin, Al De Lory, Ray Johnson, Gene Garth, Lincoln Mayorga, and me. Guitars: Glen Campbell, Barney Kessel, Tommy Tedesco, Al Casey, Carol Kaye, Ray Pohlman, Russ Titelman, Billy Strange, Louie Shelton, Jerry McKenzie, Don Peake, James Burton, Jerry Cole, Mike Deasy, David Cohen, Ben Benay, Howard Roberts, Bill Pitman, Dennis Budimir, and Lou Morell. Bassists: Joe Osborn, Carol Kaye, Max Bennett, Chuck Berghofer, Ray Pohlman, Larry Knechtel, Lyle Ritz, Jerry Scheff, Jimmy Bond (007), and Harvey Newmark. Drums: Hal Blaine, Earl Palmer, Johnny Guerin, Richie Frost, Sharky Hall, and Jim Gordon. Sax: Steve Douglas, Jay Migliori, Jim Horn, Plas Johnson, Harold Battiste, Gene Cipriano, Nino Tempo, Jackie Kelso, and William "Bill" Green. Trumpets: Roy Caton, Tony Terran, Ollie Mitchell, and John Audino. Trombone: Lou Blackburn, Richard "Slyde" Hyde, Lew McCreary, and Frank Rosolino. Percussion: Julius Wechter, Gary Coleman, Frank Capp, Gene Estes, Alan Estes, Emil Richards, Milt Holland, and Bobbye Hall. Violin: Leonard Malarsky, Israel Baker, Darrell Terwilliger, Sid Sharp, William Kurasch, Bobby Bruce, and Jimmy Getzoff. Viola: Norman Botnick and Harry Hyams. Cello: Ray Kelley, Jan Kelley, and Jesse Ehrlich.

What a group of really fabulous musicians to be a part of and each session was always a thrill. Not all of us would be on a single date, but a good many from this group were always booked on these recording dates.

A few of the artists that I recorded with at Gold Star Studios were: the Righteous Brothers, Sony and Cher, Herb Alpert and the Tijuana Brass, the Baja Marimba Band, Darlene Love, the Ronettes, Bob B. Soxx and the Blue Jeans, the Crystals, the Cascades, Tommy Roe/Boyce and Hart, the Ramones, and Leonard Cohen.

Many more artists and producers had Wall of Sound/Wrecking Crew musicians as their studio band, recording all over Los Angeles. I was in a great many of these sessions, but Gold Star was where it all started for me, with Phil Spector.

Guitar Master Tommy Tedesco

Tommy Tedesco was an exceptional musician and guitar player and he was such a funny guy! His wit and humor were always making us laugh on dates, and I would say his antics helped the Wall of Sound band get known as the Wrecking Crew for some of the things he did. I wish Tommy was still around. He passed away in 1997, but his legacy lives on. His son, Denny Tedesco, has produced a documentary film, *The Wrecking Crew*, which highlights Tommy and many of the studio musicians (including me) who were a part of the group of top session musicians.

One recording date we had with producer Dick Glasser and arranger Jimmie Haskell had Tommy on guitar, Hal Blaine on drums, Carol Kaye on bass, and me on piano. I recall a full string section there, too. This session was scheduled for noon to three o'clock in the afternoon. Some of us had another session to do starting at four o'clock at another studio, but we didn't think that we would have a problem getting to the next session, because the other studio was close.

Everything was going great; we had three songs done and were working on the fourth song. Well, we had gone through a few takes on this song and the time was ticking. At 2:45 p.m. we finished a great take and Dick Glasser said over the PA, "That was it; you guys nailed it." We start packing up to go, but Jimmie (who was in the room with us) said, "Guys, let's do another take." We all sighed and then Dick spoke over the PA: "Jimmie, it's not necessary; the last take was the keeper." Jimmie was looking at the clock on the wall and he knew he could get one more take in, but meanwhile those of us who had to get the next session were packing up quickly so we could get out of there. Jimmy said to Dick, "We have time," and insisted we do one more take. If we went past 3:00 p.m. it would put the session into overtime pay. Hal had started to break down his cymbals, so he was setting back up. Tommy had already put his guitar in the case, so he went to get it out again, and while he was getting set up, he said, "Hey, Jimmie, when we get started again, how do you want me to play that part starting at bar fourteen, you know that part where I go . . ." (he played his guitar). Jimmie replied, "Just play it the same way, Tommy" (tick tock). Then Tommy said in the most sweet and innocent tone, "What if I change guitars? I could use my Tele, or do you want me to use the Gibson?" (tick tock). Jimmie was getting frustrated and said, "Just use the same guitar, the same guitar, Tommy." Meanwhile, Hal was trying so hard not to laugh and tried to hide his face behind his cymbals. I was biting my lip trying not to laugh and Carol had to be pinching herself, too. We all knew what Tommy was doing and this kept going with Tommy until it was about 2:57 p.m. and we would probably go overtime if we did another take. So, Dick came out of the control room and said, "Hey, guys, that's a wrap; we are going with the last take." We could see Jimmie shaking his head at Tommy. And Tommy, with an innocent look on his face, shrugged his shoulders and said, "Whaaat?" We couldn't hold back any longer and just exploded laughing. I think Jimmie thought we all were in on this, but it was all Tommy.

Incidentally, when producers or music directors addressed the musicians with the word *guys*, they weren't excluding Carol Kaye. She was considered one of the guys in the band because she is a talented and creative professional musician. Carol did not let stereotypes or gender hold her back from a successful career in a profession that was dominated by men in those days, and she is not only a great bass player, she's also a terrific guitar player.

Another funny "Tommy" story was when we recorded Mike Nesmith's solo album *The Wichita Train Whistle Sings*. (Michael Nesmith was one of the members of the Monkees.) The four recording sessions for this record were really exceptional in that they were scheduled on a weekend, Saturday and Sunday, when we would get paid double and triple scale. It was also catered by top restaurants, like Chasen's in Beverly Hills and Musso & Frank Grill in Hollywood, which was unheard of at that time. The great Shorty Rogers wrote some of the arrangements and in the band we had Wrecking Crew regulars: Larry Knechtel on piano as well as me, Carol Kaye on bass, Tommy Tedesco on guitar, and Hal Blaine on drums. We were working at RCA Studios in a room that had a really high ceiling.

We were recording the song "Don't Call On Me" and after a take that I thought was really great, Mike Nesmith came out and told us all to improvise the last few bars and do whatever would make this song really different. Shorty Rogers (Mr. Cool) said, "Ah, Tommy, man . . . can you do something outrageous for your solo?" and Mike said, "Yeah, do something really crazy." Tommy replied, "You got it." So, we got going again and were really grooving and improvising, and when we got to Tommy's solo I was waiting to hear what he was going to do. Tommy took his guitar and threw it straight up in the air. I mentioned that the room had high ceilings, so you can imagine what we all witnessed . . . it seemed like the guitar was a rocket with a long cord attached. The guitar dropped to the floor, but it didn't break (it was damaged, but contrary to what was said in other accounts of this story, it was still playable). Tommy picked up the guitar and kept playing it. Ha ha! Yes, the guitar was badly out of tune and sounded weird, but amazingly it was still playable. When Tommy finished, he asked, "How was that?"

Tommy Tedesco was on almost every date I produced and arranged. He was one of the best guitarists of all time and could play any music style and genre. For example, I was hired to score a movie titled *Stacey*, directed and produced by Andy Sidaris. Andy, as I mention in the story I tell about my work with James Garner, was a director and producer for ABC Sports, but he also made a few action movies that would be labeled as "B" movies. *Stacey* was one of those movies, about a sexy female private detective played by Anne Randall, and her shady adventures. Actor Nick Georgiade, famous for his work in *The Untouchables*, played the bad guy in this movie.

There was a big car chase scene in the movie, which was the best part of *Stacey*. Andy Sidaris and Nick Georgiade were both of Greek heritage and good friends. Andy wanted me to compose the music for the chase scene in a Greek style for Nick and him. The movie was shot in Los Angeles, so this didn't make much sense to me, but Andy insisted. Naturally, if this music was going to sound Greek, we were going to need someone to play a bouzouki (a guitarlike instrument from Greece). Of course, I hired Tommy for the job, but he didn't own a bouzouki at the time. I got panicky because Andy wanted this music to sound authentic. Tommy said, "I'll play a mandolin and it will sound just like a bouzouki." I was not convinced and was expressing my doubts, when Tommy in his usual humor and confidence said, "You'll know the difference and I'll know the difference, but no one else is gonna know, Don." I had to go along with him.

The day of the session arrived and we had a full orchestra along with the usual session players I liked to work with, including Tommy Tedesco. I was having a run-through before we recorded the chase scene music. Tommy was sitting there, mandolin in his lap, calmly smoking a cigarette. In fact, he looked like he was not paying attention, just taking a break. I was getting annoyed and asked Tommy to run through the music with us because I want to hear his part with the orchestra at least once before we recorded. Tommy kept telling me no and not to worry about it. I was bothered but I didn't know what else to do, so we ran through the song a couple of times without him.

We started to record a take. Tommy was ready, and when we got to his part he played flawlessly and amazingly. It went great until the very end, when a string player made a mistake. Oh man, I was about to lose it because Tommy's part was awesome. So, I looked over at Tommy and he said, "Let's go." We did another take and Tommy was brilliant again, but that first take had more magic. Fortunately the engineer had saved Tommy's first take and we edited the music so that great part was in the movie.

I also produced and cowrote the theme song for *Stacey*, "Hidin' from Sunshine," with Bob Silver and Pete Willcox, who sang the song as well.

Tommy was playing guitar in the session I scored for the TV series *The New Mike Hammer*, which starred Stacy Keach. One of the music cues I wrote was for a scene that took place on the Venice Beach boardwalk. If you've ever been to Venice Beach in California or have seen footage of the place, you know that the area has a diverse variety of interesting sights, characters, styles, and sounds. It's a lively, bohemian zone with a blend of many elements. The feeling is a mixture of ethnic, rap, gypsy, rock, and pop, and I had arranged a very intricate cue that had all of those elements. In the recording session, we were running through the cue when the music coordinator came out and asked, "What's this? The scene is at the beach, so the music should be surf music, Beach Boys." At first I could not believe what I was hearing, then I got angry and insulted that this guy didn't appreciate my work and thought what an idiot he was to think surf music went with this scene.

I started walking out really pissed, but Tommy Tedesco grabbed my arm and stopped me. He pulled me aside and said, "Mr. Randi, did you fall in love with your cue? Get over it, it doesn't matter." Tommy was right.

A Beach Boys sound-alike band was hired to record the cue and the music coordinator was happy. This change ended up costing three times more for the session and licensing rights of the music than they would have paid for my arrangement, but in the end we did our job and got paid. That is something that Tommy Tedesco did well: he showed us all how important it was to keep that perspective.

Because of these types of gigs we did to make our living, I often felt like I needed to just play the music I love with my friends. That was a core reason I opened my club, The Baked Potato. The scoring gigs we did for the studios were done during the day, much like a regular day job most people have. After work, we also liked to unwind and we did that by playing jazz or going out to hear great live music. On one occasion Thumbs Carllile was playing at my club, The Baked Potato, so I invited Tommy and the other guitarists working with us to come see him that night. Thumbs was a unique guitar player because he played the guitar on his lap and picked the strings with his fingers and thumbs. Dennis Budimir (guitarist), Howard Roberts (guitarist), Tommy Tedesco, and I were standing at the bar watching the great Thumbs Carllile play. He was electrifying! The crowd went wild and so did we. Once the cheering subsided, Tommy turned to Howard Roberts and said, "Wouldn't it be something if he's right and we're wrong?" That's Tommy!

Ray Pohlman and Carol Kaye

Ray Pohlman and Carol Kaye, both great bassists and equally great guitarists, were part of the Wrecking Crew.

Most of Carol's session work was playing bass and her performance was always outstanding. She has written several music instruction books for playing bass that are wonderful.

Ray Pohlman, besides being great on both the bass and guitar, was also an accomplished arranger. Ray was always a delight to be around.

Joe Osborn, Bass

Joe Osborn is one of the top bassists in music. His credits are very long and he is also known for discovering the duo the Carpenters. I have played with Joe on many recording dates, and this story takes place on a date with arranger Jimmie Haskell and producer Dick Glasser.

Joe is fine with chord charts and lead sheets but he's not as strong at sight-reading music notes. In most sessions he'll pick up the tune through the chord chart and just improvise his part, and he's so talented and creative at that. On this session Jimmie had given us written music parts for the tune and we ran through the song, which we thought was a great take. But Jimmie asked us to take a ten-minute break so he could make some adjustments in the arrangement. Joe asked me if I would stay with him to go over his part. I helped him out by playing his bass part on the piano and we ran through it one time only and he had it, but he probably didn't need me to help him. Joe, a perfectionist, wanted to get his part down perfectly.

So, the rest of the guys come back from break and we got back to the song. Jimmie asked us to play exactly as he wrote it, which wasn't a problem for Joe now. We were running through the song and it was feeling really good and we were all just cookin' on this tune. Joe nailed his part, hitting every note just as Jimmie wrote it. I thought it had to be "the" take, it was that good!

We looked up at Jimmie and he said, "Let's do another take." He looked over at Joe and said, "I don't like the bass part I wrote. Can you make up your own part this time?" I was surprised and so was Joe. In frustration Joe replied, "Well, why the fuck did you write it, then?" Oh man, we all exploded in laughter right then. It was a duel of two perfectionists—Jimmie was second-guessing himself and Joe was proud that he had nailed his part just as Jimmie wrote it. He was expecting Jimmie to compliment his precision, so Joe couldn't hold back his outburst.

More Jimmie Haskell

Jimmie Haskell is a very talented composer and arranger and has Grammy Awards and an Emmy Award among his accomplishments, but he does take his time to go over every note many times to perfect every song he works on. I have another hilarious story that includes another renowned bass player, which took place several years after the Joe Osborn story.

It was either 2003 or 2004 when I was hired to play piano on a recording date for Jimmie Haskell that included Hal Blaine on drums, James Burton on lead guitar, Michael Hakes on rhythm guitar, and Leland Sklar on bass. Leland Sklar is one of today's top bass players in recording and has played on over a thousand hit albums from the '70s through to today, and he has toured with famous artists like James Taylor. You have seen Leland Sklar, even if you didn't know his name, because he's also appeared on television series and on award shows, playing bass in the band. You'd recognize him because Leland has a very full and very long white beard. It's his signature look.

The session Jimmie hired us for was for a male singer, but I do not remember his name. He was a tall guy, nice looking, and I remember he had a white Rolls-Royce, but he never left the booth the whole time we were there. The session was scheduled to start at 10:00 a.m. We all showed up on time and Jimmie was already there in the booth, going over the arrangement with the producer and the artist. Jimmie came out to greet us and said he had an idea of what we were going to do, but he wanted to make sure everything was right, so it would be a few minutes before we could start. Then he went back into the booth.

We hung out and talked and joked and got warmed up a bit just to pass the time while waiting for Jimmie to be ready to go. He came out of the booth a couple of times to play something on the piano, made some notes, and then went back to the booth.

This session was scheduled for 10:00 a.m. to 1:00 p.m., and around 12:45 p.m. Jimmie came over the PA and said, "We're still working on things in here, so why don't you guys go have lunch and come back at 2:00 p.m. We should be ready when you get back." This meant that we'd now be working into a second session and be paid union scale for the first one as well as the second, not too bad for all the waiting. We went to lunch and came back at 2:00 p.m., but Jimmie said there were still a few things that they need to work on, so we waited again.

Another two hours passed and we were all going insane waiting and I was getting agitated. I hate just stilling around, waiting. Finally Jimmie Haskell came out of the booth and apologized to us, telling us he was going to call the date because the arrangement still needed work. Jimmie said, "Guys, thank you so much for your patience. I know you have been waiting all day and I'm sorry to have held you here for so long." Leland answered back, "Jimmie, do you know we've been here so long that I was clean shaven when I arrived?" Everyone, including Jimmie, just roared laughing at Leland's comment. Thank goodness, Leland broke the tension with his very sharp wit.

Drummer Hal Blaine

I met Hal Blaine when I started doing recording sessions for Phil Spector at Gold Star Studios, but I didn't become good friends with him until I ran into him in Chicago in 1962 at the Saharan. Gene Autry once owned the Saharan, but sold it to Manny Skar, who was known to be associated with organized crime.

My trio was doing a gig, playing jazz in the main dining room that was a very large and elegant room for the guests. One night between sets, I was walking through the backstage area to get to the lobby and was about to pass by a guy when I recognized him as Hal Blaine. We were really surprised to run into each other in Chicago. We both stopped in our tracks and pointed at each other with surprised looks on our faces and we laughed! Hal was playing in the nightclub of the hotel with Patti Page. Ever since that coincidence, we became good friends, and of course we did many sessions together and still do to this day.

One thing that impressed me about Hal, as a drummer, was that he paid very close attention to details. He would tune his drums at every recording session or before a live show, and he went further in a session by actually tuning his drums to complement the tones or notes in the song we were playing. This practice, along with his talent for putting the right feeling in his performance, made it easier for producers and engineers to get the best drum sound for the song and became a reason Hal got called to do so many top recording sessions.

As a joke, Hal Blaine had a small rubber stamp made with "Hal Blaine Strikes Again," and he would stamp the drum charts he would get on recording dates and live shows. Later, if the song was performed by another artist or even the same artist, but a different drummer might be playing the date or gig, the original charts were often used for the song. The drummer would know Hal played the song originally because "Hal Blaine Strikes Again" was stamped on the music.

Hal Does Sinatra

We were working for Nancy Sinatra, and for some of the tours we went on with her, Hal Blaine was the drummer.

In 1968 Hubert Humphrey was the Democratic candidate for president, running against Republican candidate Richard Nixon. Frank Sinatra wanted to support Hubert Humphrey by doing concerts with Nancy, Dean Martin, Sammy Davis Jr., and himself. They were really fantastic shows and Hal Blaine was part of the tour for the first two weeks we went out on the road. We continued the tour for six more weeks after a short break but Hal didn't join us for that leg of the tour.

We were in Minneapolis and had just played the show and gotten back to the hotel. It was a Sunday and in Minnesota they have a blue law where establishments cannot serve or sell alcohol. It was also late and the hotel room service had just closed. All the other guys in the band had already left to try to find a place to eat, but Hal Blaine and I were tired and were sharing a room. We didn't feel like going out to find a hamburger joint, so we had a plan . . . Knowing that Frank was out at a restaurant and it was only a few minutes after room service closed, I phoned room service anyway. Fortunately someone answered the call and I told the person this was Frank Sinatra's room and I needed to order dinner for him and me—could the kitchen open for him? The guy said, "Hold a minute," and the chef came on and said of course he would open the kitchen for Mr. Sinatra and what did we want? I ordered a couple of steaks with baked potatoes and rolls, salad, and a couple of Pepsis.

So, now the order was in and I asked Hal, "How the fuck are we gonna pull this off?" He said, "I know what to do." When the knock on the door came, Hal jumped into the bathroom and turned on the shower and started singing "Come Fly with Me." The chef himself delivered the order because he wanted to meet Frank, but with Hal (Frank) singing in the bathroom, the chef was a little disappointed he wasn't going to meet him. I was asking for the bill when I noticed that the rolls weren't on the cart. The chef said, "No worries," that he would get them and be right back. The chef left and Hal came out. Within minutes the knock came again and Hal jumped back into the bathroom and turned on the shower and started singing again, "Come Fly with Me." The chef was at the door with the rolls and he could hear Hal (Frank) singing in the bathroom. He again looked disappointed but I said, "Frank takes a long shower after a show, but he knows that you have been so great to accommodate him and wanted me to say thank you on his behalf." Hal could pull this off because he has a great voice and he can mimic Frank Sinatra fairly well.

Hal and I had our delicious steak dinner, but after we were done, Hal said, "If we put this cart outside, the rest of the guys are going to know we had room service." Well, we had to put it out there, and yes, the guys gave us shit for having steak dinner when they only got hamburgers and fries. We never had to pay for the dinner, though, because the chef refused to let me sign for it or pay cash. And we didn't let anyone else know the details of what we did. After all these years, we still laugh when we tell this story.

Hal and I see and call each other often and it's usually a joke fest as we reminisce about all the crazy, funny stories we both have. Here is another funny story that Hal and I reminisce about when we get together . . .

Las Vegas Winning Streak

When Hal and I were touring with Nancy Sinatra and were playing at the Las Vegas Hilton, on our breaks between the first and second show, we would go have some fun in the casino and play quarter slot machines. We were still dressed in our tuxedos because we had to be ready for the next show, so we looked like a couple of "high rollers," but we only looked the part. Hal and I never gambled very much money on our break. We would play together on one slot machine and take turns putting in the quarters and pulling the handle. If we won twenty-five cents, we would whoop and holler like we just won a million dollars and the other slot players around us would look over to see what we were winning. It was fun for us and we didn't expect to hit a jackpot.

One time we did hit it big! Hal put in five quarters, I pulled the handle, and we won a jackpot of five hundred dollars! This time we really whooped and hollered and the machine was ringing, the lights on it were flashing, and the coins were flowing out into the bin, making a lot of noise. All of the people around us came over to see what we won. When the slot machine attendant came over to make sure the jackpot was the correct payout and reset the machine, she asked us to play off the jackpot, meaning to play one more pull to clear the machine. So, Hal put five more quarters in the machine and I pulled the handle, and the machine hit again for five hundred dollars! We'd won one thousand dollars from the two jackpots and there was a crowd around us, cheering. Hal and I were screaming and jumping up and down like a couple of kids, as though we'd won ten million dollars. The attendant said in all the years she worked there, she never saw that happen before. We got all the quarters and went to the cashier and even she said in the years she'd worked there, that never happened before. It was the best time I've ever had in a casino and the only time I felt like a real "high roller" in one.

CHAPTER 2

Judd for the Defense and Randy Newman

I was hired to work on a scoring date at Twentieth Century-Fox Studios for a new dramatic TV series, *Judd for the Defense*, on ABC. This was a weekly series starring Carl Betz, who played the role of Clinton Judd, a flashy attorney in Houston. Randy Newman was the composer for the music and I had been working with him on other projects, so he requested me for this job as a specialist. My friend Paul Humphries was the drummer in this session, too.

The session started and it was not going well for Randy. Some guy kept coming out and stopping him every time Randy got us going. It just wasn't going anywhere and the guy kept coming out and scolding Randy over and over and over again, saying, "No, no, no, no! Why did you do that?' I'm thinking, *Jeez, this guy's being a jerk to Randy.*

Randy called a ten-minute break and we all went out and came back. I remember it was a pretty sizable orchestra. We were getting settled and I noticed again that guy was really on Randy's case. I was not paying close attention, but I was hearing it, because the guy's voice was loud. The whole orchestra was hearing it, too, but the musicians seemed to be ignoring it, so I tried to do the same.

So, now they started to run a cue and we went back working on the project again. I'd worked for Randy Newman on other recording sessions but I'd never worked before for Randy doing a scoring gig or, for the guy who kept interrupting. This guy was never introduced to us at the beginning of the session and I guess it was because all of the other musicians working this gig already knew him. I was just trying to go along with it all. The guy came out again to talk to Randy Newman. While they were straightening out another cue we all took off our headphones. When you work recording sessions, everyone takes them off when we can because it gets uncomfortable.

Finally the guy said, "All right, let's get going here." We put the phones on and the thing that you don't want to happen, happened. Evidently, the sound man accidentally turned the dial way up on the click track (a click track is a click sound that goes in a steady, timed beat that is synced to the frame rate of the video or film that is being scored, so we can play in the correct timing), and when it came on it was like a bullet shooting through my ear! I yelled out, "OH!" and pulled off my headphones, like everyone else did. That was for the pain piercing through my ears. All of a sudden I heard, "Who said that?" I looked over and replied, "I did." The guy said, "Well, watch it!" I asked, "What do you mean, watch it?" He said, "I told you, shut up!" I replied, "Are you talking to me?" He said, "Yes! Do you know who I am?" And that's when all hell broke loose, because I said, "No, I don't know who you are and I don't give a fuck who you are." And he lost it. He went completely berserk because I didn't know who he was: Lionel Newman, the famous conductor and composer. He was also Randy Newman's uncle. Oy!

It continued . . . Lionel screamed, "I want you off the lot! I want you outta here now!" I said, "Come on, throw me out. Take your best shot!" "Urban! Urban!"—Lionel started screaming for Urban Thielmann, the music contractor—"Where's the contractor? Where's the goddamn contractor? Where's Urban? I want that guy off this date right now," he said, pointing to me. Poor Randy Newman had tears in his eyes. He was standing there in the middle of it and I felt so bad for Randy.

I was walking out when I suddenly realized something and said, "Where's my W-4?" I hadn't signed the federal form to give to the union. Lionel came back at me, screaming, "What the hell? Get outta here!" I said, "You better be very careful, sir, because you're really pushing it now!" The musicians were silent and in total shock. You could cut the silence with a knife, that's how quiet they were.

Urban, the music contractor, came through the door, running. Someone had gone to get him because he was outside at another stage handling another production. The contractor is supposed to be present during the session, so Lionel started yelling at Urban, "Where the hell were you? Give him his goddamn W-4 and get him outta here!" Lionel pointed at me and said, "I'm taking you to the union board." I said, "Come on."

I signed the W-4 and left the studio. A week later I got a call from the union to inform me that Lionel Newman wanted to file charges against me. In the meantime, I was getting phone calls from musicians that were on the date and some that weren't on the date but had been working for Lionel Newman for twenty years, all thanking me for standing up to him because they'd been mistreated for so long and nobody had ever had the balls to stand up to him. People sent me letters with four stars on them, like a rating for my "performance." Artie Kane, who was one of the best studio pianists and composers, called me on the phone in hysterics. He said, "Don, the only thing I'm so sorry about is that I wasn't there, because you said everything I've always wanted to say to Lionel."

It is ironic that the TV show we were working on was titled *Judd for the Defense*, because in my defense, all the musicians who were union members were calling the union in my favor and someone advised Lionel that he'd better cool it because he was opening up a can of worms. So, nothing ever happened to me for that incident, except I got a call from Quincy Jones to do a date at Fox but wasn't allowed to do the date, though I got paid for it anyway. And a Lalo Shifrin date came up for me at Fox some months later, and I got paid for that also but didn't work the date. Basically, while Lionel was there, I was blacklisted from the Twentieth Century-Fox lot but not from the income from bookings.

CHAPTER 3

James Garner's Theme

In 1969 I worked on a score for a docudrama directed by Andy Sidaris, whom I knew from working on other TV show scores on ABC, like *Wide World of Sports*. The film, *The Racing Scene*, was about James Garner's connection with auto racing and his formula cars. Garner had three or four race cars at that point. It was really heavy-duty stuff for those days. It was filmed mostly on the Can Am Tour: Sebring, Lime Rock, St. Jovite, and the Daytona 500, which is the last race of that Can Am Tour.

James really loved it and he loved to drive. I went for a ride with him in his custom Shelby Cobra from Gower and Sunset over to Sunset just past La Cienega Boulevard and I was hanging on the whole time. He drove from one place to the other as if he was at Le Mans. I said, "Jim! What are you doing?" He said, "We're fine, we're fine." It was scary and we went screaming all the way there. I kept saying, "If a cop stops us, we're in a shitload of trouble," because he was doing 65 and 70 on Sunset!

So, anyway, I was hired to score this film. Pete Willcox and Bob Silver wrote the lyrics for the theme song, "Why Does a Man Do What He Has to Do?" and it was based on something that Garner said to me. I asked him why he raced cars and his answer was, "It's like if you could look at a buzz saw and think you could touch it and nothing would happen." I replied, "Oh-kaaay."

We finished doing the score and Pete Willcox, who wrote the theme with me, sang the demo and it was really good. Garner listened to it and said, "You know who my favorite artist is?" I said, "No, who is it?" He said, "Joe South," and asked, "Do you think he'll sing the song?" I flat-out said no. Joe South sings his own songs. He won't sing anybody else's. Then Garner handed me five hundred dollars and said, "If you can pull it off, give somebody this cash. If they want more, let me know how much." So, I said, "Jesus Christ, it's worth a shot!"

I thought of a producer I had just finished working with at Capitol, Wayne Shuler, who had just moved out here from Texas. Wayne was a hell of a producer and knew everybody in Nashville, Memphis, and Atlanta, including Billy Joe Royal and Joe South. But to actually get the song into Joe's hands and have him seriously consider it, I needed Bill Lowery, one of the biggest publishers in Nashville, who handled all of Joe's stuff. Since I had only met Bill once, I needed Wayne Shuler to help me, as he was a good friend of Bill's.

I met with Wayne and asked him if he could help me get the song into Bill Lowery's hands for Joe South. He said the same thing I told Garner, that Joe South would not do anyone else's songs. I told him that this was for Jim Garner and his film, if that would make a difference. As far as Wayne knew, Joe South had not done a song for a movie yet. Wayne was hesitant, but I handed him the five hundred dollars. Wayne tried to push it back, saying he didn't want the money, but I told him to take it anyway. "Whatever happens, it's still yours. Just get something for your kids with it," I told him.

Wayne was able to get the song to Bill Lowery and talk to him and Bill agreed to talk to Joe. About a week later, we were in the studio, editing the song with Pete singing it. We couldn't keep waiting for Joe's answer in case he said no. Then my wife called to let me know that I was going to get a call from Joe South. He had just called the house from Memphis, looking for me. So, the call came in and Joe said, "Hello, you Don Randi?" I said yeah. He said, "Well, this is Joe South and listen to this . . ." All I could think of in the few seconds before the music started was, *I hope he didn't write a new song because he won't sing ours.* But what I heard was our song, sung by him and performed by his band! Joe South had liked the song, so he went ahead and recorded it for us.

Joe South's version of the song ended up being in the movie after all and

Garner couldn't have been more excited. I was in awe that it all worked out. To top that off, Joe South had toured that year and played the Greek Theatre in Los Angeles. He closed the show at the Greek, performing "Why Does a Man Do What He Has to Do?" and announced, "That song was written by Don Randi, one of your local boys, and is the only song I do that was written by someone else." Stupid me, I did not go to that concert but I read a review of the concert in the *Hollywood Reporter* that quoted Joe saying this. It was quite an honor and evidence that you can't ever say never! I regret I never met Joe South in person.

CHAPTER 4

The Time I Had Bell's Palsy

In 1968 I came down with Bell's palsy. It is a facial paralysis resulting from a dysfunction of the seventh cranial nerve, or facial nerve. Though I never found out exactly why it occurred, I thought it was from a recent dental procedure, but the dentist swore it did not happen from his work. Even though the condition went away completely after a few months, it was scary and I felt and looked grotesque. It affected half of my face and for some time I had to tape my eyes shut so I could sleep.

A week after the Bell's palsy came on, I was in the breakfast nook at home and Norma, my wife, was standing at the kitchen sink. She started talking and my jaw dropped—well, half of my jaw—because she was talking as though she also had Bell's palsy. At first I thought, *OH MY GOD, I gave her this, too!* which wasn't possible. It's not contagious. She continued and saw the horror in half of my face and then she started laughing. She was just playing a joke on me, which was pretty much the funniest joke Norma has ever played on me. She was able to pull this off because Norma is not a joking person.

At that time, I was working for Nancy Sinatra and had just got back from doing the first leg of a fund-raising concert tour with Nancy and her father, Frank Sinatra, for the Democratic presidential campaign for Hubert Humphrey, so I had to tell her what had happened to my face. I was certain that I would not be able to work for a while, even though it did not affect my playing. I tried to phone her but my speech was garbled because I could not move my mouth properly. I had to hand the phone to my wife so she could explain my condition to her.

Nancy asked Norma to hand the phone back to me and I listened to her say, "You've gotta play at my engagement party!" I wasn't sure I wanted to play with Bell's palsy affecting half of my face. I tried to reply to her question and I am sure Nancy understood my hesitation. She said, "You have to be at my engagement party and I don't care what you look like!"

Nancy Sinatra had recently become engaged to Jack Haley Jr. (a director, producer, and writer, and the son of Jack Haley, who played the Tin Man in *The Wizard of Oz*). Their wedding never happened, but the two remained good friends and continued to work on projects together. Anyway, Nancy would not take no for an answer and I didn't want to let her down.

On the day of Nancy's engagement party at her house in the Hollywood Hills, as I was setting up Nancy's mother walked in and saw me. She screamed, "Oh my God! Are you okay?" in that dramatic Italian mother from Hoboken, New Jersey, kind of way. I explain what it was and calmed her down and told her I was taking my medication and going to the hospital every day for therapy.

My trio set up in the foyer with Harvey Newmark on acoustic bass, John Clauder on drums, and me on piano, of course. I arranged us so when I sat at the piano people could see my good side. When I turned to face the guests, that's when I looked like Quasimodo on one side.

Finally the boss—Frank—arrived. I recall his driving up in a Mustang with Tuesday Weld. He saw me and said, "What's wrong with you?!" So, I gave him the whole story. "We're going back on the road next week for Hubert Humphrey," Frank said, but I didn't know what to reply because I didn't really want to go in this condition. He asked Dean Martin and Sammy Davis Jr. to go on tour with us and, of course, his daughter Nancy. It was a really big deal!

A while later we went on a break and Frank's secretary, Shirley, came up to me; apparently they (Frank and Nancy) had already had a meeting about me. She said that whatever I needed to do therapeutically here could be done on the road and that she would make all of the arrangements for me. Since my condition did not affect my playing, it seemed that I had no reason to decline this tour. So, Shirley contacted my doctor and they made the arrangements for my therapy with hospitals on all of the stops on the six-week tour.

Wherever the tour took us, there was a car available to take me to the hospital every day for my therapy session. And, of course, I never had to worry about having my medication available. I didn't lift a finger to make any of this happen and I am so grateful to the Sinatra family for treating me like family. They have always been more than kind and generous with me throughout the years.

The tour itself was very interesting and fun. Dean Martin, Sammy Davis Jr., and Frank Sinatra together were phenomenal and it was a thrill for me. In Houston, at the Astrodome, LBJ (then president Lyndon B. Johnson) and Humphrey walked around the track before the show and waved to the sold-out crowd. There was a really powerful energy in the air that night; you could have sworn that Hubert Humphrey was going to be the next president of the United States. Certainly we all thought our campaign efforts would have pushed through his election.

In St. Louis I received a call from Hubert Humphrey's wife, Muriel, who asked if I would meet with her secretary to discuss something she would like me to consider. Her secretary asked me if I could take Douglas Humphrey, who was around twenty years old at the time, with us and let him hang out with the band. She said Doug thought it would be really exciting to be on the tour with us. I didn't really know what to make of this kind of request, but I told her it would be my pleasure.

Doug Humphrey joined us, just as arranged, and he was a delightful young man. I noticed he was shy, but that didn't keep him from becoming just one of the guys for the rest of the tour. He spent a lot of time with the band; he was laughing and swearing just like us and he generally had a great time. Not sure why Mrs. Humphrey wanted her son to hang out with us, but at the end of the tour she was very appreciative that I took him under my wing and thanked me personally. I also received a thank-you letter from the Democratic National Committee for being part of the fund-raising tour.

It was really a once-in-a-lifetime experience despite my having Bell's palsy, which was almost completely healed by the end of the tour. This was just one of the many opportunities I would have never imagined could be part of my life, if it weren't for Nancy.

CHAPTER 5

Nancy Sinatra—It All Started with Boots

T he first time I met Nancy Sinatra was at that momentous session where she recorded her first and signature hit, "These Boots Are Made for Walkin'." Lee Hazlewood wrote and produced the song and Billy Strange did the arrangement. I was called in to play piano; Bill Pitman played electric bass; Chuck Berghofer was on acoustic bass and Richie Frost on drums; Billy Strange, Al Casey, Tommy Tedesco, and Don Owens were on guitars; plus Ollie Mitchell, Roy Caton, and Lew McCreary were on horns. Eddie Brackett was the engineer. My first impression of Nancy was that she was so petite, gorgeous, and delightful. She is a warm and kind person, but can also be as tough as her father when she needs to be.

Most people don't know that there was a chance that Nancy Sinatra's signature song, "Boots," was not going to be recorded by her. I overheard Nancy and Lee discussing the song while we were standing by . . . Lee said, "You shouldn't do this song." Nancy replied, "Why not?" Lee said, "It's a man's song" Nancy replied, "It is not! No, no, this is a little girl's song." Nancy was standing up for herself even though she was still a young artist, not yet at the level (like her father) to call the shots. Fortunately Lee agreed and Nancy's instincts were proven when "Boots" went to number one in the US and UK in 1966.

That signature bass line in the intro of the song and played throughout was the brainchild of Chuck Berghofer, playing the acoustic bass. Lee Hazlewood was looking for something different for the song, a really catchy hook. It seemed to take Chuck about a minute of thought, then he said, "Well, Lee, try this," and started playing the walking line, consisting of quarter-tones all the way down. That was it, and it became one of the classic bass lines of all time. That hook made Chuck one of the hottest bass players in town, getting calls for numerous gigs. To this day, people ask him to play it and he does! In the '60s, when "Boots" came out, it was a groundbreaking song. Most women were still in traditional, subordinate positions in relationships and the workplace. The statement the song makes is that women can be empowered to call the shots and don't have to stick around to be mistreated by a jerk. Nancy had a great instinct about how she performed the song on TV and in shows as well. It's truly her signature song, and it will always have a special place in my heart as it reminds me of the first time I met her.

After "Boots" I did countless other sessions with Nancy; Lee Hazlewood and Billy Strange would pick the bands and they usually included me. I'd say I did about 90 percent of her recordings. Even though "Boots" is the most popular hit that Nancy did, I have many other favorites she recorded. Some weren't big sellers but they were great songs! Besides her solo recordings, Nancy did several duets with Lee that are still admired today by generations of music fans. In fact, just about every time a girl with a pretty voice sings a duet with a guy with a deep voice, they're compared with Nancy Sinatra and Lee Hazlewood.

One song I love to play with Nancy is Lee's "Arkansas Coal (Suite)," a fantastic duet she did with Lee. In just over five and a half minutes, this mini-epic goes through several musical changes, making it a very challenging but such a rewarding song to play. It's also a very emotional song for Nancy to sing. In fact, she stopped singing it live because she would get so caught up in the song that she would cry. She really gets into the song, telling the story, and you can hear that she really believes in the story like she is living it right there. This is something she learned from her father, how to express the meaning of the lyric.

"Some Velvet Morning" and "Jackson" are also beautiful duets with Lee Hazlewood. There are so many Lee and Nancy favorites of mine that it's hard to not list every one.

Another song I love that Nancy is famous for is "You Only Live Twice," the theme from the 1967 James Bond film of the same name. This song, written by John Barry and Leslie Bricusse, is much loved by Nancy's fans. Over the decades it has been covered by a diverse list of artists, like Robbie Williams, Björk, and Coldplay. When we did it in Nancy's shows, I played a big piano intro and the moment I started to play it, the audience recognized the song and applauded.

I arranged a version of the Moody Blues classic "Nights in White Satin" for Nancy. We did it with synthesizers instead of an orchestra, which turned out very interesting.

In the early days on the road with Nancy, Billy Strange was the musical director and the main arranger of her music. Billy played guitar, I played piano, Hal Blaine was on drums, and Jerry Scheff (who later played with Elvis Presley) played bass. These guys were the best rhythm section in the business.

People in general may not know that Nancy loves good jokes and pranks, which inspired us to do outrageous ones when we toured. Generally, it was the last show on a two- or three-week engagement. On one night, I decided to mess with Billy's guitar. When Nancy performed the song "Bang Bang," Billy would strum his guitar, *brrriiiinnng*, and in the pause Nancy would sing her line "I was five and he was six . . ." etc. Before we played that song there was a short break, so Billy would always set his guitar in the curve of my grand piano, then walk offstage. On one closing night, while he was backstage, I quickly picked up his guitar and detuned it. Billy came back onstage and we were ready to start the song. Billy picked up his guitar and strummed that first chord. Instead of that beautiful *brrriiiinnng*, there was a horrible out-of-tune noise. Billy started frantically to tune his guitar and meanwhile Nancy, the rest of the band, and I were hysterical! Billy shot me a mad look and whispered, "You son-of-a-bitch," except his whisper was picked up on the mic of my piano and everybody in the audience heard it. This made us all laugh even harder!

Years later the song "Bang Bang" was in the movie *Kill Bill*, and so it became Nancy's current signature song, which presented her to a new base of fans.

On another closing show we played, I was in a full tuxedo but with bare feet and my pants rolled up. Nancy could not see that because she stood in front, but as she performed the fans in the front rows were laughing and she couldn't understand why. I was wiggling my toes and moving my feet around in a crazy way. The people who could see what I was doing were really laughing hard and some pointed at me. Nancy kept on singing, but eventually turned around and saw my bare feet going crazy and she broke out laughing, too!

Billy Strange remained Nancy's music director and for a few more tour dates, but he left eventually and I became her music director and have been ever since. When I started going on tour with Nancy, she would hire my whole band. One of my favorite bands with Nancy was with Bobby Economou, Al Criado, and Rob Whitsitt. They were so much fun.

The best drum solo ever on "Drummer Man" (other than Hal Blaine's) was done by John Sumner. "John Sumner, my drummer," Nancy used to say. He could tear the house down every time he did it. The audience would go crazy during his solo because his performance was something magical.

Norma Randi, my wife, was also a part of the tour when we did a run of shows at Resorts International in Atlantic City. She was a backup singer along with Phyllis Battle and Anita Cortez.

Nancy took off a few years when she had children, but when she was ready to start again, her dad asked if she would open for him. So, that's how we started opening for Frank Sinatra and toured with him for a couple of years.

The shows Nancy did as an opening act for Frank were really memorable and always sold out. Frank Sinatra was one of the most professional performers one could work with. His shows ran like clockwork . . . unless he had his talented daughter opening for him.

Nancy was supposed to perform for twenty minutes and then comedian Charlie Callas would come out and do his bit for fifteen minutes, then Frank would come on. Well, everyone just loved Nancy, and so she stretched out her set, adding a song or two so her set would go to twenty-three minutes, twenty-eight minutes, etc. This would annoy Frank to no end! One night after we were done with our set, Frank's conductor and pianist Joe Parnello came up to me and said, "The Boss wants to talk to you." I went to his dressing room and Frank said, "Shut the door." He started shouting, "Goddammit, her set is supposed to be twenty minutes, Don! Not twenty-two, not twenty-five or twenty-eight! You have to talk to her and get some control of this!" I thought to myself, *He's really pissed.* I stared at him for a minute, then said, "What's her last name?" Frank's angry face slowly relaxed and then he said, laughing, "Get the hell out of here." He realized that he was going to have to live with Nancy's timing.

Nancy brought her daughters on tour with her at times, and usually her husband was there with them when she was rehearsing and such, but one time when we were in Atlantic City, Hugh Lambert, her husband, could not join us. Her daughters, A.J. and Amanda, were there, but they stayed in their room and I knew it had to be boring for them. A.J. and Amanda were six and four years old and I thought it would be nice to give them a break from being in the room all day and take them outside to the beach to play, so Nancy told the bodyguard I was taking them out for a while. I took them down through the kitchen for an extra measure of security.

We were walking on the boardwalk, each girl holding my hand, when I noticed a woman following us. I recognized her as a woman who stalks Frank Sinatra. All of his security crew had strict instructions to not let her get close to him or his family. I was not sure how she slipped their watch, but my heart was beating like crazy, because I didn't know what she would do. At one point I just stopped and pushed both girls behind me and confronted the woman. In a soft voice so the girls could not hear me but loud enough for the woman to hear, I told her to back off. And I said it with enough fierceness that the woman stared at me, frightened, then turned around and took off. I turned around and said, "Come on girls, let's go." We continued to the beach as I intended and the three of us had fun collecting shells and enjoyed being out by the shore. It ended up being a nice time for the three of us, and the girls were really happy and excited when we went back to the room.

Later I told Nancy what had happened and she was okay with how it turned out, but she was worried about the stalker getting that close to us. Later after Frank found out what happened, he found me. Frank said, "That's why I have all this security, so that doesn't happen. I told the security guard the girls should stay in the room."

Snowball Fight in Tahoe . . .

We were with Nancy in Tahoe as the opening act for Frank. My wife, Norma, was also on tour with us, singing backup. It was February and there was quite a bit of snow up there. Six o'clock in the morning, the phone rang. I said, "Who is this?" It was Shirley, Frank's assistant, and she said that Frank wanted me to meet him downstairs in an hour. I asked what was going on and she just said, "Frank wants you downstairs by seven a.m." I had just gone to bed when this call came! She hung up the phone, then two seconds later, the phone rang and it was Hugh Lambert. He said, "My father-in-law wants us all downstairs. I'm going, but the girls won't go unless you go." I said okay, then I got dressed. Hugh said to wear warm clothes, so I put on all my winter clothes.

I got downstairs and Frank was half awake but he'd got his overcoat and cap on and said, "Let's go!" The group was Jilly Rizzo, Frank, Hugh, Nancy's two girls, and me. (Nancy joined us later.) We hopped in this big limo and went half a mile to Bill Harrah's mansion, which was closed, but they opened the gates for Frank. We drove in and got out of the car in front of the mansion. Frank had us choosing sides for a snowball fight! It was about seven thirty or eight o'clock in the morning, and for the next three hours we had a blast! I said to Frank at one point, "You're not going to be able to sing tonight!" He replied, "Fuck it!"

We had a hell of a time. We also had these big snow disks to slide with and the girls made snowmen and joined us in the snowball fight. By the end of the morning we were all soaked and freezing. The entire time we were having fun, there were security men positioned in various spots. There was always protection wherever Frank went.

Nancy in Vegas

Nancy did a lot of shows in Las Vegas. Most of these shows were produced by Hugh Lambert, her husband. We played the Riviera, Caesars Palace, and the Hilton. I remember we followed Elvis at the Hilton. That was one of the hardest gigs we ever played because we did five weeks in a row, without a day off.

Nancy incorporated comedy into her shows, too. One hilarious bit she did was with Arte Johnson. She would come out in a beautiful gown and walk up to a podium that was set up onstage. Nancy would have some papers and put them down on the podium and put on her glasses, then Arte Johnson would come walking out in character, like a professor who just came from Sweden. Then he would start talking Swedish gibberish and Nancy would translate. It was a hilarious bit and the audience loved it.

In Nancy's show, Arte Johnson also did a version of his "dirty old man" bit that he made famous on the *Laugh-In* television show. When he walked out onstage in the "dirty old man" character, he walked past the piano where I was sitting and every time he would say something dirty to me like, "What you looking at, you dirty bastard," which would get me laughing. His bit was even more hilarious in Nancy's show than it was on television.

These Vegas shows were really big productions with a huge cast; at different times the bill might include the Osmonds, the Muppets, Sugar Ray Robinson, and Frank Sinatra Jr. The Blossoms or Sweet Inspirations would sing background for Nancy. Those shows were amazing. Some fans would start to get pissed off because they wanted to see more of Nancy Sinatra than the other acts, but the second the bass player started playing the "Boots" intro, the audience went wild and the fans were happy again.

Sugar Ray Robinson was one of my favorite costars in Nancy's big shows. I am a big boxing fan and of course a fan of Sugar Ray Robinson. When we were at the Las Vegas Hilton, our rooms were next to each other, so I would walk to the shows with him. From our rooms we'd start walking to the elevator and Sugar Ray's wife would call out from their room, "Sugah? Do you have your cufflinks?" Sugar Ray would answer, "Yes, dear." She would ask again,

"Sugah? Did you get your tie?" Sugar Ray would answer again, "Yes, dear." And this continued all the way to the elevator. When we got to the elevator, I would mock-spar with him and I would ask him, "Come on, hit me one time, Sugar." Sugar Ray would point and shake his index finger at me and say, "You don't want that, Don." This continued for many days because we were booked at the Las Vegas Hilton for five weeks. At the end of the third week, I said to Sugar Ray, "Just hit me one time, Sugar, just one time." We were backstage and Sugar Ray gave me a light jab to my chest, just above my heart, and I thought I would die. The best way to explain how that jab felt is to imagine a cartoon where a character gets hit and the character crumbles into a pile of a million pieces. From the look on Sugar Ray's face, he knew what his jab did to me and he said, "I told you, Don."

One highlight of our Caesars Palace shows—which at the time was the biggest production that Caesars had ever put on—was when little Jimmy Osmond would walk onstage wearing a fedora, his thumb hooked under a trench coat that was draped over his shoulder, put one foot on a tiny stool, and start singing "That's Life." The only thing that was missing was a cigarette, but it was just like Frank would do and it was brilliant. The audience loved it and it was a hard act to follow.

During one of those Vegas extravaganzas, Nancy introduced the Muppets to Vegas. Shortly after that, she introduced them to network TV and they became hugely popular with adults and kids.

The Muppets shows were big productions. Even when Nancy would go offstage, someone else came on for a number, so the band had to keep going. It was hard work, but it was an opportunity to meet Jerry Nelson, Frank Oz, and Jim Henson, and a friendship formed.

A very memorable part of the Muppets show was in the big finale when Nancy introduced all of the characters. When she got to Thog, a nine-and-a-half-foot blue monster played by Jerry Nelson, he came out and bounced around Nancy and sang with her. The musical arrangement in this part of the show left four bars open for him to scat sing over, and he killed it every time. He never once repeated the same scat. It was unbelievable and the whole band looked forward to that part to see "what's Jerry gonna do to-night?" His performance would drop-dead knock us and the audience out every night.

After shows, we often had dinner with Nancy. One of these times, all of us were standing in Caesars Palace near the area where the restaurants are, deciding where we were going to have dinner, when I saw a guy approaching us. I had to look twice because he looked like Frank Sinatra, but he turned out to be an impersonator-performer. He went straight for Nancy, so my protective side came out and I went to grab him, but Nancy waved and said it was okay. The guy started out complimentary and told Nancy he was a fan, etc. But then he started into his spiel . . . how everyone said he sounds just like Frank and he has so much talent, yada, yada, and he took a cassette tape from his pocket, gave it to Nancy, and told her to listen to it and get in touch with him soon. Nancy was so polite to the guy and thanked him and he left. After he left I asked Nancy how she felt about what just happened because, to me, it was a rude way for the guy to approach her. Nancy's matter-of-fact response was, "Well, I feel that he should eat shit and die." The way she said it so flatly just made me burst out in laughter.

On the Road

Nancy Sinatra went out on concert tours several times over the years. I continued as her music director for all of her tours since I took the job after Billy Strange left to do other projects. We toured all over the US and Europe, but there is a story I want to share that happened during a concert tour Nancy did on the East Coast in 1995.

When we traveled on tour, we had a large luxury tour bus to get to each date. Everyone in the show traveled together on the bus, including Nancy. This tour was a string of one-nighters, so we had a tight road schedule, but as we traveled we had time to take meal breaks and stretch our legs. When we did, we usually stopped at truck stops because Nancy liked them for the good food and the gift shops they usually had. On this occasion we were at a truck stop just outside Hershey, Pennsylvania, and had finished our lunch and the band was already back on the bus. Nancy, John Dubuque (tour manager), and I were the last ones of our group in the truck stop, but I still wanted to check something out in the store, so I was a little late getting back to the bus. Just as I was walking out a man stopped me and asked, "Was that Nancy Sinatra?" The guy was tall and had a large frame, but wasn't threatening. When I confirmed it was Nancy, he asked me if he could speak to her. By this time, John was standing by the bus and I could see him waving me over. I told the guy Nancy was already on the bus and we had to leave to get to our next show. The man told me his story and why he wanted to see Nancy . . .

When he had been in the military, his legs had been very badly injured. When he was brought back home for surgery at the VA hospital, the doctors told him that he would not be able to walk again. He was feeling so much despair lying there in the hospital, on a day Nancy Sinatra happened to be there visiting the veterans. When she walked into his room and saw that he was distraught, she sat in the chair next to his bed and asked him to tell her what was wrong. She encouraged him, cheered him up, and gave him hope when she told him, "Don't believe them; you'll walk again." He told me he wanted to thank her and show Nancy she was right.

I told him to come with me and when I got to the bus, I asked John to tell Nancy to come out; it was important. John looked at this big guy next to me and said, "Don, we need to get on the road." I said, "It won't take long; it's important." When Nancy came to the door and saw the man, it took her only a couple of seconds to recognize him. She came out and the guy proceeded to tell her how he not only recovered and could walk but he was doing very well as a truck driver now, making a good living. He thanked Nancy and said this would not have happened if she had not visited the hospital that day and taken the time to listen and give her support and encouragement. The three of us were in tears.

Nancy Sinatra has been an active supporter of veterans for many years and still visits VA hospitals where ever she is, because she knows how important it is to give hope and comfort to the men and women that serve in our military. Nancy's support of veterans also goes back to the USO shows she has done along with her father. The USO was so grateful to Nancy Sinatra for her support that it honored her with an award.

Another show we did a few years later was at the Little Steven's International Underground Garage Festival at Randalls Island, New York. We had an incredible time doing the festival and Steven Van Zandt was the best host. His wife is a choreographer and dancer, and as a surprise for Nancy Sinatra, she choreographed eight go-go dancers to dance onstage while Nancy sang "These Boots Are Made for Walkin'." There were about five thousand people in the audience and they went wild during that number.

The Touring Bands

We always managed to have the best rhythm-section musicians playing in the show bands. Piano, bass, drums, and at least two guitars and sometimes a percussionist. In the beginning, we would usually augment a large orchestra. For a tour with Nancy Sinatra and Lee Hazlewood where we played in Europe and the USA, the great violinist Bobby Furgo, Miles Robinson on drums, Tom Lilly on bass, and Mike Faue on percussion joined the band. When Nancy opened for Frank, we would use our rhythm section with his big band.

Recalling all those great gigs I had with Nancy, the last touring band that we assembled was incredible. In 2004 and 2005 we were very fortunate to have two great drummers, Clem Burke (drummer with Blondie) and Pete Thomas (drummer for Elvis Costello), who alternated the gigs between them. Trent Stroh played bass and also sang harmonies with Nancy, Danny B. Harvey (Mr. Rockabilly) played guitar, and John DePatie also played guitar. John still plays guitar with me in my band, Quest, and remains a very good friend of mine. For two years, on and off, we were more than just a band; we were a traveling family working for Nancy. In talking with other band members, we all agree it was the best of times because of Nancy Sinatra.

Traveling with Nancy's Tours

Traveling all over North America and Europe, touring with Nancy Sinatra, was more than a thrill for the band and especially me. Because Nancy was so kind and supportive of everyone who worked with her and the fact that she is so respected and loved all over the world, we were always treated well and had the best experience in every city we played. And there were so many places we performed. (For a US tour schedule and show itinerary, see Appendix B.)

Here is a list of the cities we traveled to on tour with Nancy Sinatra.

USA:

Anaheim, CA

Beverly Hills, CA

Hollywood, CA

Los Angeles, CA

Palm Springs, CA

Petaluma, CA

San Diego, CA

San Francisco, CA

Santa Cruz, CA

Washington, DC

Oahu, HI

Boston, MA

Detroit, MI

Pontiac, MI

Minneapolis, MN

Las Vegas, NV

   Hilton International

   Caesars Palace

   Riviera

Atlantic City, NJ

   Resorts International

   White House Subs

Hoboken, NJ

Buffalo, NY

Long Island, NY

New York, NY

Raleigh, NC

Portland, OR

Hershey, PA

Philadelphia, PA

Houston, TX

Richmond, VA

Seattle, WA

Milwaukee, WI

Canada:

Montreal

Toronto

Europe:

Vienna, Austria

London, England

Manchester, England

Newcastle, England

Shepherds Bush, England

Helsinki, Finland

Bourges, France

Paris, France

Berlin, Germany

Hamburg, Germany

Ludwigshafen, Germany

Munich, Germany	Edinburgh, Scotland
Rotterdam, Holland	Glasgow, Scotland
Budapest, Hungary	Madrid, Spain
Venice, Italy	Stockholm, Sweden
Porto, Portugal	Zurich, Switzerland

Nancy and Brian

I've continued to work with Nancy on and off through the years. We've had so many memorable shows, like one we did a few years ago at B.B. King's Blues Club in Universal CityWalk. That is about a block from my club, The Baked Potato, in Studio City.

At our rehearsal Nancy told me that Brian Wilson was going to come to the show and she wanted to do "In My Room" for him. She loved that song and we did it occasionally in her shows. When it came time to do the song, Nancy announced, "Brian, this is for you. We are going to do 'In My Room.'" Well, it turns out that we were the ones surprised because Brian jumped up and said, "Oh! I'll sing it with you," and came up onstage.

I was sitting there in a panic, thinking to myself, *Is this going to work?* This was a time before Brian got back into touring and was just starting to get out again. But we got started, and after a short intro, Brian began singing. First he sang the high part and then he took the middle harmony while Nancy sang lead. Then he sang yet another harmony part with her at the end. The audience was on its feet and cheering and applauding! Nancy and Brian were brilliant together and we were all treated to a once-in-a-lifetime live performance. As Brian walked by the piano he leaned over to me and said, "Don, I remembered," which filled me with emotion and nostalgia and made me cry. It was an amazing night!

Nancy is more than just one of the artists I worked with. She and I are really good friends and we go to Dodgers games and other events together. In 1970 Nancy married Hugh Lambert, who was an extremely talented producer, dancer, and choreographer. Hugh was also one of my favorite people of all time, so my wife and I often did things with Nancy and Hugh and it was like we were one big family because my kids and hers were often included. I would sometimes bring my kids to her recording sessions.

Of all the people I've worked with, the most outstanding in my mind will always be Nancy Sinatra. She is one of the few stars to whom the musicians, backup singers, and crew came first. We are always taken care of and I didn't have to worry about bringing up any problem that might arise. She is always considerate and fair in dealing with any challenge and she celebrated us in our successes. Because of all she does, Nancy inspires a deep respect and loyalty in all of us who have been fortunate to work with her. Nancy Sinatra is one of a kind. A true genuine person!

CHAPTER 6

Raquel Welch—Who Knew?

It was in the autumn of 1969 that David Winters and Burt Rosen asked me to write and arrange the music for an upcoming TV variety special starring Raquel Welch, titled *Raquel!* Tom Jones, Bob Hope, and John Wayne were also slated to costar in the special, and it would be filmed in several locations: London, Paris, Mexico City, Yucatán, Big Sur, and Los Angeles.

David Winters is an award-winning producer, director, actor, and choreographer, and Burt Rosen (who passed away in 2008), his partner in Winters/ Rosen Productions, was also a well-known and award-winning television producer. I have worked on several TV projects they produced, including *Spring Thing* with Bobbie Gentry and Noel Harrison, *Once Upon a Wheel* with Paul Newman, *Travelling Sunshine Show* with the 5th Dimension, and the *Nitty Gritty Hour* with Sonny and Cher.

I was pretty excited about working on this project. Both Raquel Welch and Tom Jones were at the height of their careers and undeniably the world's sexiest celebrities of this time as well. If that wasn't enough, Bob Hope and John Wayne were confirmed for cameo appearances in the special. Big-money cosponsors were tapped in: Coca-Cola and Motorola. By all indications it looked as though this was going to be a top-notch production and a smash of a success!

Once I completed all of the music arrangements, I recorded demo tapes of all of the songs with piano, bass, guitar, and drums. These were just basic tracks so Raquel could use them to rehearse, but they had the cues in there for her to know when she needed to come in on vocals and dance. I gave her the tapes at one of the preproduction meetings in LA and I found her to be a little uptight. She was cool toward me and maybe a little terse. I didn't think too much about her behavior because I was certain that she would warm up once we started production. After all, I was looking for ward to recording with the full orchestra in London.

We arrived in London on New Year's Eve and rang in not only a new year but a new decade, 1970. I was so full of great anticipation that nothing could have convinced me there was trouble ahead.

David, Burt, and Raquel were staying at the Dorchester, which could be compared to the Plaza in New York. I stayed at a different hotel but it was still a very fine one, and was given a limo and driver to shuttle me back and forth to the meetings and studio. The funny thing is the limo they gave me was an American car, a Caddy, but the limos used by everyone staying at the Dorchester were a British make (Hackney) and these cars kept break-ing down so often my limo was sent to pick up the others. Good old reliable American Cadillac.

Once I started working with Raquel in production meetings, going over segments that were being scored, it was apparent that she was more than a diva and we didn't get along. One of the features in the special was Raquel globetrotting to the various locations with exuberant, adoring fans and paparazzi fawning over her, vying for her attention. David Winters choose Harry Nilsson's hit "Everybody's Talkin'" for this scene, which I did the orchestral arrangement for. While we were reviewing the tape of the filmed segment, Raquel kept making snide remarks toward me regarding the music and production, and her face was in a constant scowl. At the end of the playback she suddenly snapped and shrieked, "So, what happens now, Roy Rogers and Dale Evans ride in on their horses?!"

I had tried to suppress my annoyance and frustration up until that point. When she made her outburst, it pushed me too far and I stood up and glared at her while thinking to myself, *You're an idiot! This arrangement fits in the scene and the producers love it!* When I stood up, she caught the look in my eyes, which conveyed my anger and disgust. I guess it frightened her, because she jumped up from her chair and ran out of the room, slammed the door, and didn't come back.

With Raquel out of the room, I walked over to her husband and manager, Patrick Curtis, and told him directly and without editing my language exactly what I thought of Raquel's insulting behavior. I was expecting the worst in response, like getting my face punched, but he just looked up at me and said sadly, "I know." Then I turned to David and Burt and said, "I quit," and walked out of the room. David and Burt came running after me and begged me not to leave. Burt said, "I promise, I'll straighten it all out." David and Burt really respected my work and I liked working with them, but Raquel Welch was impossible. Despite the way I was feeling, I said okay, I would stay, and David and Burt were relieved.

I was still fuming and had to take a walk or something to calm down. I got in the elevator and pushed the button for the lobby. When the doors opened I went bursting out, and in my rush, I knocked down a man who was trying to get in the elevator at the same time. I realized it was my friend Lou Rawls. We were both shocked to run into each other in London (me literally running into him) and Lou asked, "What the hell is going on, Don?!" He could see I was very pissed about something. He said, "Let me buy you a drink at the bar." Thank God, Lou showed up when he did, because I really needed a good friend to turn my anger around.

Things were never agreeable between Raquel and me, but I did my best. The rest of the crew was fantastic and we had a great time working with each other, especially when Raquel wasn't around. By the time we started recording, we figured out she didn't sing well. Evidently Raquel chose to heave all her insecurities at me, the music director.

Burt leaked a story to the press that Raquel had issues with me and gave them a few tidbits from the incident that happened in London. I guess he was trying to control the press in case bystanders and production staff who had witnessed some of her behavior started giving stories to them that he could not control. And, of course, it generated buzz about the show. My friends and reporters started calling me and asking what was going on, but I kept telling them nothing.

In the recording sessions, Raquel would exclaim that the music the orchestra was playing didn't sound anything like the demos I had given her. Well, of course it didn't! I recorded the demos with piano, drums, guitar, and bass. The demos were stripped-down versions and now we were recording with a full orchestra. But one thing that was the same in the demos was the timing and the breaks in the songs. Raquel could not understand this concept, but most likely she was making a big stink in an attempt to mask the fact she had never rehearsed appropriately and couldn't sync in with the timing. Plus her vocals were off pitch. She would walk out of the studio in a huff.

In addition to her solo pieces, Raquel was to sing a duet with Tom Jones on a couple of numbers, including a Little Richard medley. Tom is a great guy and was a pleasure to work with. He was very impressed with my rearrangement of his hit "I (Who Have Nothing)," which was a welcome appreciation compared to the insults I would get from Raquel. Tom Jones would have nailed his part of the duet in one or two takes, but Raquel was off pitch and off timing and we went take after take.

After several hours of trying to get the duet recorded, Tom was beyond his limit and he asked me if I was up to going to shoot some pool and having a couple of drinks with him. He needed a break and so did I! He said this to me in front of Raquel, who had been flirting with him the whole session. The look on her face was priceless as she watched Tom leave with me, the person she hated.

When I got back to LA to record the session with Bob Hope and Raquel, I was really stressed. Tom Jones' vocals were perfect and all the backing tracks were great, but I was trying to think of something that could remedy the situation with Raquel's dreadful tracks. Plus I was sure that the session with Bob Hope and Raquel wasn't going to go very well, either.

The duet with Bob and Raquel was to the tune of the Beatles hit "Rocky Raccoon." In the skit, they were dressed in western costumes and sing to each other. As we were preparing to record, I noticed that Raquel was chewing and smacking gum while telling lame jokes to Bob Hope. Meanwhile he was sitting there looking bored and not warming up to her at all. Bob turned to me and said that he had rehearsed his part and wanted to get started right away.

If dealing with Raquel Welch wasn't difficult enough, a major glitch occurred. I had prerecorded the intro for the song, which was a cue for them to come in on the vocals. Without this it would have been very hard for them to come in at the right time, especially for Raquel. I was scrambling to find it on the tape as quickly as possible when Raquel pointed her finger at me and called out, "See, I told you he doesn't know what the fuck he's doing!" I was angry and mortified that all this shit was happening in front of Bob Hope. Then a miraculous thing happened . . . Bob stood up, pulled me aside, and said, "Look, I have to go to a party for Bing Crosby, but I'll be back in a few hours. Don't have her around when I get back, okay, son?" Right after Bob left, we found that intro at the end of the song. One of the engineers had put it at the end instead of the front by mistake! The only good thing about that was it gave Bob and the rest of us the opportunity to work without Raquel.

Just as he promised, a few hours later, Bob returned with a few of his good buddies. He was in a great mood and we were ready to go. Bob nailed his vocals on the first take. David Winters bought a bottle of top-shelf scotch and brought it to the studio for Bob, in apology for the mess that happened earlier. Bob opened the bottle right then and invited us all to drink with him, and it turned into a mini wrap party with Bob Hope telling one hilarious story after another. We were laughing so hard and it felt so good after the tension we went through earlier. As Bob was leaving he thanked me for keeping Raquel away from the session.

A couple of weeks later it was time to do vocal overdubs with Raquel. By this time her meanness extended to just about everyone, and we spent an excruciating two days in the studio without a good vocal part to show for it. When David reviewed the recordings, he was horrified. He called me to say, "I'll never be able to work in television again if we can't fix her vocals!" He decided to "augment" Raquel's vocal parts. David knew a professional singer who agreed to help us. It took over sixty hours of working on the vocals to get them right and she did an exceptional job.

Raquel! aired in April 1970 on CBS and was a big hit! The ratings were through the roof (51% of US, source: ARB) and the network and sponsors were very pleased with the show. I was pleased, too. Pleased that I got through this project with my sanity.

CHAPTER 7

Linda Ronstadt and the Stone Poneys

L inda Ronstadt is a kind and talented woman. I worked with her early in her career when she was in the Stone Poneys, at Capitol Records. She was discovered when the Stone Poneys were playing in a club in Topanga, California, and the producer, Nik Venet, decided to sign them. He produced their first album, which introduced Linda and her fellow Poneys, Bob Kimmel and Ken Edwards, to the many music fans that fell in love with their music. Incidentally, the guitar players in the Stone Poneys were fantastic musicians and they impressed me with their talent as folk guitar pickers.

For the next album Nik said, "We're going to bring them in and put an orchestra with them." It was a bold move for their style of folk-rock songs and it worked. Jimmy Bond led the session and did many of the song arrangements, and I helped a bit on some of them.

Linda came into the studio and she was scruffy, the image of a hippie. But when she sang, it was just beautiful. Linda Ronstadt is a truly talented singer. She would sing live with the orchestra and was perfect. We were recording the song "Drifting" when Jesse Ehrlich, the cello player, made a mistake and we stopped. Linda looked over and then Jesse stood up and said, "I'm sorry, sweetheart, I made a mistake." Linda very matter-of-factly said, "It's okay; everybody fucks up." There was a brief hush and you could hear the band take a quick intake of breath in the studio. The shocked reaction by the string section was hilarious. They weren't used to hearing a woman say a "dirty" word. It was probably the first time many of those classical musicians had a chance to work closely with a young artist like Linda in the rock music genre. It was 1967, so there were many things we were trying in the way we were recording, but it forged new connections between the generations of musicians and artists.

I played on several songs that were featured on two top-selling Stone Poneys albums on Capitol Records, *Evergreen Vol. 2* and *Stone Poneys Vol. 3*. They were: "Different Drum," "December Dream," "Morning Dew," "Orion," "Stoney End," "Hobo," "Go Back Where You Stayed Last Night," "Some of Shelly's Blues," "Driftin'," "Autumn Afternoon," "Star and a Stone," "By the Fruits of Their Labors," and "Wings."

One of my highlights from that work was playing the harpsichord solo on "Different Drum." I was so touched to receive fan mail through Capitol Records back then from people asking who played the harpsichord solo. Jimmy Bond started kidding around with me, calling me "Wanda" for Wanda Landowska, who at the time was a famous classical harpsichordist.

One of the nicest things artists can do is give credit to the session players they work with and Linda did it on her *Greatest Hits* album. She thanked every musician that worked with her on each song. What a wonderful and classy thing to do! Linda really respected the musicians she worked with, and I will always respect her for being such a kind and thoughtful person and a talented artist.

Update

As I was working on this book, a journalist doing a story for the *Wall Street Journal* about Linda's book *Simple Dreams* contacted me for an interview. In her book and the article she talks about my harpsichord playing in her story about "Different Drum." I also learned that Linda has Parkinson's disease and it has affected her voice. What a loss to the world that we won't hear her perform live or on new recordings anymore. I hope someone will discover a new medication or a cure for this. I feel very fortunate to know Linda and I wish her well.

CHAPTER 8

Lynda Carter—No Wonder

I had been in and out, doing loads of gigs, when I was contacted by Ron Samuels, who was manager and married to Lynda Carter. I knew him since he was a gofer and did the errands for Julie Sharr, who was Nancy Sinatra's manager.

I was at Raleigh Studios rehearsing when Ron came by to say, "I want to use your band's rhythm section with Lynda." It was a great band that had Chet McCracken on drums, Dave Coy on bass, Bobby Torres on percussion, Chuck Camper on reeds, and Randy Strom on guitar and Chapman stick, plus the Faragher Brothers.

Visually and musically, that show was one of the best shows you could ever see. Lynda has talent as a singer and danced well, too. Johnny Harris, who did a lot of Tom Jones' arrangements, did the arrangements for Lynda's show. Johnny is a great English guy! He led the orchestra and, of course, my band as well.

We did several shows on tour with Lynda Carter. The production included some great background singers and a brilliant production of laser lights in the show. When the curtains opened, you couldn't see her because the dancers surrounded her. Then a cloud of fog would rise and out came Wonder Woman, Lynda Carter. Then the lasers, one by one, would pull up and the dancers performed in sync with the laser show. It was absolutely beautiful! They were bouncing lasers off mirrors to create all the effects. In those days you could do it that way because safety regulations weren't in place yet regarding the danger of blinding someone if the laser went astray.

Lynda Carter was religious, so there were times we'd go to open our music and we would find a little book in there about Christianity. She appreciated us and was always nice to the band. I loved working with Lynda Carter, but Ron Samuels became one of my least favorite people (to put it mildly).

From the get-go he and I were at odds, but it was in Reno, our last gig on the tour, when Ron informed me that he was not going to pay us that night. We got paid weekly, but Ron said, "We'll send you the checks when we get back to Beverly Hills."

All of the guys were going to be splitting up after that night, going to other gigs and tours, so we weren't all going back to LA after this show. And I knew Ron had the checkbook with him! This conversation was taking place before our first show of the night, and I told him we needed our paychecks that night. Ron said, with no remorse, "Sorry, you'll have to wait."

So, we did the first show and went on break. Chet McCracken discovered he'd torn his clothes, so they sent the wardrobe mistress up to fix Chet's tear. This woman was the number one gossipmonger of all time and worshiped Lynda Carter. She would report everything and anything to her. So, we were sitting there and Chet asked me, "Are we going to get paid or not?" The other guys started in on me, too. "Are we going to get our checks?" And I said, "Look, I really don't know." Then it hit me. I said, "Fuck this! I know he's got the checkbook!" The wardrobe mistress was there working on Chet's costume, so I knew whatever I said to Chet was going right back to Lynda and Ron. I said, "Chet, you know, if we don't have our money before we start the second show, we're not doing the second show. That's the way I feel. I'm the leader of the rhythm section, it's our band, and I don't think we should play." The woman finished sewing very quickly and left.

We had less than an hour before the next show when, all of a sudden, in came Ron Samuels with a security guard. "Don, I need to talk to you," said Ron, trying to be tough. I said, "Fine," and I walked out the room with Ron and the guard. Ron said, "I told you I'll pay you when we get back." I said, "No, you won't; you and the guard can do whatever you want, but I guarantee if you put one hand on me, you'll never be able to breathe through your nose again."

And now the guard was looking like, *What the fuck did I get into?* I said, "We need our checks now, so don't bullshit me. I know you have the checkbook. If we don't have our checks, we won't do the second show." I continued, "I feel sorry for Lynda because I'm sure if it was up to her, we'd be paid right now." The guard and Ron left, and I went back into the break room. The guys had heard everything I said to Ron. Dave Coy said to me, "Goddamn, Don! I thought you were gonna open up a can of whoop ass!" I'd never heard that line before, but it was just the thing to break the tension for me and the rest of the guys, and we all laughed.

A few minutes later, in came the security guard with the checks. The checks weren't handwritten; they were already printed out! And the date on the check was the current date. Proof positive that Ron was a major asshole because none of this needed to have happened.

Before the second show I went to see Lynda because she was upset and I told her this situation did not reflect how I felt about working with her. I explained that it was just her husband/manager I had a problem with, and she accepted that and was fine with me. Lynda and Ron were only married for another year after that.

CHAPTER 9

Laura Nyro—The Stoned Soul Session

I was on a recording session for Laura Nyro at RCA studios in 1968. She usually recorded in New York, so this was a rare opportunity. Laura was a very talented composer and artist whose songs were recorded by many different groups and artists. She released a few very popular albums of her own, as well. One of the many big hits she wrote was "Stoned Soul Picnic," which was recorded by the 5th Dimension.

On this session I worked to record the song "Save the Country." After the morning session, the band went on a lunch break and we came back a few minutes early. Laura had baked some brownies and brought them to the studio, so she shared them with us. She also brought some milk to go with them. Wow, those brownies were delicious, and with ice-cold milk, it was a perfect treat to get the session started again, or so I thought . . .

We were all sitting around at first, enjoying the brownies, and then we had to get ready to start playing. After a few minutes I started feeling funny, light-headed and spacey. I felt like everything was going in slow motion and I think the other guys were feeling it the same way. All the guys, including me, were just sitting there, spaced out. Laura was sitting there, too, with a big smile on her face. She had baked marijuana into the brownies. No wonder we were trippin'!

The producer was Bones Howe. Bones is not only a great record producer, but he was also a top recording engineer. I also worked sessions with him when he was either the engineer, producer, or both on projects for the Association, the Mamas and the Papas, and more.

Bones had a couple of brownies, too, but he still wanted to finish the session. What a joke. There was no way we were going to be able to function for hours—these brownies were potent! Under the haze, Bones kept asking us to get it together. We just laughed. I don't know how Bones could even remember what song we were recording because we were all zombielike. Eventually he called the date (ended the session). At least we got one song recorded for Laura Nyro that day.

CHAPTER 10

The Dale Evans Story

I have been asked to tell the "Dale Evans story" so many times over the years that even new people I meet in music circles ask me, because this story has been passed around the industry as one of those "funny shit that happens in the studio" stories. In writing this story, I take a different approach than when I tell it, so you can truly appreciate the hilarity of the situation without my voice and mimicry. You'll understand what I mean as you read on.

In 1967 I was hired to do a session for Dale Evans at Capitol Records to record her Christian music album *It's Real*. The music director was the fabulous Anita Kerr, and members of her famous Anita Kerr Singers were among the twelve chorale singers for this session. Anita Kerr has a very distinguished career in music as a singer, composer, and arranger and was awarded a Grammy for Best Vocal Group Recording.

Dale Evans became famous on TV for starring with her husband, Roy Rogers, in *The Roy Rogers Show* during the 1950s. Dale Evans wrote the well-known, iconic song "Happy Trails" that she sang with Roy at the end of each episode of the program. Dale Evans and Roy Rogers remained very popular and were beloved as a wholesome, American couple. Wearing matching western outfits, Dale was the "Queen of the West" and Roy was the "King of the Cowboys." She also wrote and recorded many Christian songs. "The Bible Tells Me So" is among her most popular religious compositions. Imagine Dale Evans in your mind as I tell you the story.

The studio band was a trio: Earl Palmer on drums, Carol Kaye on bass, and me on piano. For the song we were about to record, Anita wanted just piano with Dale and the chorale singers, so Earl and Carol went out into the hall and took a break while we worked on this song. Because this was a session for a religious album with Dale Evans, the atmosphere in the studio was very respectful and courteous—the usual joking around or coarseness was not going on.

We got started on the first take and I noticed Dale, who sang with a VERY pronounced vibrato all the time, sang off-key in different parts of the song. Anita stopped us and asked us to go again, but she didn't mention to Dale that her part was sounding off-key. On take two it happened again. I was listening to her sing through the headphones while I was playing: Dale was sometimes flat, sometimes sharp, and her vibrato accentuated and amplified the notes that were off. Anita asked us to go again, still not saying anything to Dale Evans about being off-key. Take three, same thing happened, and I started to wonder, *Why doesn't anyone say something to her?* All of the chorale singers had headphones on as well, and these singers were the best vocalists in Los Angeles. They must have been hearing the same thing I was. Since I was not the music director, and Anita was, I did not overstep her authority and speak up about Dale's not hitting the notes, even though it was killing me to keep it inside.

By the fourth take, the chorus of the song was starting to strike me as funny. The lyrics of the chorus were: "He's coming, Jesus is coming, I know he is coming, Jesus is coming someday," and Dale's vibrato was so heavy you could row a boat through it, not to mention it was up and down (literally), sharp and flat, along with the chorale singers who repeated the words as they sang in response to Dale. For example, Dale would sing solo "He's coming" (flat-sharp), then the chorale singers would repeat the "He's coming" but in perfect tune, and it would go back and forth like that for each line of the chorus. The repetition of lyrics, Dale's over-the-top vibrato and singing off-key, the chorale singers' responding, all combined to start a storm of laughter inside me. I wondered why none of the chorale singers were laughing or saying something to Anita.

We went take after take on the song, yet Anita never told Dale she was singing sharp or flat. I think Anita didn't want to embarrass Dale and hoped she would just hit the right key eventually, but in the meantime it was torture to keep myself composed. For the next two takes, every time we got to the chorus I was biting my lips, squinting, holding my breath, trying to think of sad stuff, you name it, to keep from laughing out loud. I started sweating and silently pleading for Anita to tell the "Queen of the West" that her singing was horribly hilarious before I did.

Then it happened . . . on the seventh take, I lost it! I burst out in the most explosive howl of a laugh ever in the history of laughing, right in the middle of the sharp-flat, overvibrating vibrato "He's coming" that Dale sang and I could not stop. I was doubling over trying not to pee in my pants, my side hurt, and tears were streaming from my eyes, I was laughing that hard. Until that moment, the mood in the studio had been reverent and serious. Anita, who was shocked and appalled that I was laughing, said, "How dare you disrupt the session like this, Don!" I could barely talk and when I did, it just made it worse because I couldn't talk, I only laughed more. Anita was so mad and embarrassed she told me to get up and get out. She said, "If you don't mind, I will finish this myself!" I thought to myself, *Good, and you try to keep a straight face while doing so*, while I laughed all the way to the door.

When I went out into the hall, Earl and Carol wanted to know what happened and I told them (still laughing) that I got fired for laughing. I told them the whole story, which got them laughing, too. Earl Palmer started telling other musicians that I got fired for laughing in the Dale Evans session, and that is how my "Dale Evans story" started to spread, and it got so popular among all of the Wrecking Crew players, producers, and friends because they all wanted me to tell the story.

I still got paid for the session, actually for two sessions, which I was contracted for, because the record company didn't want to have to explain to the union that I had been fired for laughing.

CHAPTER 11

Marilyn Chambers—Looking at Her Differently

M arilyn Chambers was a famous adult film star and is best known for her role in the X-rated film *Behind the Green Door.* She also had a modeling career prior to that film and was pictured on the box of Ivory Snow laundry soap as a young mom holding a baby. This brought her even more attention because this picture was still being used on Ivory Snow when *Behind the Green Door* came out. Along that wide spectrum of fame, Marilyn Chambers had many talents and opportunities to show her versatility before her passing in 2009.

In 1974 I discovered how multitalented Marilyn was, when I worked with her on a live cabaret show she did at the Riverboat Restaurant in the Empire State Building in New York. Marilyn Chambers was a smash and her show at the Riverboat went on for four months.

The producer David Winters, who I worked with on many TV projects, hired me to be the music director and arrange all of the music for her live show. When I met Marilyn the first time, she asked me if I had seen *Behind the Green Door.* I told her I hadn't, which was true, and she urged me to go see it.

I was impressed with Marilyn from the start. She was not only beautiful, she was focused and hardworking, taking the preparation for the show very seriously because she wanted to prove she was more than an adult film actress. Marilyn had a good voice, but she wanted to sing perfectly, so she had a voice coach working with her. She also rehearsed every day with her choreographer, Joe Cassini, to perfect her dance routine. Marilyn had a delightful personality and a great sense of humor.

She would come to my house to go over the music with me and we'd enjoy having tea with my wife in our kitchen, chatting like we all had been friends for years. We learned that she was a junior Olympic gymnast in high school, and before we knew it, my sons, David and Justin, who were twelve and nine at the time, were getting tumbling lessons from Marilyn Chambers in my living room!

While we worked on the song arrangements for her show, Marilyn would ask me if I had seen *Behind the Green Door* yet. I told her I didn't have time to go see the movie; I only had a few weeks to do the arrangements and then rehearse the show with her and the band. But really, I didn't want to see the movie because I didn't want to change how I saw her.

One time Marilyn asked if I could come to her house to work on the music because her schedule was so busy she didn't have time to come to mine. She said she had a piano at her house, so I agreed. I arrived at her house, rang the bell, and Marilyn opened the door naked. I was speechless, and Marilyn said, "Oh, I was having a photo shoot here and we just finished." I didn't make any comments to her about her nudity, but I saw that she was very naturally beautiful. She led me to the room where her piano was and put on a robe. We tried to work on the music, but her piano was in terrible shape, so out of tune, and it had other problems. I told Marilyn I couldn't work on that piano and we had to resume work at my house. Before I left, she asked me again if I had seen her movie and again I told her I didn't have time. We had been working together for five weeks and only had a couple more weeks to work and rehearse before the show opened.

Later that evening my brother-in-law Jim came to my house to tell me *Behind the Green Door* was playing in Beverly Hills and I should go see it. I told him that I didn't want to see it, but he kept pushing me, saying, "Come on, I'll go with you!" Between him and Marilyn's nagging, I gave in and went with Jim to see *Behind the Green Door* that night.

Two days later, Marilyn came over to work on the music. I was at the piano, playing, and she was standing next to me, singing. When we stopped so I could make some notes on the music, she leaned over and whispered, "You saw it." I replied, "Yes, but how did you know?" Marilyn said, "You're looking at me differently." Busted!

CHAPTER 12

Cher and Sonny

I remember the day I met Cher. It was in 1962 and I had arrived at Gold Star Studios for a session with Phil Spector and was walking from my car to the studio, when a VW van pulled up and stopped next to me. It was Frank Baldwin (who managed songwriters) and he opened up the van door and said, "Hey, Don, this is Cher; would you take her in? Phil is expecting her." I said, "Sure," and I introduced myself to her. Cher had a sweet smile and looked very young. Later I learned she was only sixteen years old, but she seemed older, confident and shy at the same time, and I saw a twinkle in her eyes. Cher followed me into the studio and I took her to the booth where Phil was. I introduced her to Phil and he pointed to a chair in the booth, indicating she should sit there.

Cher started working on Phil's record projects as a background singer and that is how she met Sonny Bono, who was the promo man for Philles, Phil's record company. Cher sang background on many of the big hits Phil Spector produced that I played on, like the Ronettes' "Be My Baby" and the Righteous Brothers' "You've Lost That Lovin' Feelin'."

Cher became friends with Sonny Bono and not long after that, they got married and Sonny started to produce himself and Cher as a duo, Caesar and Cleo. I played on those first sessions, and when Sonny decided they should go out as Sonny and Cher, I was there on those sessions as well, playing on "Baby Don't Go," "I Got You Babe," and "The Beat Goes On."

In the very early part of their career I was booked to play in a huge concert in San Francisco that took place at the Cow Palace. Tom "Big Daddy" Dona-hue and Bobby Mitchell were popular DJs on KYA (now KOIT) and friends of Phil Spector. Phil had a promotional idea to produce a big concert with several of his artists and a few others like Sonny and Cher on the bill. For the weeks leading up to the concert, Tom, Bobby, and the other DJs promoted it on KYA, and this also made certain that they played all of the current hits by the artists in the concert very heavily.

I was the music director and one of the keyboard players in a very large, thirty-piece band that included a full horn section for this concert. It was a very challenging gig compiling and handling all of the charts and arrangements for all these different artists that were going to perform. One of the artists performing that day was Dobie Gray, who was going to sing "The In Crowd." Well, I never got the charts for it in advance, so the band could not rehearse the song. I asked Dobie if he brought the charts with him and he replied, "No, Don, but everybody knows that song." Regardless if it's a song that everyone knows, for a professional gig and for a band that has not played the song together, we needed the charts. But somehow we managed to get through it. Anyway, for Sonny and Cher, it was their first major concert in front of a huge audience and the crowd loved them.

I also worked on a TV special called *The Sonny & Cher Nitty Gritty Hour*. It was a Winters/Rosen production, and I was hired by David Winters, who I worked with on the *Raquel!* TV special and others. Sandy Baron was the writer and Joe Cassini was the choreographer. This show came out prior to their very popular weekly TV variety show, *The Sonny & Cher Comedy Hour.*

Throughout the years Cher and I have been good friends, whether working on projects or just out and about. There have been many times I have run into Cher at the airport, especially when I was touring with Nancy Sinatra. I also saw Cher quite often in Las Vegas when she was performing there at the same time I would be in Vegas with Nancy Sinatra. When Cher sees me, I'm always greeted with a big hug.

I might have worked with Cher after she went out as a solo artist, but timing never worked out for it. There was one time when Nancy took a break for a few years to have her two daughters and Sonny approached me to be their music director for a tour. Sonny was a penny-pincher when it came to salary. He offered me five hundred dollars a week but I had to decline his offer; even though I would have loved to work with Cher, the pay was way too low.

A few years later, I was hired for an overdub session to play piano on a song Cher recorded as a duet with her son, Elijah Blue Allman. The song was "Crimson and Clover," which is on the soundtrack for the film *A Walk on the Moon.* Cher told the producer that she wanted a certain sound for the piano that only Don Randi can do. I am very flattered that she thought of me for the song.

Cher has always been a faithful supporter of the musicians who were part of the Wall of Sound and the Wrecking Crew, and we all continued to work with her throughout the years. I am very delighted that Cher became so successful in many ways and continues to record hit albums and perform in concerts.

CHAPTER 13

Darlene Love and the Blossoms

D arlene Love was the consummate background singer for so many hit recordings, but she has always been so much more. Without question, her
voice is like an angel's, but what makes Darlene one of the best vocalists of
any day is her natural talent to pick up on a song and musical arrangement
immediately and enhance it. Music fans have connected with so many of the
songs Darlene has sung because of her soulful delivery and ability to sing in
just the right style for the music. In fact, Darlene has such an amazing ear
for vocals that she has helped many times with the vocal arrangements on
several hit songs.

The day I started working for Phil Spector on recording sessions was
when I met Darlene, who sang lead on the number one hit "He's a Rebel," but
the song was credited to the Crystals. I was amazed at how calm she was with
Phil even during his most demanding moments. There were plenty of times
that could have been very stressful during these sessions, which was why Hal
Blaine, Tommy Tedesco, and I would cut up for fun. Though Darlene is a little
shy at first, soon she opened up and her warm personality kept things easygo-
ing and friendly. Darlene has a wonderful laugh, which I enjoy hearing.

Darlene sang background on nearly all of the hits that Phil Spector produced, which meant that she and I worked a lot together. And, of course, she
worked closely with the artists that we recorded, and formed friendships
with a few of them. One friendship she had was with Bill Medley of the Righteous Brothers, and she worked closely with him on their songs, including

"You've Lost That Lovin' Feelin'." I played on several Righteous Brothers songs, but one song, "Brown Eyed Woman," written by Bill, was probably for Darlene Love.

As a member of the Blossoms (with Fanita James, Gracia Nitzsche, and Jean King) Darlene has performed background vocals on most of the songs I have also played on. The Blossoms also toured with Nancy Sinatra as her background singers for several dates. She really loved having the Blossoms singing background for her because they were so terrific. On one leg of a tour with Nancy, we had an unexpected delay at the Cleveland Airport. Fanita James had family in the area, so she phoned one of her sisters and soon there were twenty of her relatives there in the airport terminal with us. We all had a wonderful time visiting with them, laughing, and the time went by so fast that soon we had to say good-bye and get on our flight. Nancy, being the generous person that she is, gave Darlene and the Blossoms a segment of the set to perform a few songs of their own.

One song that is most recognized by music fans being a Darlene Love hit is "Christmas (Baby Please Come Home)" that is included on the hit album *A Christmas Gift for You from Philles Records*, which is probably the best rock 'n' roll Christmas album of all time. I played on every song on the album and Darlene sang lead on nearly every song, except the ones with the Ronettes.

Darlene Love and her sister Edna Wright came into my club, The Baked Potato, one night after we had been working on a recording of her group, the Blossoms, in a studio. I mentioned to her I was performing with my band at my club if she wanted to come out. I wasn't sure she would stop by, but when I saw that she had made it to the club, I asked her and Edna if they would come up and sing with the band. Darlene is a little shy so she declined, but I didn't want to miss an opportunity to have her sing at The Baked Potato, so I put a really long cord on the mic and took it to where she sat and I asked her to sing "Amazing Grace." We were treated to an AMAZING performance! Darlene and her sister were singing in harmony and they were making key changes to higher and higher keys and you could feel the energy of the moment, like the roof of the club was lifting off. Incidentally, Edna Wright was the lead singer in the trio Honey Cone in the early '70s among other record projects she has done.

There were a few years that Darlene stopped working in the music business, but I am so happy that she decided to perform and record again.

CHAPTER 14

Bobbie Gentry

B obbie Gentry, who rose to fame with her single "Ode to Billie Joe," was a neighbor of mine. She and Kelly Gordon lived up the hill from me on Nichols Canyon Road, which was convenient when I worked on her *Local Gentry* album because I could walk to her house to meet with Bobbie and Kelly, who was the producer. The songs I played and arranged were "Fool on the Hill," "Casket Vignette," and "Recollection."

I also was the music director and played piano in the band on a television music variety show that starred Bobbie Gentry and featured Noel Harrison. *Spring Thing* was produced in 1974 and I remember the taping of the opening of the show, which featured Bobbie singing, dressed in a tight white jumpsuit. The opening was probably the sexiest scene on TV at that time. The music began and the camera was focused closely on Bobbie Gentry's legs and then moved up her body very slowly, while she sang the song. As the camera shot moved closer to her face, the shot started to pull out a little and once the camera was on her face, the camera pulled out to show her standing on the stage.

Though I wasn't aware while we were in production how the camera shot was being directed, later David Winters, who was the producer of the show, told me how surprised he was that the opening was approved for air. As required, the show was submitted to S&P (Standards and Practices) before it could air on CBS in prime time. S&P is the legal department that reviews programs to make sure there isn't any inappropriate content in a show before it airs on public television. S&P did not require the opening to be changed.

However, another change was requested by S&P: A comedian that was on the show was told by S&P to edit his material to remove the word *hell* from his comedy monologue. The comedian edited his monologue, but I heard that he complained that the word *hell* was not nearly as inappropriate as the very provocative close-up of the camera slowly traveling up Bobbie Gentry's body.

CHAPTER 15

Cass Elliot

C ass Elliot, who was a member of the Mamas and the Papas, was also my neighbor. Her home was up the hill from mine, near Woodrow Wilson and Mulholland Drives in the Hollywood Hills. I played piano on her 1972 album, *Cass Elliot*, produced by Lewis Merenstein.

The album was such a joy to do and Cass was an amazing singer. The songs on the album were standards beautifully arranged by the fantastic jazz musician Benny Golson. Benny played the saxophone and wrote one of the all-time jazz hits, "Killer Joe." I felt the album showcased Cass Elliot as a consummate solo vocalist and I'm sure she would have gone to new heights in her career and life. It's so sad that Cass Elliot, at thirty-two years old, passed away just two years after that album was released.

CHAPTER 16

Elvis Presley—A Little Less and a Lot More

People often ask me, "Did you ever get to work with Elvis?" Well, yes, I did! In 1968 I did several sessions with Elvis. One project was for the NBC-TV *Elvis' '68 Comeback Special*, playing piano with an orchestra in the scoring sessions. Tommy Tedesco, Mike Deasy, and Hal Blaine, my friends from the Wall of Sound band, also played in this production.

Some of the music for this show was prerecorded in the studio, but Elvis liked to sing live with the band, so my story with Elvis starts one Saturday evening when we were recording "Jailhouse Rock." FYI, in a union gig, if you work on a Saturday you must get paid time and a half and working on Sunday is double scale. Some of us in the group were being paid at a higher scale, as well.

We recorded at United Western Recorders in Hollywood. United Western is still there today as East West Studios. This is one of the top recording studios in Los Angeles. It's where the Beach Boys' *Pet Sounds* was recorded, Frank Sinatra and his daughter Nancy recorded "Something Stupid," the Mamas and the Papas recorded "California Dreamin'," and many, many more well-known records were cut.

The session started around 4:00 p.m. and everything was going fine until around 11:15 p.m. when we were trying to get the vocal tracks with Elvis down, but he was having trouble coming in on cue. He came over to the piano and asked me to listen to the playback in his headphones. Man! No wonder he couldn't hear his cue; the engineer had every track coming through the headphones.

So, we started going back and forth with the engineer to adjust Elvis' playback. We did a few more takes. Meanwhile, the clock was ticking . . . it was 11:20, 11:40, 11:50 p.m., and we finally got the mix right in the headphones and Elvis was happy and ready to go again on the song. The cue Elvis sang was only ten seconds and he sang it live with the orchestra.

It was about 11:55 p.m. when the production manager came in with a frustrated expression. He was literally tapping his foot and pointing to his watch. He said to Elvis, "Can we get this wrapped up?" This did not sit well with Elvis. In fact, I did a quick look around the room and it seemed all of the guys' attention was on Elvis, waiting for his reaction. Elvis glared at the production manager, then after a pause he turned to me and asked, "Don, you hungry?" I said, "Yeah." Elvis said, "Me, too." Elvis then walked into the booth, and after a few seconds one of the producers said over the PA, "Lunch." So, the whole band went on break and the production manager couldn't do anything. Going on break also meant that we were still being paid.

Around 1:15 a.m. Sunday morning we all, including Elvis, came back from our break and got to the vocals and Elvis nailed it! It took less than five minutes to do the take. If the production manager hadn't pulled his impatient stunt, we probably would have finished just before midnight. Thanks to Elvis, the musicians, including me, got paid so well on this one gig that it was equivalent to working a week at regular scale. Not to mention a thrill to work with the legendary Elvis Presley.

Another Elvis project I worked on that year was for the film *Live a Little, Love a Little*. It was a musical that was released late in 1968, but it didn't do very well at the box office. One of the songs we did for this film was "A Little Less Conversation," written by Billy Strange and Mac Davis. The story behind this song is that the producer of the film came to the studio (MGM) where we were working on the other songs for the film. He told Billy Strange that he needed one more song for the film, so Billy came out into the studio and told us to take a thirty-minute break. We came back from break and Billy and Mac had just finished writing the song. They had the lyrics and the base melody written, so we, the band, came up with the arrangement on the fly.

Elvis was great on the vocals and I would estimate that we had that song cut in about two hours. The band featured Al Casey on guitar, Hal Blaine on drums, Larry Knechtel on bass, and me on piano.

"A Little Less Conversation" became much more popular than the film it was for. Almost thirty years after the film, "A Little Less Conversation" was rereleased as a remix with Elvis and became a global number one hit. The song has also been featured in a number of TV shows, films, and commercials. Recently the song was used in another remix format, by Junkie XL in the film *Megamind.*

Over the years I have received checks for the reuse and new use of the recording, which amounts to a lot more than I made for that day's session. The latest payments I received in 2014 were for the use of the song on Elvis-themed slot machines in Las Vegas. I'm a winner in many ways because of Elvis.

CHAPTER 17

Neil Diamond—Cracklin' Rosie

One of the very popular songs that Neil Diamond recorded and released was "Cracklin' Rosie." Its distinctive arrangement was my idea, but the song might have had a very different arrangement if it weren't for Hal Blaine.

I was in an overdub session with Hal Blaine for Neil Diamond to record new drum and piano parts for "Cracklin' Rosie," and while we were running through the song I was singing it to myself. I had a very strong feeling on how my part could be arranged that would really improve it. We finished the overdub in under an hour and the producer, Tommy Catalano, said we were great. While I was still sitting there I turned to Hal and said, "I know exactly what to do with this song, arrangement-wise." And that's all I said to Hal.

Next thing I knew, Hal went into the booth while I was sitting there writing a couple of notes for myself on my arrangement ideas. Then I looked up at the booth and saw through the glass that Hal, Tommy Catalano, and Neil Diamond were discussing something. Then Tommy came out of the booth, walked over to me, and asked if I wanted to go to Neil's house that afternoon and write the arrangement with him. I said, "I sure do!" That afternoon I worked with Neil and wrote the arrangement and the next day I recorded it.

The whole time I heard the song in my mind with Neil singing it and knew it was going to be a smash hit, and it was. "Cracklin' Rosie" was the first hit song I arranged and it was a number one hit on *Billboard* in 1970. I'm very proud of the arrangement I wrote and recorded for the song and it still thrills me today to hear it. Thanks, Hal!

CHAPTER 18

Dennis Cole

I produced a few songs with Dennis Cole that record company executive, Mike Curb was going to release on a record label I was involved in, Winro Records. Dennis was well known for being the handsome lead actor in the TV series *Felony Squad*. He also appeared in several popular series, like *Charlie's Angels*, *Three's Company*, and *Murder, She Wrote*, and he played Lance Prentiss on *The Young and the Restless*. Dennis was dating Mike Curb's sister at the time we recorded the songs. Three of the songs Dennis recorded were written by Christopher Kingsley. Unfortunately, Dennis Cole's album was never released.

Dennis Cole became a good friend of mine and he was also one of my neighbors on Nichols Canyon. Dennis was also a very good trumpet player and for a time he tried to get the rights to produce a movie on the life of the great trumpet player Chet Baker. He wanted me to work with him on the project as his technical adviser. It's a shame that Dennis never got a chance to produce a movie on Chet.

After his son, Joe Cole, was murdered, Dennis was devastated and didn't work as much in TV and eventually moved to Florida. He stayed in touch with me after he moved and would call me a few times a year to talk. Dennis Cole passed away in 2009 and I miss him and our friendship.

CHAPTER 19

Dean Martin

Working for Nancy Sinatra and her dad was good luck for anyone, but through them I had even more when I met Dean Martin and worked with him as well. One highlight with Dean was playing piano on his hit "Everybody Loves Somebody." I also played on a few other songs Dean recorded: "Everybody but Me," "Somewhere There's a Someone for Everyone," "Little Old Wine Drinker Me," and "I Will."

Here's a story about a recording session with Dean Martin. I believe this was in 1964, but I do remember this session took place a few days before Christmas. The record company's PR person arranged a stunt with KLAC-AM radio station in Los Angeles. It ran a call-in contest on-air during DJ Danny Dark's show to award ten seats at Dean's upcoming recording session. The winners were selected and they showed up at the studio on the day arranged. Jimmy Bowen was the producer and we were recording at Western with a full orchestra. The contest winners were seated in the studio with us and their chairs were not far from the piano I was playing. I noticed that most of the winners/fans were a mature group of mostly women around Dean Martin's age. Though Jimmy and the rest of us thought it might not work out with them in the studio, these fans were very respectful and they stayed very quiet when we recorded.

The part that was funny to me is probably a reason this wasn't the best PR idea the record company had. In recording sessions, Dean and the rest of the crew joked around and the language was often coarse. I watched as Dean, who might have been "relaxed" by a cocktail or two, start telling very adult and off-color jokes. I looked over at the fans. Some of the older ladies were obviously in shock. They were all still thrilled that they were in a Dean Martin recording session, but I am sure they all went home and told their friends how "wild" and foul mouthed the musicians and singers are in recording sessions.

Another story was a time that I played in the band on *The Dean Martin Show*, which was a weekly TV variety show that aired on NBC from 1965 to 1974. I played on a few of the shows, filling in on keyboards when needed in Dean's band. On one occasion the contractor, Al Lapin, called me at home around 12:30 p.m. and asked if I could come in by 2:00 p.m. because the show would start taping at 3:00 p.m. This was incredibly short notice, but I lived only ten to fifteen minutes from the studio, so I said yes to the job. Al said I would be playing the Hammond B3 for Olivia Newton-John. I quickly changed into my standard dark blue suit, white shirt, black tie, and black shoes and drove to NBC as soon as I could so I'd have enough time to go over the music and rehearse to be ready to play on time. I drove up to the gate that Al told me to check in at and the guard said he didn't have my name on the list. I told him I was there to play on *The Dean Martin Show* and the contractor, Al Lapin, was expecting me. This guard had a tough attitude and said he didn't care and my name was not on the list, so I couldn't enter. I asked the guard to call Al Lapin and he'd clear me, but he refused to do it. I stressed very strongly that I needed to be in the studio that instant, so we could start taping at three o'clock. The argument continued for a few more seconds, but it was a waste of time. I asked the guard for his name and left. I drove back home and as I walked in the door, my phone was ringing. It was Al and he asked, "Why aren't you here?" I told him about the guard and not being on the list, so Al told me to come right back and he'd have this cleared up. If only we had cell phones back then! Anyway, I hurried back to the studio and got to the gate and there was a different guard there. This time my name was on the list, but before I drove in I asked, "What happened to the other guard?" This guard said the other guy was new, that it was his first day. I think it may have been his last day, too.

I got into the studio and saw Al waiting for me, but he gave me a stern look and I couldn't figure out why. I got the music from the band's conductor and he gave me a rundown of the show and when my part on the B3 was going to be taped with Olivia Newton-John.

Before I arrived, Al had let the band know I would be there to play the B3. The trumpet players, Pete and Conte Candoli (the Candoli Brothers), were friends of mine, and Pete, who was known as a practical joker, had an idea to have Conte set me up with one of his practical jokes. Al Lapin was an efficient contractor who took his job very seriously and did things by the book (union rules), and that's why things ran smoothly without major problems or incidents when he was there. When he had a chance, Conte pulled Al aside and said, "You know about Don, don't you?" Al said, "Yeah, I know Don, but what, Conte?" Conte said, "Well, Don is a flirt and hits on all the pretty ladies and he tries to get their phone numbers." (I don't do this, by the way.) Conte added, "You better keep an eye on him with Olivia." Al said, "Thanks," and told Conte, "Don't worry; Don isn't going to flirt with the talent on THIS show." Al didn't suspect this was a joke because Conte was the more low-key and serious of the two brothers. Pete and Conte knew Al would be proactive to prevent an incident between Olivia Newton-John and me and told the whole band about the prank, so they were in on it and sat back and watched Al be a pain in my ass.

I rehearsed my part with the band and we had a short break before starting the segment with Olivia. Al came up and scolded me, "Don, you better watch yourself tonight. You don't talk to the talent, okay?" I said, "What?" Al said, "You know what I mean!" I didn't and was confused because I couldn't figure out why Al was being so tough on me. I looked over at the band members and they shrugged. It was turning into a nightmare of a gig, starting with the mix-up at the gate. When I was introduced to Olivia Newton-John, Al was there looking at me with a warning stare. I was thinking, *What the hell is Al's problem?*

After we finished taping the song with Olivia, I got up with the band and we all walked toward the break room. Pete, Conte, and the other band members started laughing and they told me all about the joke. Yeah, Pete and Conte got me that time!

A couple of weeks later I was called again to play on Dean's show and it all went great. We had a fifteen-minute break before taping the second half of the show and, as usual, the band went to the musicians' break room and in there are three phones on the wall. Two of the phones were direct lines to the musicians' exchanges (Arlen's Answering Service and Your Girl Answering Service), so band members could check messages and get important info on new gigs that were being offered. The other phone was just a regular line for other types of calls. Anyway, this time both of the exchange lines were dead and the only phone that was working was the regular line, so it meant that we'd have to line up and dial to our exchange to get our messages. This was aggravating enough, but one of the guys on the production crew, a grip, was using the only working phone.

This guy was a bit older than we were and was probably one of the production crew who had worked at NBC for years. He was dressed in the typical work pants, work boots, chambray shirt unbuttoned, and white T-shirt, and was unshaven. As the band (fifteen members) filled the break room around him, we were in sharp contrast, wearing our dark blue suits, white dress shirts, black dress shoes, and black ties. We heard him having an argument with his wife and it got pretty bad. He would say a couple of words like "yes dear" and "no dear" in a sarcastic tone, then hold the receiver away from his ear and we could hear his wife yelling at hm. While he held the receiver out, he looked at us, rolled his eyes, and made other facial and hand gestures (the finger) toward the phone. It was quite a show we were getting, but we didn't utter a word. After about five minutes the guy said, "OKAY!" and slammed the receiver down. I flinched and hoped he hadn't broken the only phone we had to use. He turned around and paused for a couple of seconds, as he realized he'd had a big audience for his "performance." We all stood there in silence, staring at him. Then he said, "You know, all cunts are pricks!!" We couldn't hold back. We all busted up laughing hysterically!

A Father and a Friend . . .

Dean Martin was a proud father and did everything he could to support his kids when they wanted to follow their dreams, especially in music. His son Dean Paul Martin was in the group Dino, Desi and Billy, and I played keyboards on their hit recordings. His daughter Deana Martin takes after her father as a wonderful singer and has recorded jazz CDs.

Dean's other daughter Gail also had a desire to sing and start a music career, so Dean got Jimmy Bowen to produce an album for her and asked him to hire me to come to his home to work with Gail on her vocals. This was a huge honor for me because Dean Martin was protective of his family's privacy and he invited only trusted friends to his home, especially if it involved his kids.

Dean had a grand piano in his living room. For a few weeks I came to his house to work there with Gail, playing piano while she learned the words and arrangements to the songs Jimmy Bowen chose for her album. As we worked, Dean would often pop his head in and give me that smile and a thumbs-up. I knew what he meant by that. He was glad that his daughter was happy doing what she loved. Even though the album did not become a hit, Gail was such a nice, down-to-earth person and worked really hard.

Dean Martin and Frank Sinatra had a very close friendship, as was evident to the public in the many performances and movies they did together. What really demonstrates how close a friendship can be is the way two friends can joke and be 100 percent supportive of each other at the same time. Next is a funny story of that support and humor that I saw between Frank and Dean . . .

This happened on the tour Nancy Sinatra did, opening for her dad. When we were playing at Caesars Palace in Las Vegas, many of Nancy's and Frank's friends and family came to the shows. When Frank asked Dean what night he would be coming to the show, Dean said he wasn't sure which night he could make it but would definitely let him know the date beforehand. With Frank not expecting to see him, Dean had a prank in mind and contacted Nancy to let her know that he was coming that night but to not tell her dad and be sure to watch from the stage during his set.

After Nancy's set and while comedian Charlie Callas was doing his bit, she told me to stay onstage with her and watch Dean Martin surprise her father.

She said Dean had something planned, but didn't know what it was going to be. Frank's set started and we stood in the wings, watching. Norma, my wife, and others joined us, watching and waiting. Frank did three songs in a row but Dean still had not done anything and we were getting anxious. I asked Nancy, "When is Dean going to do this?" She said, "I don't know, but if I know Dean, it's perfectly planned."

For the next number, all the lights went out onstage for several seconds, then the band started playing the intro to "One for My Baby." It was also completely dark in the house, except for candles on the tables. A pin spot (single spotlight) went on directly above Frank Sinatra, who was sitting on a barstool. He lit a cigarette, let the smoke swirl up into the spotlight, and then he began to sing . . . "It's a quarter to three. There's no one in the place 'cept you and me." There was a short, very dramatic pause at that moment in the song, leaving the audience mesmerized and completely silent. In that pause Dean Martin yelled out, "Who the fuck cares!" The band and the audience sat silently, shocked, for a few seconds, then Frank said, "There's only one person that could be! Can I have the house lights, please?" The lights went on in the room and Frank yelled out, "Dean, where are you?" Dean stood up from where he was sitting in the audience. Everyone, including Dean Martin and Frank, started to roar laughing. From where Nancy and I were watching, we could see just how Dean's surprise joke was not only funny but also a sign of friendship and appreciation to Frank from Dean.

A 1965 Wall of Sound recording session at Gold Star Studios in Hollywood. Don Randi is standing in the upper left corner. (Photo by Ray Avery/Getty Images)

Don Randi, Leon Russell, and Al De Lory in a recording session at Gold Star Studios. (Photo by Ray Avery/Michael Ochs Archives/Getty Images)

Tommy Tedesco and Don Randi in the studio at a Nancy Sinatra recording session in 1969. (Photo by Michael Ochs Archives/Getty Images)

Glen Campbell and Hal Blaine at a recording session. (Photo by Michael Ochs Archives/ Getty Images)

Anita Cortez, Al Criado, Bobby Economou, Norma Randi, Don Randi, Rob Whitsitt, Nancy Sinatra, and Phyllis Battle pose while on tour. (Author's collection)

A group shot of band members and dancers with the Nancy Sinatra show. Nancy herself is in the front row, fourth from right. (Author's collection)

Frank Sinatra and granddaughter Amanda Lambert enjoy an early morning of sledding in Lake Tahoe. (Author's collection; Frank Sinatra courtesy of Frank Sinatra Enterprises)

Don Randi and Amanda's sister, A.J. Lambert, build a snowman on the same Lake Tahoe outing. (Author's collection)

Dean Martin, Sammy Davis Jr., and Frank Sinatra in Palm Springs for a benefit concert. (Author's collection; Frank Sinatra courtesy of Frank Sinatra Enterprises)

Don Randi, Hal Blaine, Duane Eddy, John Garnache, Steve Douglas, and Ry Cooder playing the opening night of Duane Eddy's tour at The Baked Potato. (Author's collection)

Don Randi and Duane Eddy backstage at the Hollywood Bowl for the 50th Anniversary of Rock 'n' Roll at the Hollywood Bowl on June 20, 2008. (Photo by Mathew Imaging/ WireImage)

Phil Spector, Darlene Love, and Sonny Bono recording *A Christmas Gift for You from Philles Records* in 1963 at Gold Star Studios. (Photo by Ray Avery/Getty Images)

Bobby Hatfield and Phil Spector at a 1965 Righteous Brothers recording session at Gold Star Studios. Don Randi is at the grand piano, rear left. (Photo by Ray Avery/Getty Images)

Don Randi, Nancy Sinatra, and Phil Spector at The Baked Potato's thirtieth-anniversary event in 2000. (Author's collection)

Lee Hazlewood in front of a recording studio in Paris. (Author's collection)

Don Randi, Keely Smith (back to camera), Lou Morell, Jimmy Bowen, and Buddy Green at a recording session circa 1966. (Photo by Michael Ochs Archives/Getty Images)

Don Randi and David Axelrod in a recording session at Capitol Records Studios. (Author's collection)

CHAPTER 20

Neil Young and the One That Got Away . . .

E verybody's got a fishing story and I certainly have mine, but this one includes a twist and the brilliant artist, Neil Young.

In 1967 I was working with Neil Young in recording sessions produced by my good friend Jack Nitzsche, when Neil was still with the Buffalo Springfield. The album was *Buffalo Springfield Again*, and I wrote and played the piano solo on "Broken Arrow." Working on the project with Neil and Jack was very rewarding for me because they are as passionate as I am about the creative process of collaboration and improvisation in recording.

After the many hours of hard work in the studio that week, I suggested to Jack and Neil that we take a Saturday afternoon off and go out on my boat for some much deserved R&R. Jack thought it was a great idea and Neil was excited about it because he had never been out on the Pacific Ocean before. We went out of Marina del Rey, where my boat was docked, cruised a few miles north, and anchored about a half-mile off the Malibu Beach shore. I brought fishing poles and bait for us to use just for fun, so we cast out our lines and set the poles in the holders around the boat's rail, waiting for a catch. However, fish wasn't our priority for the location where I anchored the boat. We had another catch in mind that could be found with binoculars . . . girls on the beach.

The three of us were enjoying the view of the Malibu Beach shore, which was peppered with beautiful sunbathing ladies in bikinis. Neil commented that he had not truly understood how enchanting the California beach scene really was until now as he experienced and enjoyed the sun, the water, and the beauty all around. I loved to go out on my boat with friends, so this was a real treat for me, too.

After an hour of binocular passing, great conversation, and laughs, I heard one of the fishing pole's lines zinging. A fish must have taken the bait and it was Neil's pole, so I told him to grab it and get ready to reel in the catch. He was so excited, though a little nervous because he had never done ocean fishing before, but Jack and I coached him.

I told Neil to let the fish take the line out and when the fish stopped, that was when to start reeling it in. Neil did just as I instructed him to do and I could tell this must have been a large fish on the line by how far the pole bent when Neil was reeling in the line. He got the hang of the technique quickly and kept at it for quite a long time, reeling in the catch little by little. Even though Neil was getting tired, he was determined to bring that fish in.

After nearly an hour of Neil's persistence, the catch was close enough for us to see what kind of fish it was and its size. To our shock it was a blue shark. I was surprised that the fishing line held all this time, because it was a ten-pound line and it was evident that the shark was much heavier than ten pounds. Neil nearly dropped the fishing pole when he saw the shark, but Jack and I cheered him on to reel that shark in.

It took another half-hour but Neil did it . . . he reeled the shark close enough to the boat that we could clearly see it was about eight feet long and probably weighed more than a hundred pounds. I knew it had to be eight feet long because my boat was twenty feet long and the shark was nearly half the length of the boat. The shark looked like it was almost dead in the water, comatose from exhaustion. I didn't have anything on the boat that we could use to pull it up onto the deck, the shark was that big. Plus I didn't have anything to knock it out with if we did get it on my boat, so it would certainly thrash about and could capsize the boat and/or bite us. As Neil held the line, Jack and I tried to figure out what to do. Suddenly it jumped straight up out of the water right next to the boat in front of Neil, who was still holding tight to the pole. For a couple of seconds the shark and Neil were face to face. I wish I had a camera at that moment. Neil's face was white because all the blood drained from it as the shark looked right at him. A second later the shark jerked its head, which broke the line, and then it fell back into the water and swam away. When the shark broke the line, Neil fell back onto the deck of the boat, still holding the fishing pole, in a daze. The whole scene was incredible, a hundred times more exciting than any special effect that movies could achieve because it was real; you couldn't repeat what happened in a million years.

This is one of my favorite stories and I've told it many times because everyone loves it. A few years ago I was performing in Palm Springs, California, and told this story during a Q&A session between sets. A reporter from a local Palm Springs newspaper wrote a very nice review of my performance and added that I told the best fishing story she'd ever heard.

Bobby Furgo's Story

That Palm Springs gig I did included Bobby Furgo (violin) and John DePatie (guitar), and Bobby told me a funny story that happened to him at another gig. Sometimes, at gigs that musicians end up taking, they often feel unappreciated. He was playing at a restaurant/club, and what often happens when the audience is eating and drinking is they don't pay much attention or show appreciation for the performance of musicians playing for them. While Bobby was playing he noticed a couple seated at a table a few feet away from the stage. They would smile and nod at him while he was playing and they seemed to be really enjoying his performance. They didn't talk while he played and Bobby felt that was so nice of the couple to be so polite during the show. After his set, he went over to the couple to thank them and when he got close to the table, he realized the couple was using sign language to communicate with each other. Bobby Fargo laughed and smiled to himself, thinking this nice couple didn't hear him, either.

CHAPTER 21

Duane Eddy

The "twangy guitar" sound played by Duane in his hit recordings of "Peter Gunn" and "Rebel Rouser" is his signature sound and famous for it. That sound became the "Duane Eddy" guitar sound among record producers and professional session guitar players. Duane Eddy has been an inspiration to many young musicians. I want to start my chapter on Duane Eddy with a story he told me a few years ago . . .

Duane told me this happened in Valley Arts Guitar music store, which was a well-known full music store that specialized in guitars; they also repaired many types of instruments as well as guitars. I used to go there myself to get my keyboards worked on by Doug Walraven. The store, owned by Al Carness and Mike McGuire, was located on Ventura Boulevard near Laurel Canyon. Many top guitar players back then (1970s through the late 1980s) would go there to have custom work done or repairs on their guitars, and it was a hangout for many of them as well.

One day, Duane went to Valley Arts to get some work done on his guitar when Lee Ritenour and Tommy Tedesco happened to be there. Tommy and Lee were good friends and were talking about various gigs they had just played, etc., while they were picking up some parts for their guitars. Just before Duane arrived, Tommy was sharing with Lee how on his last session the producer kept asking him to give him more of the "Duane Eddy" sound. When Tommy saw Duane walking into the store, he yelled out, "Hey, Duane," to get his attention and everyone in the store turned to look at Tommy. Then he said, "Hey, Duane, does anyone ever ask you to play like me?" This caught Duane totally off-guard, but all he could do was laugh because of the way Tommy looked as he said it.

It was in the early 1990s when Duane Eddy was living just outside of Nashville that Steve Douglas, a close friend to both Duane and me, talked Duane into forming an all-star band to do a short concert tour of ten dates on the West Coast. The band included Steve Douglas on sax, Ry Cooder on guitar, Duane on guitar, Hal Blaine on drums, John Garnache on bass, and me on keyboards. We opened the tour at my club, The Baked Potato, for two nights.

On the opening night, the club was sold out and the audience was filled with many music greats. Linda Ronstadt, Larry Carlton, Tom Petty, Jackson Browne, Joni Mitchell, James Taylor, and Lee Ritenour were among the guests packed into the club for the show. Before the show Hal Blaine and I were out back in the parking lot, talking, and Duane came out to find us.

Duane was wearing a silk shirt and when we saw him, it was soaked and stuck to his skin. I asked Duane, "What was wrong?" He said, "Did you see who was out there?" Duane's wife, Deed, was with him and said, "Take it easy, Duane." Apparently Duane got nervous seeing our peers, who were renowned music artists, there to see our show and especially him. I had never seen Duane like that, ever, and the silk shirt he wore couldn't hide it. He didn't have anything to be nervous about because he is so talented and the show was brilliant. Duane's performance was incredible, and Ry Cooder played solos that were out of this world!

I really enjoyed playing with this group and the whole tour was great! Every concert was sold out and the fans really loved the shows. It was one of the best and most fun tours I've done. I had the time of my life performing with my best friends who are also phenomenal musicians.

In 2008 I had another once-in-a-lifetime opportunity to perform live with Duane Eddy and the Hollywood Bowl Orchestra at the 50th Anniversary of Rock 'n' Roll at the Hollywood Bowl. We did Duane Eddy's and Henry Mancini's versions of "Peter Gunn" and it was fantastic. The audience loved it.

CHAPTER 22

Phil Spector—Tomorrow's Sound Today

I had met and became good friends with Phil when I was playing at various clubs around Los Angeles with my trio. That was before I started working regularly on recording dates. The first time I worked with Phil Spector on a recording session was when I was hired by my friend Steve Douglas (sax) to play piano on "He's a Rebel." From that day forward I became one of the regulars on Phil's Wall of Sound band and played on many of the hits that he produced in the 1960s.

When we met, Phil already had a hit record with the Teddy Bears, "To Know Him Is to Love Him." This song was released on the label Doré Records and was Phil's first number one hit. The title of the song came from what is written on his father's gravestone. Phil wasn't twenty-one yet and his mother, for reasons I don't understand, blocked the royalty payments from the record company to Phil. Phil wanted his royalties, so he filed a lawsuit to prevent his mother from being able to block payments from Doré. Phil asked me to testify for him as a character reference.

At the court hearing Herb Newman, one of the owners of Doré Records, was there along with Phil Spector, his mother, his sister, and me. I was really nervous, so in my head I kept going over what I was going to say because I didn't want to blow it and prevent Phil from getting what he deserved. His mother testified ahead of me and went on and on about why she did not want Phil to get this money. After she finished her rant, the judge ruled in favor of Phil and said, "If this young man wrote and performed the song on this recording, then he has a right to receive his share of the royalties." The judge struck his gavel. The whole thing had happened so fast it confused me. I said, "Wait, I didn't get to speak." Phil turned to me and said, "It's over; you don't have to. I'm getting my money." I was relieved! And with the money Phil got from Doré Records, he was able to start his own label, Philles, and produce artists independently.

Before session work with Phil and other producers filled my schedule, I played in Las Vegas with my trio. One time, when I got back from a really successful gig in Vegas, I had an idea to form a casual band for a lounge act at a Vegas casino with Phil Spector playing guitar. I told him about my idea and he really liked it, so we formed the band and started rehearsing. Most people forget or don't realize that Phil is a great guitar player and singer. The band we formed was: Mike Bermani on drums, Steve Douglas on sax and flute, Phil on guitar, and me on piano. There was also a tall female singer in the group and a bass player, but their names escape me. Though we rehearsed, had fun, and put together a great set, we never did take the show to Vegas because recording sessions were starting to take over our lives.

I worked often on Phil Spector's sessions, and the roster of hit songs I played on with many terrific artists grew quickly. "Da Do Ron Ron" by the Crystals and "Be My Baby" by the Ronettes were the next two big hits I played on after "He's a Rebel." I also played on hits produced by Phil for artists and bands, like the Righteous Brothers, Ike and Tina Turner, Bob B. Soxx and the Blue Jeans, the Checkmates, Darlene Love, and the Blossoms. At the end of the book I've added a list of popular artists and songs I have played on.

At the end of a recording session, Phil invites the band members to listen to the playback in the booth. I always appreciated that about Phil because it is hard to know how the song really sounds when you are playing. It might have been on the session when we were recorded "Be My Baby." It was a session that spanned nine and a half hours, so we were pretty tired, but when we heard the playback in the booth, all of us knew this was a hit song. It was mind blowing and we were excited about the work we just did. After all of the pats on the backs, the guys started to pack up to go home. I was still in the booth when Larry Levine, the engineer, discovered the Record button had been pressed during that playback and erased the whole song. I saw Larry felt awful and I felt bad for him because he is a top-notch engineer and this was just a crazy mistake. Then I looked at Phil and was waiting for him to explode, but he didn't. Phil uttered a couple of expletives, but he remained calm and just said, "Get everyone back in here and let's do this again." It took another two hours to record the song again, but it still came out fantastic.

It was on recording sessions with Phil Spector that I met Sonny Bono, who was Phil's promo man for his record company. The promo man makes sure that the radio stations played the current record releases by the label. In the early '60s payola—paying cash to radio station managers to play certain songs more often—was a common and accepted practice. Sonny always had a big wad of money with him for that purpose. Sonny also wanted to be a part of the music Phil was producing, so Phil would occasionally have Sonny play tambourine on songs.

Phil was a maniac about checking radio stations to make sure they were playing his records. In his car, he had every radio station that played pop, rock, or R&B music set to the buttons on the radio. In the early '60s it was common to have three or four different Philles Records singles from different artists out at the same time. If you were riding in the car with Phil, he was constantly pushing the buttons to hear the songs being played, and quite often every station was playing one of his releases. If he landed on a station and it wasn't playing one of his songs, he'd say to Sonny, "What happened to my station?!" It was Phil's cue to Sonny that he needed to make a visit to the station manager.

This radio habit of Phil's gave Sonny an idea for a prank. Phil had a trip to New York coming up and he asked Sonny to drop him off at the airport on that day. His flight was scheduled for Sunday morning and that is when a few radio stations in LA aired religious programs. We called them the funeral shows because mortuaries would sponsor these programs. Sonny's plan was to change all of the buttons on Phil's car radio to be tuned to these programs, so when he pushed the buttons all he'd hear would be religious music and funeral home ads. Steve Douglas, Jack Nitzsche, and I were also in on the prank. All of us were in the car when we picked Phil up for the airport and Phil was none the wiser because we were buddies and often all went out together. As usual, Phil was pushing buttons, but as he kept changing the stations he got progressively infuriated. He kept asking Sonny, "What happened to my stations?!" By the time we got to the airport Phil was livid, thinking none of his records were being played. Sonny and the rest of us were getting more than an earful from Phil, but we kept from laughing or telling him it was a prank.

At the airport in those days (before all the security checks) you could walk to the gate with passengers and see them off. So, we all walked with Phil to the gate and watched him get on the plane. Once he was on the plane we let out a gut-busting laugh together and stood by the window so we could watch the plane move out on the runway and take off. We watched the plane get backed out, away from the passenger ramp, and set into position to proceed to the runway. Then it just sat there, and after a few minutes the plane was brought back to the gate. We looked at one another and knew Phil had something to do with this. Phil got off the plane really pissed. We asked him, "What happened?" Phil said, "I told them I'm not going to fly with a bunch of fucking losers." He had pitched a fit, so they brought the plane back to the gate and let him get off. He was so angry about the plane and the radio stations that we just took him home.

The "A" Side and the "F" Side . . .

On 45 rpm singles there's an "A" side and a "B" side, but Phil called side two of a single the "F" side because he always put a "bad" song on that side, to make sure radio stations didn't play the "B" side of his records. Occasionally a station in a small town would actually play the "F" side. By now you probably know how Phil reacted to something like that. On many occasions I helped write and record the "F" side of the hit singles Phil produced, and Phil usually gave himself writing credit for these songs, so even if these songs got played or sold, Phil would receive the royalties.

The "F" side song titled "There's a Woman" was on the flip side of the Righteous Brothers' "You've Lost That Lovin' Feelin'." The full title of the song was "There's a Woman in a Bar Playing Piano." I know this because I wrote that song with Bill Medley and Bobby Hatfield and we recorded it with my trio. We never used all of the band members that played on the "A" side song, and on that particular session we had a new engineer, Doc Siegel. Doc, awestruck at getting his chance to work on a Phil Spector date, was trying hard to impress Phil and not make mistakes. The song was sounding too good, so Bill, Bobby, and I had fun with him because he didn't know the song was supposed to suck. We kept changing the song, rearranging parts, and telling Doc to make adjustments on levels, which made him uncomfortable because he knew it didn't sound good. We could see Doc was taking this all too seriously, so we finally told him about Phil's "F" side songs. Doc Siegel became a staff engineer at Gold Star Studios and worked there for many years.

The Righteous Brothers' "You've Lost That Lovin' Feelin'" became a number one hit in the US and UK in 1965. In 1999 BMI (Broadcast Music Inc.) proclaimed it the most played song on radio and TV in the twentieth century. The Recording Industry Association of America (RIAA) lists "You've Lost That Lovin' Feelin'" as one of the Songs of the Century and it is number thirty-four on the list of the "500 Greatest Songs of All Time" by *Rolling Stone* magazine. In 2015 the song was added to the National Recording Registry of the Library of Congress. All of the success and accolades the song has received since its release in December 1964 could scarcely be imagined when we were recording it. However, Phil Spector believed in the power of the song from the moment he finished writing it with Cynthia Weil and Barry Mann. Gene Page did the arrangement for "You've Lost That Lovin' Feelin'."

Phil Spector is a mastermind of recording and "You've Lost That Lovin' Feelin'" is his masterpiece. The song is actually 3:45 long, but Phil would not cut the length. He told the record company to put 3:05 on the label so the radio stations would play it. In those days AM radio stations didn't want to play records longer than three minutes long because they programmed lots of ads between two- or three-song sets; longer songs = fewer ads per hour. The Wall of Sound regulars on this date were: Earl Palmer on drums, Tommy Tedesco on guitar, Carol Kaye and Ray Pohlman on bass, Steve Douglas on sax, and me on piano.

When "You've Lost That Lovin' Feelin'" was released in the UK, Andrew Oldham (manager and producer for the Rolling Stones) took out an ad in a popular music magazine and wrote, "This is Spector's greatest production, the last word in Tomorrow's Sound Today, exposing the overall mediocrity of the Music Industry." Wow, what a powerful statement, yet it was so true, and I am fortunate to be one of the musicians that played on that song.

After three more hits Phil produced for the Righteous Brothers—"Just Once in My Life," "Unchained Melody," and "Ebb Tide"—Bill Medley and Bobby Hatfield left Philles and signed with Verve/MGM Records. They tried and succeeded to re-create Phil's sound on their next record, "Soul and Inspiration," which was also written by Cynthia Weil and Barry Mann. It was arranged by Jack Nitzsche, who also arranged many hits for Phil. For this date Bill and Bobby hired me as well as many of the other Wall of Sound regulars. When Phil found out I had done this session, he got angry with me and didn't speak to me for a long time. Phil took this personally and he felt it was a betrayal on my part to work with the Righteous Brothers after they left Philles. I worked recording sessions for many different producers and artists, and this session had nothing to do with Phil personally. Phil's decision to turn his back on me really hurt, especially because Phil and I were friends before I started recording with him.

Phil's scorn found a way to reach me after that incident. Later that year, I was dropping off some charts to Lester Sill as a favor to Jack Nitzsche, since Lester's session was on my way to another session I was doing. When I got to the studio where Lester was, he took one look at me and said, "What the hell are you doing here?!" I said, "I'm just here to drop off these charts." Lester shouted he didn't want anything from Phil Spector. I said, "These are from Jack," and set the charts on the desk next to the console and got out of there. Later Lester called me and apologized. He said he just had a huge argument with Phil on the phone when I walked into the studio. Lester went berserk because he knew I was such a close friend to Phil that he took his frustrations out on me. But I told Lester that Phil wasn't even talking to me anymore.

Since the Last Time . . .

When Jack Nitzsche passed away in 2000, many of my friends and colleagues I had not seen in years went to his funeral. Nancy Sinatra and I went to the funeral together. Phil Spector was there and when we saw each other, Phil came up to me and gave me a hug, and we happily reconnected and mourned our friend Jack. I was asked to speak at the service, and when I went up to say a few words about Jack, I began my speech with, "As I look around I am happy to see so many friends of Jack's that I haven't seen or spoken to in years. It's a shame that it takes a funeral to get us all together again."

Phil and I caught up with each other after Jack's funeral and renewed our friendship. I was telling Nancy Sinatra that I wanted to write a song about the whole experience and she said Lyle Lovett already wrote it; the song is "Since the Last Time."

Phil came to the thirtieth-anniversary party for my club, The Baked Potato, that same year, and he asked me if he could come to the studio where I was rehearsing with Nancy Sinatra for an upcoming tour. I told him I would have to ask Nancy and when I did, she said of course.

In February 2007 my family threw a big surprise seventieth-birthday party for me, and Phil Spector was there with his wife, Rachelle, and his two bodyguards. It was very rare for Phil to leave his home during that period, which was just prior to the start of the murder trial for the death of Lana Clarkson. This was a huge gesture of friendship to me. When the trial began in March of that year, the producers at Court TV asked me if I would agree to be interviewed about Phil Spector at the courthouse. I did three interviews as a friend of Phil Spector, to support him.

Through all of the tragedy and complications he's gone through, Phil's wife, Rachelle, has remained devoted to him; she is constantly by his side in her thoughts and she visits him often. Rachelle is a sweetheart and she updates me on how Phil's doing.

How can a guy so groovy be so misunderstood? Phil Spector's bark is a hundred times worse than his bite and if you don't know him well, you won't realize this. Come what may, I am looking forward to seeing Phil again soon.

CHAPTER 23

Brian Wilson—Good Vibrations

When Brian Wilson heard "Be My Baby" by the Ronettes on the radio for the first time, it inspired him to learn more about Phil Spector's recording method and in doing so, he learned that a regular group of studio musicians (the Wall of Sound band) played on all of the records produced by Phil Spector, which included me. Brian began using the same session musicians on the Beach Boys records and became an innovator and pioneer in recording when he produced the *Pet Sounds* album and released the extraordinary single "Good Vibrations." There are hundreds of brilliant recordings that I have played on, but I am always amazed that I got to play on both of those remarkable songs and have the lifetime honor to be a part of music history with Brian Wilson and Phil Spector.

Both are brilliant producers, but a major difference between a Phil session and a Brian session is that you generally finished a song in one day with Phil, but Brian often took several days, up to weeks, to complete recording a song. "Good Vibrations" took months to record and I was on most of those recording dates.

Brian really impressed me with his creativity, brilliance, and talent. It was evident Brian learned a lot about recording techniques and producing from Phil Spector, but Brian had so much more to add to what he learned.

Also a keyboard and bass player, Brian Wilson knew what he wanted and would sit with me at the piano as we worked out an arrangement. His mind never stopped working and he certainly wasn't bashful. He would say straight out if he didn't like something, and when he liked something you played he'd get that warm smile and you could tell he genuinely loved what he heard.

Hal Blaine and I became friends with Brian early on and we made Brian laugh and had fun with our jokes during the long recording sessions. On one interview he gave about the Wrecking Crew (Wall of Sound) players, he called Hal and me the "cutup" guys.

One of the earliest sessions I worked with Brian was for the Beach Boys hit "Help Me Rhonda." It was the rerecording of the song that was released as the single. I actually just found this out while verifying the facts about the song for this book. The first version was recorded a month earlier with Leon Russell on piano at that session, not me. During that session Murry Wilson, Brian's father, came to the studio and others who were there say he had been drinking. Murry criticized the production and interfered with the creative direction Brian was trying to establish. His father eventually left the studio and they finished recording a version of the song "Help Me Rhonda," which was included on the album *The Beach Boys Today.* About a month after the first session Brian decided to rerecord "Help Me Rhonda" for the single release and that is when I played on the song. At the time I didn't know the song was recorded previously, but I do remember this was the only time for a session with Brian we actually had complete charts when we started the session. The version I played on was the one that aired on the radio and sold as the hit 45 rpm single and was included on the album *Summer Days (and Summer Nights).*

As I mentioned, the recording process for Brian was a painstakingly long creative process. I recall on a long Beach Boys session, Hal Blaine, Glen Campbell, Ray Pohlman, and I snacked on pistachio nuts during the date. These were the ones with red shells and we had a big bag of them. The date went for so long that by the end of the session, the studio floor looked like a red carpet with all the shells we tossed on the floor.

While recording "Good Vibrations," Brian wanted me to play the Hammond organ and in one particular passage of the song he asked me to sustain a very low note on the foot pedals. I remember it was really late and we'd been in the studio for at least eight or nine hours already and I was very tired. Brian kept going over this part several times, trying different things to get the sound he wanted, and was close to being happy with the part. The band went out in the hall and was taking a break while I was working on this overdub with Brian. He spoke over the PA and said, "Don, can you hold that note, just keep holding it, and I'm going to be starting and stopping in here." I saw a pillow that some keyboard players used to sit on and set that pillow on the pedal that I needed to press, then I lay down with my head on that pillow, holding the note. I knew Brian could not see me because of the baffles around the organ used to isolate the sound, and I didn't think any of the guys would ever find out, but I was just so damn tired. As soon as my head hit that pillow, my eyes closed and I fell asleep. I was probably asleep for ten or fifteen minutes while Brian was working on that part, then I awoke with start when I heard Brian say over the PA, "Okay, Don, that's good; we got it." I got up and thought I pulled it off, until Hal Blaine came up to me and said, "Have a nice nap?" Brian didn't find out what I did until a few years later when Hal told him, and he thought it was the funniest thing he'd ever heard and wished he had seen me.

One of the most beautiful songs from the *Pet Sounds* album is "God Only Knows." It's really a musical masterpiece and could be used to teach harmonies in music classes. The music is very simple yet so intricate and very deep, which is the essence of Brian Wilson. During the recording session Brian tried different things on the instrumental bridge and wasn't quite satisfied with what he was hearing. I suggested to Brian that this section be played staccato and he liked the idea, so we recorded it and that version was the keeper. I also played on "Sloop John B," "Here Today," and "I Just Wasn't Made for These Times" on the album.

The US audience was not quite ready for *Pet Sounds* when it was released in 1966, and it didn't do as well in sales as the record company hoped. Brian was ahead of his time. Years later *Pet Sounds* was ranked number two on the "500 Greatest Albums of All Time" list by *Rolling Stone* magazine. It took a while for music fans to really appreciate Brian's vision.

I loved working with Brian because he wrote and produced in a jazz harmonic way. As a jazz musician myself, I really understood where he was taking the arrangements and his mind was always writing and arranging music, I could see it in his eyes. Collaborating with him was amazing. He would play chords sometimes and you wouldn't quite know where he was coming from. Then I might respond by playing something that would inspire him in another direction, but it often seemed like he had already composed it in his mind. Brian is such a hip musician, capable of anything.

After *Pet Sounds*, I played for Brian on several sessions that ended up being material that was used on the *Smile* album. "Good Vibrations," which was released in 1966 as a single only, was remixed for the *Smile* album, which was released in 2004. These sessions I did were during 1966 to 1967, at a time that's already been documented about Brian's moodiness and depression. However, I saw individuals trying to influence Brian, who encouraged him to isolate and medicate himself, which did not help his mental state. Be that as it may, I recall a few of sessions where I was in the studio and Brian would be right next to me and I would try to talk to him, or just say hello, and he would not respond. He'd look right at me, but it was like he didn't see or hear me. That was not the Brian Wilson I knew and I was very worried about him. Then one day he was on the Hammond B3 and I was on piano just a few feet from him, and he looked at me and said, "Don!" I was surprised because he had not said anything to me in two days. Brian continued, "I'm having this Brazilian coffee and it is so good! Do you want to try some, Don?" I said, "Sure, Brian." So, he poured some of his coffee into my cup and then he didn't say anything else to me the rest of the session.

In May 2005 I was invited to the dedication ceremony of the Beach Boys monument in Hawthorne, California. The monument is located in the spot where the Wilson family home stood before it was demolished to make way for the Century Freeway (Interstate 105). The City of Hawthorne hosted a delightful ceremony and celebration with a performance by the Beach Boys (Brian, Carl Wilson, and Al Jardine were there). It was a fun event and one that the Beach Boys certainly deserved.

I've seen Brian several times in recent years and months. He happened to be at East West Studios, working on his own project, at the same time I was there as a featured guest to speak at a screening of the documentary movie *The Wrecking Crew*. It was a rare coincidence that he was there at the same time, because Brian is also featured in the film. He participated in the documentary by giving a lengthy and detailed interview to Denny Tedesco (the film's producer), and he is an enthusiastic fan of the film.

Over the years Brian Wilson has remained one of the Wrecking Crew's strongest supporters. Anytime he's asked about recording the Beach Boys songs, he is quick to give credit to the studio musicians that played on the records. Brian is as brilliantly talented as he is a warm, kind, and genuine person. I'm lucky to work with him and be his friend.

CHAPTER 24

Jack Nitzsche

I met Jack when I began working for Phil Spector and he was doing a lot of arranging for him. In fact, we immediately became friends because of the instant rapport we had with each other. Jack's wife, Gracia, also became a good friend of mine and I met her on that same day I met Jack. Gracia Nitzsche was one of the Blossoms with Darlene Love, Fanita James, and Jean King, and sang background on the first hit song I played on for Phil Spector, "He's a Rebel." Jack Nitzsche had a creatively distinguished life full of the highest highs while fighting the lowest of lows.

Jack, Sonny Bono, Phil Spector, Steve Douglas, and I would hang out together even when we weren't in the studio. When I bought a house on Nichols Canyon in the Hollywood Hills, Jack and Gracia also had a house there and were my neighbors.

Jack Nitzsche was one of the most prolific arrangers in the music business during the '60s. Because he was working with so many different producers and artists, I also got to meet and work with many producers and projects with Jack because he'd request they hire me to play keyboards. Jack would often ask me to be the contractor for his sessions, so I would call the other musicians for the dates. Some of the many recording projects I played on because of Jack Nitzsche were for Neil Young, Doris Day, Petula Clark, the Crystals, the Ronettes, and the Turtles.

Lesley Gore was also an artist that Jack arranged and Quincy Jones produced. I played on her well-known hit record "It's My Party" and a few of her other recordings.

I also worked on some of Jack's own projects, like the album *The Lonely Surfer*. Jimmy Bowen was the producer, Jack wrote and arranged the music, and many of the guys that played in the Wall of Sound for Phil Spector played on the album: Hal Blaine on drums, Tommy Tedesco and Bill Pitman on guitars, Ray Pohlman and Jimmy Bond on bass, Roy Caton and Virgil Evans on trumpet, Harry Betts and Roy Main on trombone, Gale Robinson on French horn, Frank Capp on percussion, and Leon Russell joining me on keyboards. There were string players, too, which was one of Jack's signature sounds in his arrangements. He loved to add strings for a lush, deeply emotional layer in songs.

Not long after *The Lonely Surfer* was released I was playing in Las Vegas with my trio at the Castaways, which is where I met Norma, who was the lead dancer in the featured show, the Barry Ashton revue. I invited Jack to drive out to Vegas to hang out with me and relax for a couple of days, but I also wanted to give him a little surprise. Jack Nitzsche was a nerdy-looking guy, very thin, very fair skinned, and wearing black-framed glasses. Though Jack was one of the most brilliant men I knew, he was also shy and insecure. When I invited Jack to drive out, I asked him to bring a few copies of the album with him to give to a few people I knew. The night before Jack was to arrive in Vegas, I asked Norma if she would ask her friend Karen, who was also a dancer in the show, if she would help me surprise Jack. Karen agreed and once Jack arrived, I got one of the copies of *The Lonely Surfer*, gave it to her, and told her what I wanted her to do.

Karen went to the lounge where Jack was having a drink, waiting for me. When Karen saw Jack sitting alone in the lounge, she walked up to him and asked, "Are you Mr. Nitzsche?" Jack was very surprised that this pretty girl knew his name and he awkwardly replied, "Yes, yes I am. How do you know my name?" Karen enthusiastically told him she was his biggest fan and showed him that she had his album *The Lonely Surfer* and asked if he would sign it for her. Some of the people near them started looking their way to see if they recognized Jack as Karen went on and on complimenting him and his album. Jack was smiling from ear to ear and I could see he was blushing. He was very nervous; when he started to sign the album, his hands were shaking. I was standing just out of Jack's sight and watched the whole scene, but I couldn't hold back my laughter any longer. Jack turned and saw me, then figured out I set him up, but he still enjoyed all the attention from Karen.

Because Jack Nitzsche was such a close friend and I worked on many projects with him, he is mentioned throughout this book, but I reserved a few stories just for his chapter . . .

The Comeback

After I had a falling out with Phil Spector over the Righteous Brothers' leaving Philles Records to sign with Verve/MGM, several years passed and many of the other original musicians that worked with me in the Wall of Sound band had not really worked much with Phil in the '70s, either. The whole Wall of Sound era looked like it was a thing of the past, but Steve Douglas wanted to bring us all back together on a big project. It was in the late 1970s when Steve got Phil Spector to agree to produce a mystery artist and bring back the Wall of Sound, plus a few more. We didn't know who the artist was and Phil Spector did not want to tell us, but we thought it could be for Linda Ronstadt. We never found out who the artist was.

Steve asked Jack to arrange four songs to record that day. We were at the old RKO studio and there were twenty musicians on the date. Larry Levine was the engineer; he was our engineer for all those years at Gold Star. In addition to the Wall of Sound regulars, Paul Shaffer and a few other session musicians from New York were also on the date. Potentially, this was going to be a recording that would make music history.

Jack Nitzsche had spent the previous five or six years working with the Rolling Stones and Neil Young, among other successful projects, and his lifestyle dramatically changed from the early '60s. The excesses of his new lifestyle were affecting his life in a very detrimental way. Jack was excited to do the arrangements for this project and to see us all working together again, but his addictions got the better of him and he showed up to the session very late and very high, which infuriated Phil Spector. The charts Jack brought weren't even finished, except for one song. Steve Douglas was so angry with Jack that he wanted to call the date for Phil right away, but I tried to salvage what we did have since it was such a rare thing to have all of us together. I talked Phil into running through the one song we did have complete charts on. Well, it didn't work; the charts weren't good and Phil was livid. I felt so bad for Jack, but I was also angry with him for not having control over his addictions and letting Steve Douglas and me down.

While I was going back and forth between the booth and the studio, trying to fix this mess, Paul Shaffer was like my shadow. He followed me everywhere and stuck close, listening to every conversation I was having and setting up his keyboard next to me on the piano. After a while I asked Paul what the deal was. He explained, "Back in New York, we all wanted to know the secret of all those hits from the Wall of Sound. Don, we tried to emulate your sound and got very close, but we just couldn't quite get there." Paul continued, "So, I am going to follow and watch your every move to learn all I can from you." What an honor it was to hear that from Paul, who is a terrifically talented musician and director himself. Jack Nitzsche was just as important to that hit-making sound with his arrangements, but unfortunately Paul Shaffer didn't get to see that fact on this date.

After trying and trying, all the efforts we put into the song weren't working and Jack had left the studio shortly after bringing the charts, so Steve called the date and we never got back together to finish the project.

Another recording project was for Marianne Faithfull. Jack did the arrangements for the songs and we recorded at Sunset Sound with Mick Jagger producing the record. Jack told me that we were doing this date because Mick Jagger and Keith Richards made a bet that they could take anyone and produce a hit song. The arrangements that Jack did were really good. I don't even remember the name of the song because I don't think the title was decided yet.

Jack did many scores and sound tracks for films, and on one of his film projects I played keyboards. The movie was *Candy* and had Marlon Brando, Richard Burton, and Ringo Starr in the cast. Jack did a brilliant job on the score and arrangements and we completed recording all of the music for the film.

When the film's director presented the movie with the music in a screening for the producer, he hated the music and wanted everything to be rerecorded. They asked Dave Grusin if he would take the job. Dave knew Jack Nitzsche and that he had already scored the film. Dave called me to say how awful he felt because he was sure Jack's music was awesome, which it was. Dave said he felt bad about being offered the opportunity to rescore the film and that he should walk away from the job. I told Dave he was a great guy and a loyal friend of Jack's to consider walking away. "But don't walk away to be loyal to Jack; take the job for Jack, or someone else will," I said.

That wasn't the end of Jack's career in music for film. He went on to arrange music and score many films. *One Flew Over the Cuckoo's Nest, Stand By Me*, and *9 1/2 Weeks* are a few of the more well-known titles he scored. Among Jack's work for film, he won the highest honor, an Academy Award as cowriter of "Up Where We Belong" with Buffy Sainte-Marie for *An Officer and a Gentleman.*

Winning the Oscar was one of the most thrilling achievements Jack was awarded in his life and he was so proud of it, but one evening I got a call from our friend Hal Blaine, who frantically told me to turn on the TV, flip the channel to FOX, and watch *COPS*. I was confused by Hal's excitement for *COPS* and said, "What? I don't watch that show." Hal shrieked, "Just turn it on now!" When I did, I saw inebriated Jack Nitzsche being arrested for a scuffle he had with a woman he was dating. As the police were taking him away, the camera pulled in for a close-up of Jack and the voice-over announced, "Jack Nitzsche, Academy Award–winning composer." I was speechless, in shock over what I had just seen, as I held the receiver and Hal was still on the other end.

Jack worked a lot and produced many music projects through the 1970s and 1980s, but by the 1990s his health was starting to show the weaknesses of years of drug abuse and alcohol. It was heartbreaking when Jack had to go to the hospital because his health was rapidly deteriorating. Jack Nitzsche died in 2000 and at his funeral I eulogized him. It was one of the saddest days and yet it was a happy day. Friends who I had not seen in years came to the funeral. It was gratifying to see so many friends come pay tribute to him and it felt like a big reunion party. I renewed my friendship with Phil Spector and Gracia Nitzsche, whom I had not seen since she had left Los Angeles after her divorce from Jack many years earlier.

I started missing Jack Nitzsche before he passed away, imagining how much more he could have accomplished and enjoy it all with us. Jack was an immensely talented composer, arranger, and musician, but he will be most memorable to me as one of my best friends.

CHAPTER 25

Lee Hazlewood—We'll Always Have Paris . . .

Lee Hazlewood was one of the most innovative and talented producers I have worked with. Lee was also a composer and artist, and one of the most perplexing guys I've known. Perplexing because of his unpredictable personality; you never knew how he was going to react to something. *Cantankerous* would describe Lee Hazlewood.

Some people found Lee hard to work with, but I didn't have a problem working with him on projects, mainly because he needed me (I did a lot of arranging for him) and therefore he was more open to a discussion with me than he might have been with other musicians. Even though Lee Hazlewood might be known best for his music that could be categorized as hillbilly or rockabilly music, I did an interesting variety of projects with Lee, including a number of Nancy Sinatra recordings and shows, before he passed away in 2007. He appreciated my talent as a versatile musician and arranger and he often came to my live performances at the clubs in Los Angeles.

As a composer, Lee had a gift for storytelling in his songs. One in particular was "Some Velvet Morning," a duet he wrote, produced, and recorded with Nancy Sinatra. I mention the song in the chapter on Nancy Sinatra, but it's worth repeating that the recording is renowned for its beauty and intricacies. "Some Velvet Morning" is a challenging song for me to play and especially to conduct in Nancy's live shows, with several timing changes throughout the song. Lee Hazlewood also had a magical presence performing in person.

In the shows he did with Nancy, when they sang "Some Velvet Morning," Lee mesmerized the audience with his deep voice and delivery.

In more recent years (late 1990s through early 2000s) when Lee toured with Nancy Sinatra, we had a terrific drummer, Miles Robinson. Lee Hazlewood was born in Oklahoma and was raised with some old southern traditions, some of which are offensive by today's standards. Miles is African American and Lee would aggravate Miles with his "old southern ways" and they didn't get along very well. The band and I loved Miles, and we didn't want him to quit, so we were always on edge hoping Lee would not go too far with his behavior.

We were touring by bus on the East Coast. Nancy loved to stop at big truck stops for a break and food and because she liked buying local tchotchkes in the gift shops. At one stop we made, Miles came over to me and said he was about to fix the tension between Lee and himself, then he walked toward the gift shop. Later that evening I heard Lee Hazlewood laughing as loud as ever and Miles, too. I had to see what was making the two of them laugh together! "What's so funny?" I asked. Lee held up a license plate frame with a Confederate flag and the words "The South Will Rise Again" on it, while laughing his head off! I think Miles probably said something snappy to Lee that hit his humor just right when he gave him the license plate frame, and after that day they were good buddies.

In 1965 I worked with Lee on an album for the trio Dino, Desi and Billy, the sons of Dean Martin and Desi Arnaz and their friend Billy Hinsche. Jimmy Bowen asked Lee to produce their album on the Reprise label. The kids weren't experienced musicians, so the usual Wall of Sound studio musicians, including me, were booked for the sessions. "Our Time's Coming" was a top forty hit that Lee produced and I played on.

Lee also produced Duane Eddy for years, and I had the pleasure of working with them on several outstanding recordings. Two great talents, Duane and Lee, were a combo that produced some awesome music that endures as some of the greatest recordings ever done. Duane Eddy had fifteen top forty hits, and I played on the Duane Eddy records Lee produced for Reprise Records.

There are some projects that never took off . . . I got a call from Lee one day to come to his house in Toluca Lake. To my surprise, I found Lee and actor Anthony (Tony) Franciosa (who passed away in 2006) there to work on a demo of songs to debut him as a singer. Tony was already a very popular actor who had a Golden Globe Award for his role in the movie *Career* in 1959 and starred in a number of popular TV shows and movies. Lee asked me to keep this project a secret until they were ready to present the demo to record labels. We worked and worked on the demo with Tony, but it didn't come together. Tony was a great guy, though, and we all had high hopes and I never talked about the project to anyone, officially.

Lee Hazlewood's own records were quite amazing and eclectic, to say the least. He was very creative and his talents really came out when I worked with him on his recordings. As openly creative as Lee was, he was also tightfisted when it came to money. An example of this was the time he asked me to work with him on his album *Love and Other Crimes* that was recorded in Paris, France. He did pay for my travel and room.

When I arrived in Paris after a thirteen-hour flight from Los Angeles, I was exhausted. I called Lee from the airport to tell him I was in and that I was going to the hotel and get some sleep before the session tomorrow. Lee said, "Oh, no, no, you have to come to the studio and help me with the arrangements before we start the session tomorrow." So, to the studio I went, and I don't think I got much more than a couple of hours of sleep at night after that first day after being awake for over thirty hours straight.

You can see a video of footage taken during the recording of "She Comes Running" and "The House Song" on YouTube (search for "Lee Hazlewood" on YouTube.com to locate the video). In that video you will see me actually falling asleep at the piano at one point, but you will also see me writing my piano arrangement down as we were recording a take of the song.

I hope you are able to find this video because you will also see drummer Hal Blaine and a very interesting technique he used to get a tonal effect on some beats he played. You will see Lee in the vocal booth and a strange-looking, torn fabric in front of his mic. I think it was gauze threaded through a coat hanger. That was a makeshift pop filter, but back in those days we didn't have professional pop filters. A pop filter is a screen that prevents the burst air from the vocalist's breath from hitting the mic and causing a pop sound. Lee wasn't the first to think of doing this, but he did have a few innovative recording techniques that Phil Spector learned from him.

James Burton was the guitarist on this session and is celebrated as one of the top guitarists in the world. He is also one of the kindest and gentlest, most down-to-earth people you could know. Donnie Owens was also playing guitar on this date. Donnie had played in Duane Eddy's band and he also had a hit single in 1958, "Need You." Chuck Berghofer was on bass and as mentioned in the chapter on Nancy Sinatra, he came up with that famous bass line in "These Boots Are Made for Walkin'," written and produced by Lee with Nancy.

Getting back to Lee's tightfistedness, he never paid me for arranging the sessions in Paris. When the work was over, Lee announced he was taking everyone out to dinner to celebrate. Being in Paris I was excited, thinking we would be going to a beautiful French restaurant to enjoy some of the country's fine fare. Nope, Lee found the most American restaurant in Paris, where they served hamburgers and sandwiches, and when the bill came, he asked me if I had any money because he didn't bring that much cash and was short. I laugh every time I think about this!

Lee Hazlewood had his own record company, LHI (Lee Hazlewood Industries), and I played on nearly all of the twenty-plus albums that Lee released on his label. A few years ago a company called Light in the Attic purchased the LHI catalog and released a box set of the Lee Hazlewood albums on CD as well as records on vinyl. Light in the Attic sent me a copy of the box set and it is a beautifully done collection.

CHAPTER 26

Billy Strange

T he first time I met Billy Strange was on the first recording session I did for Nancy Sinatra, produced by Lee Hazlewood, and that session was for her signature hit, "These Boots Are Made for Walkin'," which Billy arranged. In that arrangement is one of Billy's iconic horns riff (musical phrase) and it became a riff every horn player knows to this day.

I didn't know much about Billy Strange when I met him, but as we became good friends and talked about our life and career experiences, I realized how multitalented Billy was. He could do just about anything! He was a musician, vocalist, composer, arranger, producer, and music director. Billy Strange was the busiest man in the music business and inspired me to try to be the same, but Billy could not be outdone. We worked so much together, whether it was on a recording date, on tour with Nancy Sinatra and Frank Sinatra, or on a TV or film scoring date. Billy Strange often hired me to work with him, or he handed opportunities to me to work on projects when his schedule got full, which was all the time. I laugh when I think about that because Billy never wanted to turn down a job, and he was so much in demand, especially in the 1960s. Because of Billy Strange, I got many opportunities to compose, arrange, record, and be music director on projects that I would not have gotten on my own.

I was amazed at all of what Billy Strange had done prior to my meeting him . . . Not only did Billy compose songs, record, and perform with bands on the road, he was on a TV variety show called *Hometown Jamboree* that aired on

KCOP-TV, then moved to KTLA-TV in 1953. The show was on from 1949 until 1960. Cliffie Stone was the producer and host of the show, which was country music oriented. Billy was a regular on *Hometown Jamboree*, in the show's band. Billy had a wonderful voice and great comic timing and performed duets with Tennessee Ernie Ford, who was also a regular on the show. Many big names in country music appeared on *Hometown Jamboree*, like Johnny Cash, Eddy Arnold, Tex Ritter, and Johnny Horton. *Hometown Jamboree* was the precursor to the very popular *Hee Haw* TV show, hosted by Roy Clark and Buck Owens, which began in 1969.

Billy Strange also appeared on the *Tennessee Ernie Ford Show*. The show was produced in San Francisco, so he had to travel back and forth to San Francisco, then back to Los Angeles to work in recording sessions. I found we had a lot in common because early in my own career, when my trio was booked on club gigs in Las Vegas and San Francisco, I also traveled back and forth, trying to maintain my recording session player status in LA.

Billy also loved to joke around and he could take a joke, too, so we often pulled pranks on each other. I wrote about one prank I pulled on Billy in the Nancy Sinatra chapter, but there's another funny prank I did to Billy during a Nancy Sinatra Vegas show . . .

Billy Strange kept a bottle of water and a drinking glass in my piano because he got very thirsty during the show. I am sure you are wondering, but there is a space inside a grand piano that was just big enough to put a glass and a bottle of water. The lid of the piano was removed and there was a microphone inside the piano, and I had monitors (small speakers) near me so I could hear my piano as I played. When Billy had a few seconds between songs, he would rush over and drink a glass of water, then set the glass back in my piano, but when he did, it made a *plink* sound in my monitors that I hated because Billy always set the glass down hard. I told him not to do that and soon he was doing it purposely.

One day I decided I was going to pull a prank and make sure Billy got the message to put his glass down carefully in my piano. Before the show I exchanged the glass with one I poured vodka into. The show started and we played a couple of tunes. In the pause between songs, Billy came over to take a big drink of water. *Glug, glug* . . . thirsty Billy took big gulps of vodka from his glass and in a second I saw his eyes practically bug out of his head and then he coughed. He tossed the rest of the vodka from the glass onto the floor, under the piano. Billy gave me a look and then we went on to do the next couple of songs. Again, Billy came over to the piano and poured the liquid from the water bottle into the glass without thinking I had put vodka in it, too. He fell for it a second time and Hal Blaine, who was in on this prank, almost blew it because he started laughing. It was hilarious watching Billy's face turn beet red, from the vodka and being mad at me. The vodka was harsh on his throat, which was already dry from thirst, so he temporarily lost his voice, but Billy didn't need to have a voice for me to know he was saying, "Don, you son-of-a-bitch!" Both Hal and I started laughing and after the show, Billy did, too.

Even though Billy was born in Long Beach, California, he was connected to country music and the guys who played hillbilly music. Billy and I were working on a recording session with Lee Hazlewood producing. The other players in the session were Billy's good buddies in country music: Jerry Reed (actor, guitar player), Glen Campbell (guitar), and Buddy Emmons (steel guitar). Of course, Lee Hazlewood was also in the "buddy group" and the jokes, sarcastic insults, one-liners, and stories that were being told during the session were hilarious, slapstick funny! I never had as much fun and laughed so much as I did with those guys, and I learned a few things, too.

During a break I jammed some bebop (jazz) with Buddy Emmons on steel guitar. Yes, Buddy Emmons can play jazz on his steel!

The drummer in the session was Hal Blaine, with Ray Pohlman on bass. What a wonderful experience that was, being able to work with such talented musicians and have the best time hanging with them, which is why I feel fortunate and appreciate my life working professionally in music with the colleagues who became close friends.

In the early '70s Billy Strange started a music publishing company with Nancy Sinatra called B-n-B Music (Boots and Billy). He also moved to Franklin, a suburb of Nashville, Tennessee, in the mid-'70s but continued to run the publishing company and semiretired from the grueling music production schedule he was used to in Los Angeles. Whenever he did come to town for business, he would stop by my club, The Baked Potato, and often would sit in with Quest and me to play guitar.

Billy lived in Franklin, Tennessee, until he passed away in 2012. His funeral took place in Tennessee, but one of his family members asked me if I would have a memorial gathering at The Baked Potato in his honor for the many producers, musicians, friends, and family members who live in Los Angeles. I was honored to accommodate the family's wishes, and many people came to remember Billy. Nancy Sinatra was among the people who attended and she sang "These Boots Are Made for Walkin'" in a tribute of songs my band performed to honor Billy Strange. Chuck Berghofer played acoustic bass for that number, and it was the first time Nancy sang with Chuck playing that famous bass line since the recording of the song. When Nancy has performed the song in her concerts and Vegas shows, Chuck was not part of Nancy's touring band because he was working in Los Angeles in film- and television-scoring sessions. This was such a sweet reunion and it was a highlight of the music we performed in Billy's tribute.

CHAPTER 27

Tutti Camarata

Tutti Camarata was not only a talented trumpet player who played in the big bands of Jimmy and Tommy Dorsey and Benny Goodman, but he was also an outstanding arranger and producer. In the late 1950s Tutti was hired by Walt Disney to start Disneyland Records as the music director and producer for the record company. I met and worked with Tutti on projects for Disney that included the soundtrack music for *The Jungle Book*.

In case you don't know the history, Tutti Camarata advised Walt Disney to build a recording studio for the record label, but Disney decided not to do it. Instead, Walt Disney urged Tutti to build his own recording studio, and that is how he came to build the famed Sunset Sound Recorders in Hollywood. When Sunset Sound opened, Tutti asked me to help him select two grand pianos for Studio 1 and Studio 2.

I had been working on projects with Tutti on and off, and I had a few recordings of my own with my trio that I had released, so he knew that I really wanted to get my own recording career off the ground. One afternoon Tutti asked me to meet with him in his office, which was common because we often discussed current and upcoming record projects that I might work on with him. In this meeting Tutti said it was time for me to record a new song and he wanted to produce it and an entire album for me. I was so thrilled and asked him what he had in mind. Tutti said he wanted me to write a Mexican song. I thought I must not have heard him correctly, and he saw the puzzled look on my face and said, "Yes, it's time for a Mexican hit and I want you to write this song." Tutti explained, "The melody should be simple, so anyone could play the tune with one finger on the piano." He continued, "It should not have a lot of notes. Think of Duane Eddy and his style." I said, "Tutti, I don't even like mariachi music; how am I going to write a Mexican song?" Tutti said, "Don, I'm going to give you some mariachi albums to listen to and you'll get ideas for the song."

I wasn't sure about it, but I took the mariachi albums home, listened to them, and still didn't like mariachi music. However, there must have been some inspiration in those albums, and while I kept Tutti's direction in mind, I wrote "Mexican Pearls."

We recorded "Mexican Pearls" and the other songs on my album at Tutti's studio, Sunset Sound. Brian Ross and Bruce Botnick were the recording engineers on the project. Bruce was the engineer on all of the Doors albums that were recorded at Sunset Sound, as well as many others. Jack Nitzsche, Ray Pohlman, and I did the arrangements for the songs. Hal Blaine played drums on "Mexican Pearls" and John Clauder played drums on the other cuts on the album. Ray Pohlman and Jimmy Bond played electric bass and Dick Brandt played acoustic bass. Tommy Tedesco and Bill Pitman played guitar and there was a full string section that played on "Mexican Pearls."

I wrote two more new songs for the album, "The Randi Sermon" and "Grampa's Still," cowritten with Dick Brandt. The other songs on the album are: "I Don't Want to Be Kissed," "A Lot of Livin' to Do," "My Funny Valentine," "John Brown's Body," "More (Theme from *Mondo Cane*)," "Bass Blues," "Thistle Down," and "Spanish Harlem."

I also recorded "Follow Me," a beautiful song written by Bronislau Kaper, from the soundtrack of *Mutiny on the Bounty*. On the day we were recording the song Tutti brought Bronislau Kaper to the studio to meet me. Bronislau was an exceptionally talented composer and pianist, and I had admired and respected him for years. Bronislau's very distinguished career included writing the music for over 150 films, and he was awarded an Oscar in 1954 for the musical *Lili*. Tutti, being the very unpretentious person he was, introduced Bronislau to me by saying, "Don, this is Bronislau Kaper. I thought you would like to meet him."

Tutti came to the sessions and he'd tell Jack Nitzsche that his arrangements were really good. Jack would thank Tutti, but when Tutti left the studio, Jack would come to me, freaking out, saying, "Tutti hates it! I know he does and he's just not telling me." I'd try to calm Jack down and tell him that Tutti was direct and honest but not overly passionate when he expressed himself. If Tutti said he liked something, he meant it. If he didn't like something, he would say so but never in an offensive way, and he never shouted. Jack was so used to working with producers and artists that were temperamental and volatile that he could not believe Tutti, an important record executive and producer, could have such a peaceful personality. Tutti Camarata was such a humble man that he didn't even put his name as producer on my *Mexican Pearls* album, even though he did produce it and it was his idea for the record in the first place. Phil Spector wrote the liner notes for the album, which was released on Palomar Records, a London Records company.

When the single "Mexican Pearls" was released, Don Graham, the promo man for Palomar Records, went to work and got my single on many radio stations across the country. In the chapter on the various club gigs I have played, I tell how he went above and beyond for me in San Francisco when my trio was playing at the Executive Suite.

In a few weeks "Mexican Pearls" was on the charts (*Billboard* and *Cashbox*) and climbing, but Billy Vaughn covered "Mexican Pearls" on Dot Records and released his version a few weeks after mine. His version surpassed my original recording on the charts and went to the number forty-five on the *Billboard* Top 100. Though it was very frustrating for me to have Billy's cover out while my original version was gaining ground, I still benefited from the record sales of Billy's version, receiving royalties as the composer of the song.

Billy Vaughn was not the last person to cover "Mexican Pearls." Forty-two other artists have released covers of my song, including Xavier Cugat. "Mexican Pearls" was also featured as the theme song for the airline Aeromexico for several years. "Mexican Pearls" is a jewel of a song for me as a recording artist and composer, and I give recognition to Tutti Camarata, who encouraged me to write a song that stretched my talent and expanded my range as an artist. These days, "Mexican Pearls" is an elevator hit.

CHAPTER 28

Jimmy Bowen

I worked with Jimmy Bowen on several memorable and significant recording projects in my career. Jimmy's talents as a producer are his versatility, limitless creative vision, and his instinct for choosing hit songs for the artist he's producing. In the late 1960s, when the population was going gaga over rock 'n' roll and the British invasion, etc., Jimmy produced chart-topping hits in the 1960s for Frank Sinatra, Dean Martin, and Sammy Davis Jr. I played on Dean's 1964 hit produced by Jimmy Bowen, "Everybody Loves Somebody Sometime."

Occasionally, I worked recording sessions outside Los Angeles and was hired on a session for Sammy Davis Jr. in Las Vegas that Jimmy produced. Sammy was booked at the Sands in his live concert show, so in order for Jimmy to get a recording session scheduled around Sammy's schedule, he had to book a studio at midnight. All of the players for this session were LA musicians, including myself, and were flown out to Vegas for the date. The Sands had rooms for us to relax and sleep in before and after the session, but H.B. Barnum, who was the arranger of the song, was staying at a different hotel.

No matter what time a recording session is booked to start, I try to get to the studio a few minutes early so I'm ready to start on time. All of us showed up at the studio a few minutes before midnight, except H.B. It was not like H.B. to be late. Jimmy checked to see if there were any messages from H.B., but there weren't. Sammy Davis Jr. had not shown up, either, and I know Jimmy was watching the clock because the studio time was booked and we were all being paid union scale starting from midnight. Delays would cut into the project's budget. After an hour of waiting, someone tried to locate H.B., which was difficult because none of us knew where he was staying. Sammy Davis Jr. still hadn't arrived, either, which was a good thing since we were waiting for H.B. to bring the music; however, we were all concerned about both of them. A little after an hour later, H.B. finally arrived. He was late because he had been up for over twenty-four hours and while he was working on the charts, his fatigue had caught up with him and he had fallen asleep at the desk in his room. We quickly started going over the charts and rehearsing, but Sammy was still not there. Another thirty minutes later, Sammy Davis Jr. arrived and we were ready to go. Even with all the efforts to make a success of the session after the delays, and we tried our best with the song recorded in those early-morning hours, I'm not sure the song was ever released.

Fortunately, most projects do go well. Jimmy Bowen produced a solo album for my very good friend Jack Nitzsche, *The Lonely Surfer*. It was one of those projects that was not only very creative musically, it was also fun to do because all the musicians in the session were good friends.

Jimmy vs. Tree

Besides being a fantastic record producer, Jimmy Bowen loved to play golf. Glen Campbell, a close friend of Jimmy's, told me this story . . .

One day Jimmy Bowen asked Glen, who is also a great golfer, to play a round of golf at the course in Griffith Park. Jimmy was really excited to play a game because he just bought a set of very expensive golf clubs and wanted to break them in. I forget what brand Glen said they were, but I do remember he said they cost more than a thousand dollars for the set, and that was expensive for clubs in the 1960s. They teed off and as the game progressed, it didn't go the way Jimmy had expected. Hole after hole, Jimmy's game was going very badly and he was getting mad. Glen said his own game was going really well, which pissed off Jimmy even more. By the ninth hole Jimmy was furious and he took his brand-new expensive clubs, one by one, and swung each like a baseball bat at the trunk of a pine tree, so the club bent in a curve around the trunk. He did that until every club was bent and then he threw his golf bag at the tree and walked off the course. Glen said he was laughing so hard he was practically rolling on the green. Jimmy really is a good golfer, but he's a better record producer.

Jimmy Bowen also had a knack for finding talent, but a few got away. I remember being at Jack Nitzsche's house in Los Angeles one time in the early '60s. It was a gathering of a few friends, including Sonny Bono and his first wife, Donna; Jack and Gracia; Jimmy; my wife, Norma; and me. Jimmy said, "Listen to this, Don," and put on a record. I said, "That is terrific! Who's the singer?" "George Jones," Jimmy said, "and I can kick myself for not acting sooner because I tried to sign him to Reprise but he already signed with another label." Of course you know the rest; George Jones went on to become a country music legend.

In 1966 Jimmy produced Harold Betters' jazz fusion album *Funk City Express*. I arranged a few of the songs, plus played piano. Harold Betters played trombone and Hal Blaine was on drums, Al Casey on guitar, and Larry Knechtel on bass.

Before Kenny Rogers became very well known in country music (Jimmy also produced him in country music), he was in the band Kenny Rogers and the First Edition. Jimmy produced its 1969 hit record "Ruby, Don't Take Your Love to Town," and I played piano on that song. I actually knew Kenny Rogers years before I met Jimmy Bowen. He played bass with my trio one night at the Melody Room in the late 1950s.

I also played on hits for Dorsey Burnette ("Tall Oak Tree"), Buddy Greco ("Love's Gonna Live Here," written by Buck Owens), and Keely Smith. All produced by Jimmy Bowen.

Speaking of Keely Smith . . . Jimmy Bowen was married five times and one of his wives was Keely (her first husband was Louis Prima), a singer famous for songs like "Old Black Magic." Jimmy and Keely had a very emotionally explosive relationship and it was never more demonstrated to me than on a day in the mid-'60s. I was working at a session in Hollywood and saw composer-arranger Bill Justis, who was in LA from Nashville, working on a few projects.

Bill Justis is famous for his song "Raunchy." Anyway, Bill and I were talking and he asked me to do him a favor and drop off some music to Jimmy Bowen, since Jimmy's house was on my way to a gig I had later. "No problem," I said, and took the music to Jimmy's house. When I walked up to the front door, I noticed that it was slightly ajar. I went in slowly, knocking on the door and saying, "Jimmy? It's Don; are you here?" I heard voices in the distance and as I entered the living room I noticed that it was kinda out of order and it looked like some furniture was missing. I kept walking toward the voices and got closer to the open, sliding glass patio door and now I saw and heard Keely and Jimmy yelling at each other. I stopped before going through the patio door when I saw Keely toss something into the pool. Just then Jimmy and Keely noticed me standing there and they stopped. I realized quickly that they were having a really big argument, so I put the music down on a table, gave them a salute, said, "See ya," and got the hell outta there! Later I found out that Jimmy had pushed some of Keely's furniture into the pool and Keely was tossing Jimmy's tapes into the pool when I got there. The two divorced shortly after that encounter.

Not all stories are melodramatic. Here's a funny story about one overdub session for Jimmy. Hal Blaine and I were in the studio together for what we thought was going to be a really quick and easy session. We had the music and Jimmy gave us a little direction, then we got started. It wasn't sounding right, so Jimmy kept stopping and restarting us several times, and he got impatient with me. At one point he said, "Don, can you just follow the music?" I was dumbfounded because I was very careful following the music and didn't know what to say to Jimmy. In fact, after the second take, I carefully looked over the music in front of me and made sure I was reading it correctly. Hal Blaine always had more guts than me when it came to disputing a producer, so Hal fired back, "Maybe that's the problem, the music!" So, then Jimmy answered, "Okay, Hal and Don, let's see . . . bring the music in here." We took the music into the booth, and sure enough, Jimmy discovered the copyist had made an error in writing out the music, and he was the first to start laughing.

When Jimmy Bowen became a producer for Warner Reprise Records, he was responsible for bringing talent in for the label as an A&R (artists and repertoire) executive. I had produced a wonderful country song, "My Little Boy's Hands," written by Irene Clifford and me, which was a heartfelt song about a soldier fighting in the Vietnam War who was reminiscing about his baby son and wife back home. It was so good and I knew Jimmy Bowen would like the song and give it the best chance of making it a hit. When I presented it to Jimmy, he immediately bought the song for Reprise to release as a country single. Jimmy's close friend Donnie "Dirt" Lanier sang the song and played guitar on it, too. Dirt and Jimmy had known each other since high school and were best friends. They played music together when they were teenagers in Texas and worked in music together after they both moved to Los Angeles. Jimmy didn't know Dirt was the singer and guitar player on the song when he first heard it and I didn't tell him until after he bought the song for Reprise. Jimmy was really surprised he didn't recognize Dirt's voice, but this just shows that Jimmy liked the song not because his best friend was on it, he liked the song because it was good. When the single was released, right away the song got airplay in all parts of the United States, except the southern part. It was late 1967 and the Vietnam War was still going on, and "My Little Boy's Hands" was a war protest song. Even though songs protesting the Vietnam War were popular in rock 'n' roll, it was not a popular thing to do in country music, back then.

Donnie "Dirt" Lanier was one of Jimmy Bowen's dearest friends and not long ago, when I contacted Jimmy regarding my book, he told me that Dirt had passed away recently. It hit Jimmy pretty hard and I am sad that we've lost another great musician and good guy who contributed a lot to music.

Speaking of country music . . . Jimmy Bowen moved to Nashville by the mid-1970s and produced many of the most successful and memorable country records of all time for Glen Campbell, Kenny Rogers, Garth Brooks, Hank Williams Jr., the Oak Ridge Boys, Reba McEntire, and many more.

CHAPTER 29

David Axelrod

D avid was born and raised in Los Angeles and grew up listening to R&B and jazz, so his early musical influences made him a very successful composer, arranger, and producer of many soul and jazz recordings from the start of his career in the early '60s. He also released his own recordings. David was one of the first artists to release records that can be considered jazz-fusion.

I started working with David Axelrod in 1966 when he produced the Lou Rawls album *Carryin' On*. From that point, I worked on many of the projects David produced from Cannonball Adderley, Letta Mbulu, Howard Roberts, and David McCallum, and on one of my own albums, *Don Randi Plays the Love Theme from* Romeo and Juliet. David produced my album because Capitol Records suggested he do an album with me; they had received so much fan mail from people who loved my harpsichord solo on "Different Drum" by Linda Ronstadt and the Stone Poneys. Ironically, I never played harpsichord on any of the songs on my solo album.

My version of "The Love Theme from *Romeo and Juliet*" was released as a single in 1969 and started climbing the charts very fast. About a couple of weeks later Henry Mancini released his version of "The Love Theme from *Romeo and Juliet*."

I was on Capitol Records and Henry was on RCA and despite the growing popularity of my version, the suits at Capitol contacted David Axelrod and told him they were going to pull my single. I was crushed! To the public and especially Capitol, Henry Mancini was well known and popular, and unfortunately for me, no one knew my history of all the famous hit songs I had played on so far. The record-buying public had heard my hands but not my name. Years later I met Henry at a recording industry event and though I was not going to mention my single, he brought it up and apologized to me for what had happened. In fact, he very kindly told me he felt my version was better than his.

In June 1968 I was working on a session with David Axelrod on Lou Rawls' album *You're Good for Me*. One of the evenings we were working was the night of the presidential primary election in California and the assassination of Robert Kennedy at the Ambassador Hotel in Los Angeles. We went on a break and heard what had happened. The whole crew was upset, as was the country, hearing of this horrible murder and the loss of the man who was certain to be nominated as the Democratic presidential candidate. I went to David to tell him what happened and ask if he was going to call the date. He got irritated with me and said, "Don't you know that Robert Kennedy was appointed by McCarthy to be the assistant attorney of the Senate committee that persecuted innocent Americans suspected of communism?" Of course, I knew. I fired back, "My father was blacklisted and questioned by that committee and nearly lost our family business, but Bobby resigned from that committee and is different now; he defended civil rights and was a strong supporter of Martin Luther King." But this information didn't change David's mind and we kept working that night.

David Axelrod's talent as a truly innovative composer and arranger was demonstrated in a groundbreaking project, *Mass in F Minor* for the Electric Prunes. I was involved as a musician and contractor for that project.

The Electric Prunes is famous for their rock 'n' roll hit "I've Had Too Much to Dream Last Night," but a song from their album *Mass in F Minor*, "Kyrie Eleison," can be considered nearly as famous. "Kyrie Eleison" was featured in the 1969 film *Easy Rider*, which starred Peter Fonda, Jack Nicholson, and Dennis Hopper. Dave Hassinger (the group's manager) was listed as the producer of *Mass in F Minor*, but David Axelrod was in control of the development of the album concept with his compositions and arrangements. David wanted an orchestra and a choir to add to the grandness of the songs, so many additional musicians and choral singers were hired for the sessions. The original band members played and sang as well: Jim Lowe, Mark Tulin, Ken Williams, Mike Gannon, and Quint Fortune. Though there was much controversy over the Electric Prunes' recording *Mass in F Minor*, there were plans for the band to go out on tour to promote this album and reach the demographic of teens and twenty-year-olds who had not embraced the concept of the album, which was the musical prayers from a Catholic Mass performed by a rock 'n' roll group. If that wasn't odd enough, we were booked at Culver City High School in a concert for the students to see if the group had a chance at a successful tour.

David Axelrod wanted the concert to be a theatrical experience, so we had to dress in costume for the show. I wore a British-style bowler hat and a cape over my suit. There was a choir of background singers dressed in choir robes. There were strings and horns in the band as well. Unfortunately, the members of the Electric Prunes did not spend enough time rehearsing with us before the show. We started with the song "Kyrie Eleison," but when the lead vocal was sung, it was off pitch and timing. The singer tried to recover and continue, but wasn't given a chance because the audience started to boo and shout. They chanted, "Play 'Too Much to Dream'!" Then a beer bottle was thrown from the audience onto the stage and it broke, spraying beer everywhere. We stopped playing, waiting for the audience to calm down, but the principal of the school got up and announced the show was over. That made the students even angrier and we got off the stage as quickly as possible. It was frightening because I thought the angry teens were going to rush toward the stage and riot, but we got out of there through the rear of the auditorium and the back of the campus. Needless to say, the tour didn't happen, and that experience has remained one of the most unusual concert gigs and the shortest I've ever played.

CHAPTER 30

Ray Ruff and the New World

R ay Ruff (who passed away in 2005) produced and promoted many top recording artists, and I worked with him on several projects. Some projects were for artists that had so much talent and potential to become the biggest names in music.

One such artist was Susie Allanson, a very talented singer and performer. Susie has an amazing voice and she had a few very successful recordings. One was *We Belong Together*, an album produced by Ray Ruff. I did some of the arrangements and performed on several of the songs for that album, which charted in the top five of the *Billboard* and *Cashbox* country charts back in 1978.

In addition to *We Belong Together* in 1978, I worked on Susie's debut album, *Susie Allanson*, in 1976; *A Little Love* in 1977; and *Heart to Heart* in 1979. All were produced by Ray Ruff and I did a majority of the arrangements and played piano on the songs.

Ray was smitten with Susie and they got married around the time *We Belong Together* was released. Afterward their relationship, both private and professional, became strained. This affected Susie's music career and projects while she was still married to Ray. One song that I arranged for Susie that Ray produced was "Unchained Melody." I had also played on the original release of the song with the Righteous Brothers that Phil Spector produced. Susie's version of the song was outstanding and it should have been a single that would put Susie on the top of the pop music charts. It would have if Ray had not held back on promoting the song, and I was disappointed.

Susie Allanson and Ray Ruff were not married for long and Susie's career in country music was short, but the country albums that Ray produced for her were excellent. In fact, *Heart to Heart* was issued on MP3 recently. After her solo career in country ended, Susie married Steve Williams, an arranger, producer, and pianist. As Susie Williams, she has had even greater success as a director and contractor of children's choirs for TV, radio, and films. Susie's talents continue to touch many people.

Tricia Lynn (not related to Loretta Lynn) was another very talented singer that Ray produced, and I worked on the project with him as arranger and player. Tricia and her parents were some of the nicest people you could ever meet. We went to Columbia, South Carolina, to record Tricia's album because Ray had a ranch there and he wanted to use a recording studio near his ranch. Ray had two homes in those days, one in Los Angeles and the ranch in South Carolina. Anyway, we got to the studio and recorded the country songs that Ray planned, but Tricia also wanted to do a couple of Elton John songs that I arranged for her. These songs were not country in style, but I thought they turned out even better than the country songs and showed Tricia's range and versatility. Everyone in the studio and Tricia loved how the Elton John recordings turned out, but Ray didn't like them. He said he'd hold on to them and maybe release them later. For some reason, Ray didn't do much with Tricia's record to promote it so her career in music never took off, and of course those Elton John songs were never heard by the public. It's a shame.

Also, the studio we recorded at in Columbia was peculiar. I saw many photos of black gospel artists up on the walls around the studio, but when we were there, which was during the day, I never saw one black person at the studio. I asked the receptionist about the pictures and she told me that after hours was when black artists could book the studio. This was the early 1980s and I thought segregation did not exist in the US anymore and was surprised to discover this.

Tricia Lynn gave me a lovely gift for working on her album. It's a western-style silver belt buckle with my initial on it and I am certain she had it custom made. I wear that buckle often. Tricia's music career didn't take off. She is a happy rancher who raises Angus steer. Tricia and her daughters are also famous equestrians, riding in many well-known parades each year.

Another project I did with Ray that went nowhere was for Pia Zadora. If you aren't familiar with the name, Pia Zadora was popular in the early 1980s as an actress in a few "B" movies and she also had a few recordings that made it to the charts. Though critics slammed her acting talent, she was a hit musically in Europe and had some success in the US. Ray Ruff was hired to produce an album for her. Even though he may have been known for producing country artists, he did produce many other projects that were not country. But I think one of the reasons the record company wanted Ray is that he really knew how to promote a record. That is, if he was inspired to. We recorded four to six songs with Pia, but I don't know if they were ever released.

One perk I took during this project was on one evening after we finished the day's session and were about to go home. Ray was going to stay for a while and work on the mix of the song with the engineer. Ray owned a Rolls-Royce Corniche and I asked him if I could drive his car. I had always wanted to drive a Rolls. He said, "Sure!" I left him the keys to my car and said, "In case you need to go and I haven't returned." Ray said, "Sure, sure." So, I took Ray's car and had a ball driving it around town. I decided to keep it over the weekend (it was a Friday evening when I borrowed it), so I drove the car home and used it over the weekend and didn't tell Ray. I was expecting him to call my house, asking me to bring back his car, but he never called. On Monday I drove the Rolls back to the studio for our session and there was my car parked right where I'd left it. I went in the studio and handed the keys back to Ray. He said, "Thank God! I didn't know what to think when you didn't come back!" I told him I was expecting him to call me, but he said he was afraid to, thinking I might have crashed.

Of course, Ray Ruff wasn't known for failed projects. He was very successful as a producer and record promoter. Some of the other top artists I worked with Ray on were Hank Williams Jr., the Everly Brothers, Pat Boone,

Michael Quatro, and Delaney Bramlett. Ray also produced one of my albums, *Bermuda Triangle*.

The musicians in Quest who recorded *Bermuda Triangle* were: Dave Edelstein on bass, Steve Turner on drums, Darryl Manninen on guitar, Luis Conte on congas, Chuck Camper on sax, and me on keyboards. Ray Lawrence, who I think was a marketing person for the record company, told Ray Ruff and me to name the album after one of the songs we recorded for it, "Bermuda Triangle," because he had a painting in mind for the album cover, which showed a stormy sea with musical instruments being pulled into a vortex. The song "Bermuda Triangle" has a dramatic, moody feeling about it and was a good choice for the title, and the album is one my best. We recorded the album at Heritage Studios, which had a really good Steinway piano. Ray Ruff was a creative producer and had a good instinct when it came to recording the best, full sound on my piano parts. *Bermuda Triangle* was released in 1978.

As previously mentioned, Ray Ruff was a very creative record promoter. I didn't work with him on this record, but Ray was famous for the promo stunt he orchestrated for the release of Debby Boone's single "You Light Up My Life." He had arranged for armored trucks to deliver the single to radio stations in the major markets across the country on the same day, creating a lot of publicity for the record and getting coverage by the local news outlets in those cities.

Ray produced one of Nancy Sinatra's albums. In fact, one of my favorite songs that Nancy sings is "Now I Have Everything," which is on that album. We recorded the album at Entourage Studios in Burbank and Ray, who spent most of the year living at his ranch in South Carolina, had to drive across the country to get to this session. He had a big RV he often drove when he did this. I arrived at Entourage for Nancy's session and as I walked through the parking lot, I saw a face staring at me from Ray's RV and it kinda scared me. As I got closer I could see it was a live mountain lion that had a big snaggletooth. I went in the studio and asked Ray if that was his mountain lion in the RV and he said yes. He could not leave him at home alone, so he brought him. I said, "But you can't just leave him out there." Ray said, "He's fine," and when the mountain lion needed to go, Ray took him out on a leash and he did his business. Of course none of us at the session thought it was a good idea to leave the big cat out in the RV, but it could not be in the studio, either. That mountain lion, or cougar, meant a lot to Ray Ruff. So much so that he started his own record label and called it Cougar Records after his beloved pet.

By now you are starting to get that Ray Ruff had a distinct, unpredictable, and often quirky personality. He was a born Texan and loved his ranch in South Carolina and he had some old southern/cowboy ways about him. One of his habits that we loathed was chewing tobacco; Ray would spit into a Styrofoam coffee cup that he carried around with him. This habit was something that we all had to bear with, but on one occasion Jerry Cole (guitar) had to deal with it in a very direct way.

On one session, Jerry was playing guitar and it was a demanding part that Ray and Jerry went back and forth on to get the right arrangement and sound. After a few takes Ray said he thought we had it, so we came into the booth to hear the playback. Jerry had poured himself a cup of coffee and brought it with him into the booth and set his coffee on the desk of the console while we listened to the playback. The song sounded great and Ray complimented Jerry on his part. Jerry was very happy and thanked Ray as he reached for his coffee, raised the cup in a toast to him, and took a big gulp. Except it was not his coffee; it was Ray's tobacco cup he'd picked up by mistake, because it was the same kind of Styrofoam cup and was next to his coffee. Jerry looked like he was gonna die and was so mad at Ray for chewing tobacco and leaving his cup there, but Ray just laughed along with the rest of us.

I did a couple of albums with Pat Boone that Ray Ruff produced. I liked working with Pat, who is a very nice and talented guy. There were a few years between the albums I did for Pat, and on the more recent session the new world of recording was making its debut to Ray.

We were at American Recording studio, owned by Richie Podolor and Bill Cooper, working on a song and Pat was singing live with the band. We were watching Ray Ruff while we were playing and noticed that he kept turning his head to one side, repeatedly. Between takes Pat asked me if something was wrong with Ray—was he having some kind of seizure?—because he also saw that jerky head-turning Ray was doing. And Ray looked really worried and kept asking the engineer, "Did you get that?" Finally, I asked Ray if there was something wrong. He said, "The damn tape is not turning! How the hell are we getting this on tape?!" He was turning his head to check on the tape machine that was not being used. This studio was one of the first to start using the newest digital recording method and had Pro Tools, but it still had the old tape machine in the booth. Ray could not fathom how we could be recording without tape. He just didn't get it and that was frustrating him. It was the new world of digital recording, and I am still amazed that my own career has covered mono to multitrack recording and now the unlimited possibilities with digital recording and editing. The recording techniques had evolved, but Ray Ruff was set in his old ways.

CHAPTER 31

Jerry Fuller—Producer and Composer

Jerry Fuller is one of the most successful and prolific hit songwriters in America. Jerry also produced many top artists and I have had the pleasure of playing on many of the hits Jerry produced. Many included songs he also wrote.

Recently, Jerry performed a one-man show at Café Cordiale, a restaurant/nightclub in Studio City, and I went to enjoy his show and catch up with him. The audience was amazed at all of the songs he played, which they knew from artists of the '60s and '70s. At the end of the set Jerry took questions from the audience and I raised my hand. Jerry introduced me to the audience and told stories of the sessions we worked on together. My response was, "I don't have a question, but I would love to have your monthly royalties statement!"

Back in 1961 Jerry Fuller's big break came when he had written the song "Travelin' Man," which was meant for Sam Cooke, but Joe Osborn (bass player), who was listening to the demo being played in the next room, took the song to Ricky Nelson and it became a huge hit.

Years later I worked closely with Ricky Nelson on one of his final recording projects. He met with me at my home in the Hollywood Hills to go over the music with me, and my family was so thrilled to meet him.

One of the many successful projects I worked on with Jerry was with Gary Puckett and the Union Gap. Jerry Fuller discovered the group in a San Diego bowling alley lounge and it became a hit rock group with the songs "Young Girl" and "Lady Willpower," which Jerry also wrote. I played on those songs as well as other songs on the group's albums that Jerry produced.

Another hit recording that I played on was "The Son of Hickory Holler's Tramp" with O.C. Smith, produced by Jerry. A year earlier I played on a version of that song for Sanford Clark that Lee Hazlewood produced. I really liked the version with Sanford Clark, but you never know what will make a song a hit. O.C.'s version was great, too, and Jerry's production of the song with O.C. became the big hit.

Jerry Fuller is one of those truly great guys and fun to be around, and we became friends while working on projects. Back in the 1970s I owned a boat that I kept at the yacht club in Marina del Rey, and one Saturday I invited Jerry Fuller and Dirt (Donnie Lanier—guitar) out on my boat for a day of fishing and relaxation. We went out and anchored about four miles to the south of the marina, just off the shores of El Segundo. There is a towerlike structure out in the ocean in this area that is a fantastic place to catch fish, and no one seemed to know this because we were the only ones there. We were out there for just a couple of hours and Dirt was catching some big fish, but Jerry was not as enthusiastic about being out in the boat. He didn't realize how the motion was going to affect him. While I was looking through the binoculars to see if there were any other boats in our vicinity, I noticed a sailboat coming toward us from Marina del Rey. Even though it was still a ways out the sailboat looked like it was going pretty fast, but I wasn't concerned about it yet. It was a large, fifty-foot power sailboat compared to my twenty-two-foot motorboat. I kept an eye on the sailboat through my binoculars and soon I started to worry because it was getting closer and not changing course, which meant it was heading straight for us. I got my air horn out and blew the horn a couple of times to get the crew's attention. By now they should be able to see my boat and change course to avoid hitting us.

They didn't turn, and I looked through the binoculars to see what the crew was doing on the sailboat. I didn't see anyone on deck. I was now in a panic and asked Dirt to pull up the anchor because we had to move. I kept blowing the air horn and yelling to hopefully get the attention of anyone onboard that sailboat. I checked on Jerry and his face was white from both fear and seasickness. That sailboat was getting closer and I was blowing the air horn and yelling out to it. Finally I could see two small hands on the wheel of the boat and then a man came out from below and took the wheel. Now I could see there was a kid steering the sailboat; he was small so I could not see him until they got a lot closer. Dirt got the anchor up and I tried to start my boat, but it would not start. We braced ourselves for a collision.

Despite the man's attempt to steer his sailboat away from us, it was going too fast and there was not enough time to steer clear of my boat. The sailboat hit the bow of my motorboat. The sailboat, which was made of wood, was damaged very badly. My boat didn't suffer any serious damage, just some scratches, but Jerry Fuller was sick thinking we were going to sink in the ocean.

The owner of the sailboat told us he was not on deck because he was using the bathroom below. He'd thought his son could just keep the boat going straight along the shoreline, but the kid could not see over the wheel. The guy who owned the sailboat was very apologetic and said he would pay for any of the damage to my boat that the accident had caused, but his boat was the one that needed a lot of repairs. We called the Coast Guard and they towed the sailboat back to the marina.

After they left I tried again to get my boat started and the motor just would not turn over. It was odd, like the motor completely died, so I had to get the Coast Guard out again, to tow us back to the marina. When we got back, it was difficult to get my boat back into the slip without the motor, and with all the commotion some of my buddies at the marina came over to see what was going on. I told them my motor would not start and we tried it. One of the guys who did repairs on boats offered to take a look to see if there was something damaged under the boat. He put on this dive suit and went into the water. Under my boat he found there was trash stuck in the exhaust of the motor, which prevented it from starting. It was a cap from a milk bottle that must have been sucked into the exhaust pipe of the motor when I stopped the engine in El Segundo. We were really lucky that nothing too serious happened to us that day, but I am sure Jerry hasn't gone fishing on a boat since our big boating adventure!

CHAPTER 32

Joe Wissert

Joe Wissert is a record producer who doesn't always get a spotlight for the many outstanding hit records he has produced, but he should. He has produced hit records for a diverse list of artists, like Gordon Lightfoot, Earth, Wind & Fire, Boz Scaggs, and Helen Reddy. The Turtles was another popular group in the early 1960s that Joe Wissert produced, and I played on their hit "You Know What I Mean."

Recently Joe and I reconnected at my club, The Baked Potato, when he came in to hear me play with my band, Quest. When I saw him sitting at the bar in my club, I didn't recognize him at first, but I knew his face was familiar to me. Joe was smiling as he said, "Don, you don't remember me, do you? We used to work together." When Joe told me his name I remembered him, but to be honest he looks very different today than I remember him; but I also look a lot different now, too. I also remembered the fine English bowler hat he gave me as a gift many years ago when I worked with him on projects. That was the hat I wore as part of my costume in the one-time *Mass in F Minor* concert I conducted with the Electric Prunes at Culver City High School. It's always great to see guys like Joe Wissert after all the years since we worked together, plus he's one of the nicest people you could know.

CHAPTER 33

Jackie Mills

J ackie Mills was not only a very successful record producer, he was also a talented jazz drummer who played in big bands for Tommy Dorsey, Dizzy Gillespie, and Billie Holiday. Jackie also was a composer and wrote songs for TV programs and produced album projects with breakout music artists from television shows.

Jackie also owned a wonderful recording studio, Larrabee Sound, in Hollywood. It was located on Larrabee Street, but the studio moved to Lankershim Boulevard in North Hollywood in the 1990s. Since the studio had such a famed reputation they kept the name.

I played on very popular songs recorded by teen idols David Cassidy, who was in the *Partridge Family* TV series, and Bobby Sherman from the TV series *Here Come the Brides*. Jackie Mills was the producer for solo albums of these two artists.

For Bobby Sherman I played on six of the songs on his hit album *Here Comes Bobby*: "Easy Come Easy Go," "Hey, Honey Bun," "La La La," "July Seventeen," "Make Your Own Kind of Music," and "Two Blind Minds."

There is a specific story I recall about when I worked on David Cassidy's album. The session was at A&M studios in Hollywood and Jackie Mills hired me to play piano on a few songs for David's album. I believe it was his second or third album release, so David Cassidy had some success in his solo career already. We were on a short break and were nearly finished with the session for the day. I thought the session was going very well and I know Jackie did, too. I happened to be sitting a few feet away from Jackie when David Cassidy walked over to him and said, "Jackie, I need to let you know that I want to produce my next project myself." I was really surprised by what I overheard and I looked over at Jackie. Jackie Mills was gracious and told David that was fine, and David thanked him, then walked away. But after David turned to walk away, I saw Jackie's reaction. He looked crushed. Jackie Mills was not only a fantastic producer and drummer, he was a sensitive person. I felt bad for Jackie because I know how he must have felt. My feelings have been hurt like that, too. Jackie always put so much of himself into a project, but I don't think David realized or meant to hurt Jackie's feelings; he just wanted to produce his own projects.

Santo and Johnny was a musical duo famous for the song "Sleep Walk." Jackie Mills also produced an album for Santo and Johnny and I played piano on the project.

CHAPTER 34

H.B. Barnum—Producer and Arranger

M y good friend Hidle Brown Barnum, known as H.B., has been successful in music since he was a child, playing piano and singing in early television and radio shows, like *The Jack Benny Show* and *Amos and Andy*. H.B. is
so musically talented that he can play many different instruments besides the
piano, and he has a great singing voice as well. In fact, H.B. recorded a few
solo albums in the early 1960s and had a top forty single in 1961, "Lost Love."
He became even more successful as an arranger and composer, and in my
opinion, H.B. is one of the best arrangers in the music business. One of his
signature sounds is beautifully impactful, soulful horns in an arrangement.

H.B. was the arranger when David Axelrod produced the three albums
Lou Rawls released for Capitol Records: *Too Much*, 1967; *You're Good for Me*,
1968; and *The Way It Was, the Way It Is*, 1969. I played piano on all those albums.

Many of you might be familiar with the actor David McCallum, who currently plays Dr. Donald "Ducky" Mallard on the TV series *NCIS*, or for his
role on the '60s TV series *The Man from U.N.C.L.E.* as the Russian agent Illya
Kuryakin. David Axelrod produced the albums *David McCallum Music—A
Part of Me*, *Music—It's Happening Now*, *Music—A Bit More of Me*, and *Mc-
Callum*. H.B. Barnum did the arrangements and I played piano for the songs
on these albums, which were released on Capitol Records.

H.B. worked for Motown Records before and after the company moved
from Detroit to Los Angeles in 1972 and he was arranging and composing

for many of its artists. I played keyboards on Motown sessions with H.B. for Brenda Holloway and Diana Ross and the Supremes.

I recall a story that happened when I was playing piano on a session for Diana Ross. Diana sang live in the studio with the band for this song and H.B. was directing. Diana was set up on a stool next to H.B. in front of the band and I was at a keyboard that was set up toward the back of the studio. H.B. is a very physically animated person who moves his body, arms, and hands a lot when expressing himself. When he's conducting, his movements are even grander. While we were recording a take of the song, H.B. was really getting into the music and his movements were even more exaggerated. So much so that he accidentally hit Diana Ross with a sweep of his arm and knocked her right off her stool. We all stopped immediately when this happened and a couple of people came out of the booth to help Diana. H.B., in shock at what he had done, rushed to pick up Diana and see if she was all right and apologized profusely. H.B. looked up into the booth to see if Berry Gordy Jr. (head of Motown Records) was angry with him. H.B. thought that this was going to be his last time working for Motown, but Diana was not injured, just shaken a little, and Berry told H.B. to continue with the session. What a relief that was for Diana, H.B., and everyone in the session.

I played on O.C. Smith's two signature hits, "The Son of Hickory Holler's Tramp" and "Little Green Apples," which were beautifully arranged by H.B. Barnum and produced by Jerry Fuller. "Son of Hickory Holler's Tramp" is still one of my favorite songs, and I think it is one of the best "story" songs recorded. O.C. Smith had such a wonderful, deep, rich voice that was perfect for the song, which was written by Dallas Frazier. Contrary to misinformation floating out on the Internet about where O.C. Smith recorded "Son of Hickory Holler's Tramp," the recording session was done in Los Angeles, not Muscle Shoals.

H.B. also wrote and produced music for television shows, which led to his stint as the music director for a UHF-TV station, KEEF, which was the first African American–owned TV station in Los Angeles. The studio was state of the art with all-new equipment and was located on Washington Boulevard near

Figueroa. Everyone who worked at KEEF—including the camera operators, technicians in the booth, producers, and directors—was black. H.B. hired me to play piano in the band for a variety show. I was the only nonblack person in the band. The station really had potential but it only lasted a few months. Perhaps one of the reasons it didn't do well was that the station was on channel 68 and was very hard to tune into if you were just about anywhere in Los Angeles. If you lived in Beverly Hills, however, the channel seemed to come in clearly.

In the late 1960s and early 1970s H.B. and I were working a lot on recording projects, many of them together, and we became good friends. I owned a boat back then and had it docked at Marina del Rey. I loved to take my sons, David and Justin, fishing on my boat, and a few times I invited H.B. and his son to go fishing with us. It was great for both H.B. and I to spend the much-needed downtime from our busy recording schedules and more time with our sons. I would pick up H.B. and his son at 5:00 a.m. and he would bring a big metal pail filled with food. This pail looked like a metal trash can with a lid, but was half the size of a regular trash can with a handle for carrying purposes, and was filled with fried chicken, coleslaw, rolls, and baked beans for all of us to eat on our fishing trip. It was all really delicious and he always brought enough food for everyone and then some. Even if we didn't catch much, we all enjoyed the food, one another, and our time out on the ocean for the day.

One Christmas Eve H.B. surprised me by arriving at my home to deliver a fruitcake as a gift. The fruitcake itself was not the best part of the gift—it was the presentation. H.B. arrived at my doorstep dressed like Santa Claus with a sack over his shoulder accompanied by his good friend Jim Alfrey, who was dressed in a green elf costume. The hilarious part of this scenario is Jim was a tall 6′7″ and H.B. is 5′10″. The sight of the two at my door was the best Christmas gift that year.

One of the benefits of being in the recording business for all these years is that I have done many types of music projects and this experience begins to repeat in new projects, even while technology has advanced and changed exponentially. Though I don't have the exact details of the songs, I have an interesting story how the past met the future with a little help from H.B. Barnum . . .

In the 1960s I played piano on many projects that H.B. Barnum produced and arranged. Nearly forty years later a young record producer who was working on an R&B/hip-hop project hired me to record a piano overdub. He got my name from H.B. Barnum, who told him I was the one who played piano on an early O'Jays single that was released on Little Star Records in 1963. When I arrived at the studio, the producer asked me if I remembered the song because he wanted me to play the same part I played on this particular record. I told him I could not remember the song because I've played on so many songs for H.B. Barnum and other artists and producers, but asked if he happened to have the record so I could hear it. He did have it! It was the 45 rpm single and there happened to be a record player at the studio with a special size 45 spindle from back in the day when you could stack several 45s on the record player to play one after the other. I hadn't seen that kind of record player in years. Anyway, when I heard the piano part, I recognized it and said, "Sure, I can play that for you." It was a simple piano line that included rolling chord changes.

I did the session in just under an hour, which included some improvising on that part to the producer's liking. Before I left, I asked him what he would have done if he could not find me to play the part, and he said he would have tried to sample my playing from the 45 rpm single. Unfortunately, I don't remember the producer's name, who the artist was, or the title of the tune, but if I hear the song . . .

CHAPTER 35

John Boylan, Dick Glasser, Richard Perry

John Boylan

I played in sessions for many different artists with producer John Boylan. John had an incredible ear and great talent for picking songs. He also composed music. My favorite project with John Boylan was with Rick Nelson. In fact, Rick Nelson came to my home to work with me on a song we did that was written by Randy Newman, titled "The Family."

Dick Glasser

I worked many different sessions with Dick Glasser when he was one of the staff producers at Warner Reprise Records. The most memorable session was for the Everly Brothers and their album *The Everly Brothers Sing*. The song "Bowling Green" was one of the songs from that album and became a top forty hit. Dick Glasser also produced one of my albums, *Live on the Sunset Strip*.

His brother, Ted Glasser, also was a record producer, and I worked with him as well.

Richard Perry

Richard gave me the opportunity to work with the Lovin' Spoonful, Tiny Tim, and of all singers, Mrs. Miller.

CHAPTER 36

Motown

In 1972 Berry Gordy Jr. (founder of Motown Records) officially moved the headquarters of the company from Detroit to Los Angeles. I started playing on Motown recordings for various producers, arrangers, and artists in LA even before they made the move here. Unfortunately, the documentation for many of these projects is missing or inaccurate. Sometimes omissions or errors on union contracts occurred due to a clerical mistake and weren't intentional. For Motown, at least in the years before and a few after it moved to Los Angeles, it was intentional.

You might have heard about a phenomenal group of Motown session musicians called the Funk Brothers, because there is a book and award-winning documentary film about their story (*Standing in the Shadows of Motown*). Essentially, these remarkable musicians, who played on every hit record Motown released in the days they were headquartered in Detroit, were never paid on a union contract; it was always in cash and most of the time very low compared to what they should have been paid based on union scale. They were never credited for playing, composing, or arranging these songs. Even though their public status was similar to the Wrecking Crew players that I was a part of, the big difference was Wrecking Crew musicians were contracted, or hired on union contracts. That means there is legal documentation of the sessions we played and songs we composed, arranged, or produced, etc. There are different pay scales based on what we did for the session, and we were paid overtime if a session went longer than a certain amount of hours, or if we worked a session on Saturday or Sunday. We get royalty payments if a song we played on airs on the radio, or is used on a television show, or an advertisement, or a film. Also, the record companies paid the fees to our health and welfare, and pension funds with the union in accordance with the union contract. Even if our names aren't listed on an album cover, the union contract proves we are entitled to our payments. This is why the Funk Brothers were not only unknown to the public, but also devastated financially after Motown left Detroit.

Because Motown Records was not "accustomed" to supplying documentation, let alone accurate documentation to the AFM (American Federation of Musicians, a.k.a. the union), it is very difficult to verify contracts of which recordings I worked on for Motown, but I can tell you how I helped push Motown toward union contract compliancy.

On the first Motown date I played, the session went smoothly and was outstanding musically. The guys on the session with me were mostly musicians I played with all the time, but there was one player that I didn't know before the session. He was a brilliant bass player from Detroit. Anyway, when the session was done, a man dressed in a suit walked into the studio with a briefcase. I noticed how he was dressed because people in music usually dress more casually and much more hip. He looked like a lawyer or some other corporate "suit" of Motown. He put his briefcase down on a table near me, opened it, and to my shock, I saw it had a lot of cash in it. The man prepared to start handing out cash to the players, which was bizarre to me. On a major-label recording date, this is not how it goes down. Then the impact of the situation hit me and I said, "Stop, wait a minute! Where are our W-4 forms to fill out? Where is the contractor?" The guy answered, "We don't do contracts or fill out forms; we pay you in cash for the date. Don't worry; you'll get a lot of cash today." Very smugly, he added, "This is how we do it in Detroit." That last bit enraged me because I knew exactly what Motown was up to . . . cheating us out of our future! I snapped back hard: "That's not how it's done in Los Angeles! If you don't get a union contractor here, right now, you can bet I will go straight to the union and expose Motown for violating pay scale and contract rules." I was so pissed that I felt like screaming and was about to say more when I was startled and jumped, because a pair of arms wrapped around me from behind in a hug. At first, I thought someone was trying to restrain me because I probably looked like I was about to punch this "suit" in the mouth. But the person was actually hugging me and saying, "Thank you! Thank you!" That person was James Jamerson, the bass player I had just met on this session. He was one of the Funk Brothers. Everyone in the studio now was glaring at the guy in the suit. The man closed his briefcase and said, "Okay, wait here," and he left the studio.

The Detroit-area Motown session players known as the Funk Brothers were: Joe Hunter, Earl Van Dyke (piano and organ); Clarence Isabell (double bass); James Jamerson (bass and double bass); Benny "Papa Zita" Benjamin and Richard "Pistol" Allen (drums); Paul Riser (trombone); Robert White, Eddie Willis, and Joe Messina (guitar); Jack Ashford (percussion, vibes); Jack Brokensha (vibes); Eddie "Bongo" Brown (percussion); and Antonio "Tony" Newton (bass).

To be honest, after that session I never expected to be asked to do another Motown session, but many of the producers and arrangers I worked regularly with on other record projects started producing Motown artists and wanted to hire me, so I played on several more Motown sessions.

Interestingly, one Motown project was for Tony Martin, who recorded a vocal version of my hit song "Mexican Pearls," which I wrote originally as an instrumental. Ernie Freeman was the arranger and music director for this project and someone wrote lyrics for my song. Tony Martin is a terrific vocalist and the arrangement was great, but the lyrics . . . let's just say they weren't my style.

A few of the Motown projects I worked on were with the talented composer, conductor, and arranger Gene Page. Gene was creative, passionate, and very detailed, and his signature sound was intricate horns and string arrangements. He also had a solo recording career, but his records were released on other labels, not Motown. I played keyboards in Motown recording sessions for Marvin Gaye, Stevie Wonder, the Four Tops, and Diana Ross, with

Gene Page, who was either the arranger or producer on those records. Again, due to poor administration by Motown on contracts, it's hard to verify exactly which songs I played on and many times I played sessions where the artist was not there because it was an overdub or the producer wanted to get the main rhythm tracks done and the vocal session was scheduled the following day. Sometimes the title of the song was not yet confirmed when I went into a session. This was common on some sessions for other record companies as well, but most other record companies updated contracts or submitted the contracts to the union after all of the details were confirmed.

Gene Page was the arranger for a Diana Ross project and I remember getting a call in the middle of the night from him. He asked if I would help sketch out the parts for the arrangement (write in the notes for the individual music parts for the different instruments). He told me a messenger was on their way to my house to deliver the music. I worked through the night to complete everything. The song was "Touch Me in the Morning," which was a big hit for Diana Ross. I also played on that song.

Gene Page expressed his passion for the music when conducting by putting a lot of physical movement into his conducting style, but he also had a unique habit. Before beginning a run-through, Gene would go over the music in detail and explain what he wanted and the feeling we should go for when playing. Then, with sweeping arm and body movements, he would count down, "One and two and . . . ," then suddenly Gene would stop and say, "Oh, hey, guys, don't forget at bar ten to . . ." But the beat after he had said, "Two and," we'd started playing the first few notes and as we stopped playing, it sounded like a circus band. Just imagine runners getting a false start and having to suddenly stop . . . it takes a few steps to do that. With his instructions done, we'd get ready to start again and Gene would start counting down like before and again he'd stop and say something like, "Oh, and don't forget at the bridge . . ." Again, we'd start and stop for Gene. He'd do this at least two or three times before we played through the entire song. Reading this description, it may sound like an annoying habit to you, but Gene was such a good guy that we laughed at ourselves and with him. Gene Page passed away in

1998 and he's very much missed, but I grin every time I remember his style of conducting.

Some of the earlier Motown sessions I did were for the Jackson 5. Even though in 1969 Motown was still headquartered in Detroit, all of the Jackson 5 records were recorded in Los Angeles. The songs I played on were for their hit album *ABC*, which became one of the group's best and most popular releases. I played on the title song, "ABC," and other tracks on the album. Michael Jackson was only eleven years old when I met him on an overdub session and noticed how interested he was in the recording process and ar-ranging. Between takes, Michael asked me several perceptive questions in regards to the way I played the music and about improvisation. He was de-lightful and though he was young at the time, Michael Jackson impressed me then as a very talented, sharp, and focused young man. Around 1984, Michael Jackson and one of his brothers, perhaps Jermaine, came into The Baked Potato on a night I was playing with my band, Quest. I noticed him sitting at the bar and he nodded when he saw me look his way. Michael and his brother didn't stay long, but I think it was his way of letting me know he remembered me and the time we spoke, years earlier.

My good friend H.B. Barnum arranged, produced, and directed several Motown record projects, as mentioned in my chapter on him.

CHAPTER 37

The Catskills—My Early Life

I was born the only child of Max and Ethel Schwartz in New York City on February 25, 1937, but before I turned one, my family moved up state to the Catskill Mountains. There I grew up in Woodridge, New York, an idyllic paradise of small-town life and resort living with all the outdoor amenities, like swimming, fishing, hunting, hiking, skiing, skating, and the excitement of the stage with the top entertainers of the time. The late 1940s and the 1950s were probably the greatest years for the Catskills, a.k.a. the "Jewish Alps" or the "Borscht Belt." The area is famous in American cultural history for being a Jewish resort hot spot. Urbanites, politicians, sports figures, comedians, music greats, and mobsters alike flocked to the Catskills resorts as their summer vacation destination away from New York City.

The larger resorts, like Kutsher's, Brown's, Grossinger's, and the Concord, attracted the popular new talent of the day, like Jerry Lewis, Buddy Hackett, Danny Kaye, Jackie Gleason, Bobby Darin, Steve Lawrence and Eydie Gorme, Eddie Fisher, and many more. I was lucky enough to grow up in the middle of it all in Woodridge.

My father, Max, was born in Romania in 1883 and though he wore many hats throughout his lifetime, his heart was in show business. Max immigrated to New York via Toronto and found his way to the vaudeville stage, tap dancing. He also directed and produced some silent films for the Jewish immigrant audience. He founded the first actors' union in New York and gained such a high level of respect and reputation in the New York theater scene that the

Roosevelt administration asked if he would become a liaison between out-of-work actors and writers and the WPA (Work Projects Administration), an agency that employed millions of people during the Depression. My father helped many starving actors and playwrights during that time.

While we're on the subject, I was watching the TV program *Real Time with Bill Maher* and Carl Reiner was one of the guests. The focus of discussion was the complicated subject of government programs and assistance. Carl Reiner's ire got raised and he spoke up. When he was seventeen, the WPA found him a job. If the government hadn't had his back, he would not have become an actor. I'm proud that my father was part of the WPA and helped many people like Carl Reiner.

By the end of the Depression, my father decided to move the family to the Catskills and open a deli and restaurant called the Actors Inn. With the hordes of vacationers and all the entertainment types in the area, the deli and restaurant was a smashing success. My father served the highest-quality ko-sher meats: pastrami, salami, corned beef. Even during the war years when it was difficult to get a supply of meat, my dad had a constant supply that came in by train from New York City from the now famous company Hebrew National. He was also known for making the best salads anywhere, before salads were cool.

Because of my father's experience in New York with the WPA and his be-ing known by many of the Jewish entertainers and agents, it was natural for him to include a spot in the Actors Inn for the talent and agents to hang out and conduct their business. He provided the back section of the restaurant with a bank of telephones and a piano, where the talent could rehearse and the agents could book their acts. The Actors Inn became the place where most of the acts in the Catskills got booked. Open late and well into the wee hours of the morning, the Actors Inn also was where the musicians, talent, and managers would meet, get paid, and hang out after the shows. Also many of the guests from the resorts would come in late to grab a bite to eat and hope to see their favorite talent and maybe get to chat with them. It was an awesome place to be and grow up!

In the late '40s, the postwar McCarthy-era paranoia against communists hit Woodridge and my family. My father knew everyone from Albert Einstein to Peg Leg Bates and he didn't have a prejudiced bone in his body, and that is how I grew up as well.

My father treated people with respect, openness, and kindness and he associated with many of the entertainers who were active in groups that McCarthy labeled anti-American or communist. If Max Schwartz liked you, he didn't decide to stop liking you because of your opinions or beliefs. My parents weren't anti-American or communists. My dad was a friend of the black actor, singer, athlete, and activist Paul Robeson, who was very popular in Russia and affiliated with communism. Because of his friendship with Paul and the many people who hung out at the Actors Inn who were being investigated by McCarthy, my father was also blacklisted and investigated. It was a time of pure hell for us and for many of my father's friends. I got harassed at school, being called a "rat pinko bastard" by kids who were once my good friends. Thankfully we came out of that dark period.

How I Got Started in Music

When I was five years old, my father asked me if I wanted to learn how to play piano. Since I was always tinkering around on the piano in the back room of the Actors Inn, my dad figured I might as well take lessons and really learn how to play. He arranged for me to have piano lessons with Milton Jacobs. On my first day of piano lessons I had been fishing with some other kids and lost track of time. As I mentioned, the Catskills is a beautiful area and a kid's paradise of wonderful outdoor adventure. When I came home with the fish I had caught and not a music book, my dad went ballistic and told me to go to my lesson anyway even though I was very late. So, I went to my lesson and that is how I got started in music and my life's path, thanks to the insistence of my father.

Milton Jacobs was one of my mentors, not only for teaching me the basic language of music and piano-playing skills, but also for nurturing my talent and helping me build my confidence. Milton was an accomplished musician, composer, and arranger. He composed under the pseudonym of Milt James and found his niche in writing choral music for high school and college programs. Later he was hired by a large publisher and became one of the most well-known arrangers in that genre.

I studied with Milton for six years and then studied classical piano with Anne Plotkin for three years. Her husband, an auto mechanic by trade, also played the piano but his playing style was contemporary. One day I was listening and watching him play and saw he was not reading regular sheet music; he was using a chord chart, which I had not seen before. I commented on that, so he showed me what he was doing: improvising. That was my introduction to playing jazz. From all this experience and instruction I became skilled enough to start playing in bands at the resorts.

I started working at a few of the resorts accompanying various acts by playing with the house bands by the time I was fourteen years old. This meant that I was the band leader for many of these acts, because I was the pianist and I knew the material. I would usually work weekends and holidays. The hotels offered three acts a night; each act was twenty-five minutes and I was paid fifty dollars per show. So, by the end of a night I made $150, which was quite a bundle of money for a teen or an adult at that time. This was a bit of a problem for me at first because I was viewed as a young punk by the adult, professional musicians. Most of these musicians were from New York and played in the pit bands for musical productions on Broadway. These professional players weren't used to being led by a teenager. They would give me a lot of grief to the point of bullying, but I didn't know how to get them off my back and accept me. A break came when I had a gig with Ethel Alshine. Ethel Alshine is a very talented signer and performer and still performs in shows at the retirement complexes in Boca Raton, Florida. Anyway, Ethel's husband saw the shit the guys in the band were putting me through. After one of these shows, Ethel's husband grabbed one of the guys by the neck and told him if he ever gave me trouble again, he would break his neck and Ethel would never perform in the Catskills again. It scared the crap out of the guy and me, and I never got picked on after that.

By now I was ready to expand my musical experience and came under the direction of Irving Hertz. Irv mentored me in technique and how to approach a passage and harmonies. He was also an outstanding musician, playing and conducting for various big-time bands and artists that came into the Catskills to entertain. Irv was offered numerous opportunities from these big names in entertainment to play in and direct their bands, which could have taken him to the top in the music business, but he turned them all down, electing to stay in the Catskills. But in the Catskills you could not get anyone better than Irving Hertz to play and lead the best acts in town.

In 1952 I was just fifteen when Irv asked me to accompany the heavyweight champion of the world, "Brockton Bomber" Rocky Marciano, at our Annual Sports Dinner, which was a very big event in the area. Not only was he a boxer, but he sang as well. Rocky was a big man and had a tenor singing voice. I was a huge fan of boxing and of Rocky, so this was a thrill, but I was nervous. I asked Irv why he would trust me to do such a big show, but he just told me that he wasn't feeling well. I found out many years later that he had leukemia and that is what eventually took Irv's life at a much too early age.

The show went very well and Irv told me what a good job I did. This was such valuable encouragement and I will never forget it or Irv. My parents were so proud of me, too! It was one of the best nights of my life.

A few weeks after doing the Annual Sports Dinner show with Rocky Marciano, my father died. My dad had health issues that were complicated by diabetes. It was a very sad and very difficult time for my mother and me to go through. Not long after my father's death, my mother sold the Actors Inn and we moved into an apartment in town. She just could not deal with all of the work of running the deli on her own, even with my help. I continued to play in the bands and also worked at the butcher shop in town during the off-season, to help us financially.

In my high school years, I did a variety of gigs all around the Catskills and one was a radio show on WVOS in Ferndale. This was a weekly, fifteen-minute classical music show with the singer Marlene Elchysen and it was sponsored by Budweiser. I got paid twenty-nine dollars a show, which I was happy to receive. Grossinger's resort was just about a mile from this radio station and had a promo show after ours to promote its acts. For a few weeks Grossinger's was promoting a young, up-and-coming singer, Eddie Fisher. These shows were popular, too. One day Eddie found out that we all got paid for the classical music show and I heard him complain to the Grossinger's guy, "How come the kids [he was referring to us] get paid and not me?" Grossinger's was already paying the radio station to air the promo, not the talent in the promo. Besides, the talent got paid when they did the show at the resort. That comment from Eddie Fisher was funny to me, thinking how he became a very famous and very well-paid entertainer not long after that.

After my high school graduation, my mother decided we should move to California. Irving Hertz was hoping I was going to stay in New York and wanted to help me further my education so he had made arrangements for me to attend both the Juilliard School's and New York University's music programs. It was overwhelming that he did this for me, so it was very difficult to disappoint him with the news that I was moving to California with my mom because we had family there. There was no better mentor and friend than Irving Hertz and I credit him for teaching me much of what I needed to know to become successful as a professional musician, composer, and arranger when I came to California. In my high school yearbook he wrote, "Don't ever be afraid to make a mistake."

It was after I moved to Los Angeles and started working in clubs that I changed my name to Don Randi and my first band was called the Don Randi Trio.

CHAPTER 38

Stock Boy and Promo Guy for a Day

W hen my mother and I moved to Los Angeles from the Catskills, I was just seventeen years old and knew I wanted a career in music, but I also wanted to complete my college education. I enrolled at the Los Angeles Conservatory of Music, but I also needed to work while going to school.

The first job I got was working for a restaurant supply company in downtown Los Angeles, but a year later I got a job as stock boy at Vox Records on Robertson Boulevard. Vox Records was a European classical record company. The pressings of these records were very high quality, and the people who bought classical recordings knew this about Vox because the sound quality of these records was superb. Many of the albums Vox sold featured music from pre-Bach composers but didn't sell as well as Bach because Bach was such a popular composer. It's a shame because these composers were brilliant— Francesco Manfredini, Arcangelo Corelli, Tomaso Albinoni, Jean-Baptiste Lully, and others.

Vox also distributed Elektra Records releases, which were folk music artists at that time. Josh White, Theodore Bikel, and Ed McCurdy were among the artists that Elektra had. I worked at Vox for only a short time but I was able to learn the ins and outs of handling the stockroom and I got to listen to many wonderful classical and folk recordings.

The next job I had was as stock boy at California Records Distribution. It was the same position I had at Vox, so I had enough experience to step into my new job without much training. California Records distributed East Coast and West Coast jazz, and some classical records. The labels they distributed were HiFi Records, Contemporary Records, World Pacific, Fantasy, Prestige Records, Riverside, Blue Note, Verve, Brunswick, and Concord.

My job as a stock boy was to fulfill the orders from sales and to receive the damaged records that came back from the record stores and department stores. In those days the big department stores—May Company, The Broadway, Bullock's, Montgomery Ward, Sears Roebuck, and JC Penney—all sold records. It wasn't a complicated job but it was very educational because while I worked there, I got to listen to a lot of jazz recordings and learned about the talented artists who played on them. One artist that California Records distributed for Blue Note was Horace Silver, who was an incredibly talented pianist and composer. Horace had a very distinctive and funky playing style that you might call hard bop and I was fascinated by it. I would listen to his records, then try to play his style when I started playing at nightclubs and at school. Being able to listen to a variety of records while I was working inspired me to learn as much as I could about jazz music in school and on my own.

Jack Lewerke was the owner of California Records, and he was a mentor to me in those days and one of the kindest persons I ever met, especially to jazz musicians.

Walt DeSilva was the promo guy for California Records, and he went around to the radio stations and the record stores to promote the latest releases and get orders for records the company carried in the catalog. Walt DeSilva was also a DJ and worked at KPPC and KFWB in Los Angeles.

When California Records started distributing Fantasy Records, the first Lenny Bruce album had just been released. What was cool about the records from Fantasy was they were pressed in clear red vinyl. Lenny Bruce was a young, hip stand-up comedian who was famous for his controversial routines that covered topics considered taboo for the late 1950s and early 1960s. When I was in the Catskills, I had seen all the great traditional comedians who performed there, but Lenny Bruce was nothing like them. He led the coming of a new generation of comics.

A promo tour was planned for Lenny Bruce to go with Walt to radio stations in Los Angeles for live interviews and appearances at record stores to promote his album. The day Lenny Bruce was scheduled to do this, Walt was sick and didn't come to work and Jack could not do it, so Jack asked me to take Lenny on the promo tour. I was very surprised Jack would let me do this, but either I was his only option or he had a lot of confidence in me. Jack added to my surprise and delight when he told me to drive his car, a beautiful Austin Healey convertible, to take Lenny Bruce to his appearances. Being the "promo guy" for a day, meeting Lenny Bruce, and driving the both of us in a flashy Austin Healey sports car was incredible for any guy, but I was only nineteen!

Lenny arrived and I introduced myself and told him I would be taking him around that day because Walt was out ill. He was really cool with that and didn't appear to be anxious about my being so young. I told him I had been listening to his album for two days and my sides were aching from laughing so much.

When we went to the radio stations, it seemed as though the program directors and DJs had not yet heard his album, because they didn't make a big deal that his material might be too coarse for the general public. Then we went to the record stores and the girls went gaga over him. Lenny Bruce was a very good-looking guy and he was smooth.

A few years later, when my trio was playing various clubs in Los Angeles, we opened for Lenny Bruce at the Cloister on Sunset Boulevard. Lenny remembered me from California Records. After our set we hung out in the wings and watched Lenny do his set. In the audience was a large group of ladies from a Hadassah (Jewish women's society) group sitting at the tables closest to the stage. I don't know why on earth the ladies chose to have their social event at a Lenny Bruce show, but they were not prepared for his style of comedy. I don't think any of them laughed, but that didn't seem to affect Lenny as he went on hilariously with his raunchy material. I think the ladies were either shocked or didn't really understand his material, but the guys and I were in stitches, laughing so hard standing there just offstage.

Back to my California Records experience . . . it was a year or two later that

I got laid off. California Records wasn't doing so well financially and had to cut back, so Jack came to me, in tears, to say he had to let me go because the business was in a slump. He apologized and said he really hated to let me go. I was so touched by his compassion. The timing of this worked out for me anyway because my trio was starting to get booked for more gigs at nightclubs.

My experience at California Records and at Vox was very educational and I am very grateful to have had those opportunities when I was just a teenager.

CHAPTER 39

The Clubs

While I was enrolled in college (Los Angeles Conservatory of Music) and worked at California Record Distributors as a stock boy, I started my own band, the Don Randi Trio.

In the beginning, my trio was John Clauder on drums, Ron Retchin on bass, and me on piano. We got our first nightclub gig at Marianne's Surf Club, which was located on Sixth Street and Manhattan Place. Marianne Kirk owned the club and her two daughters also worked there, one bartending and the other as a waitress. One of the best features in the club was the baby grand piano that Marianne had tuned every week. Marianne loved and cared about music and wanted musicians to have what they needed to perform.

We started playing Marianne's on Sundays, which was a jam session that started at 2:00 p.m. and you played till you dropped. Looking back, this was one of the best learning situations for live performances. I had to play songs that I had not played before right off the cuff, sight-read music, and improvise. A few months later, as my trio got better and more experienced playing live, Marianne took us off the Sunday jam session and we played six nights a week. She really liked us and did something that no club owner has done since . . . One evening we were playing a ballad that she really loved and as she was listening to us perform, a table of guests were having a loud conversation. Marianne went up to that table and asked them to be quiet and listen to the music.

Because I was going to school and working at the record company during the day, I had little time to grab a bite to eat before our gig at Marianne's, but the club also served Italian food and they gave us dinner on the nights we played. It was a sweet gig for young musicians like us and we knew we were lucky to have the opportunity and be treated so well.

Ron Retchin (bass) was really good at getting us gigs on our off-nights and booked us at the Melody Room (now the Viper Room) on Sunset and other clubs, but eventually he left the trio and Putter Smith joined to play bass, thank goodness.

One night, when we were playing at Marianne's Surf Club, Pat Dinnocenti from Sherry's nightclub came in to see us play. He was good-looking and sharply dressed, like a guy outta *Esquire* magazine, so he kind of stood out from the crowd, as Marianne's was not a strictly formal dress club. He came up to me on our break and offered us a gig at Sherry's to play on Sunday nights, but the gig was for a duo, piano and bass. I told him, "Thanks, but we're a trio." Pat replied in a tough Larimer Avenue accent (Pittsburgh, Pennsylvania), "If you think you can fit the goddamn drums in, try it!" His reply was funny and caught me by surprise, but we did fit the drums in and that's how we got our gig at Sherry's and replaced Marty Paich (piano) and Joe Mondragon (bass), who were getting very busy on recording dates and other live gigs. Marty and Joe were absolutely fantastic musicians, so it was a high honor to have this gig after them.

Sherry's

Sherry's nightclub was located on Crescent Heights and Sunset and was known for being a hangout for people from all walks of life. Many books and movies about the organized crime exploits in Los Angeles portray Sherry's as a club where gangsters met and conducted business. When I was playing there with my trio starting in 1957, Mickey Cohen came into Sherry's regularly. One of the books written in the late 1970s, given to me by a friend, included stories from Jimmy "the Weasel." Although some of the details were exaggerated, many of the events portrayed in the book that happened in Sherry's were in the years I played there regularly. When I brought the book home, my wife started reading it. One evening while I was in the den arranging some music, Norma, who was reading the book in our bedroom, walked into the den, and looked at me, then walked back to our bedroom. About thirty minutes later she came in again, looked at me, then went back to the bedroom. Finally, Norma again walked into the den, holding the book, and I asked her, "What's up?" Norma replied, "You were playing at Sherry's when all of these things I'm reading about were going on. Why didn't you tell me?" I replied, "You never asked."

Before you get the idea that Sherry's was a dark, smoky, seedy dive, let me describe the atmosphere . . . Sherry's was a very elegant establishment and when you walked into the club, you noticed the lighting was softly romantic and the whole place had a classy, warm, and comfortable vibe. There were candles on the tables and the bar, but what was unique for that time and place were the little twinkling lights on the ceiling to make it look like a night sky. It was amazing because back then we didn't have small LED lights, so this had to be accomplished with tiny incandescent light bulbs that were connected with thin wiring, but the wires were strung so they were almost invisible and the ceiling was painted a dark color. The entire back wall of the club had the most beautiful mosaic tile mural I've ever seen. Sherry's was not a restaurant; it was a cocktail lounge with live entertainment.

Many famous Hollywood celebrities, television and film producers and directors also came to Sherry's, which attracted gossip columnists into the club as well. I remember the first big movie star I saw in Sherry's was Jeff Chandler (Oscar nominated for his role as Cochise in *Broken Arrow*, Jeff was also in *Return to Peyton Place*). Jeff Chandler was a very strikingly good-looking man with his dark tan and silver hair, impeccably dressed, and when he walked into the club, every head turned to look at him. He came in with his beautiful wife and sat at the piano bar right next to me and I was really thrilled to meet him.

Beautiful call girls with their "escorts," a mix of neighborhood regulars, and a couple of "undercover" cops trying to blend in while watching everybody's moves also came to the club. Many of my good friends, like Phil Spector and

Don Randi as an
infant is held by
his mother, Ethel
Schwartz.(Author's
collection)

Don at ten years old.
(Author's collection)

Young Don Randi playing an upright piano in the Catskills. (Author's collection)

Don Randi at the piano, in a promotional photo for World Pacific Jazz, late 1950s. (Author's collection)

The Don Randi Trio at the Dunes in Las Vegas. Left to right: Eddie Rubin, Don Randi, and Jack Layton. (Author's collection)

Don Randi Trio at the Losers. Left to right: Gene Stone on drums, Don Randi at the piano, and Jack Layton on bass. (Author's collection)

A scene from *Fireball 500* with Fabian, Julie Parish, and Frankie Avalon, and with Don Randi behind them at the keyboard. (Author's collection)

Shelley Winters on a *Bloody Mama* set location in Arkansas. (Author's collection)

Don Randi at a film scoring session for *Circus Time*. (Photo by Greg Dinallo)

Don Randi playing at a Nancy Sinatra concert at San Francisco's famous Bimbo's 365 Club. (Photo courtesy of Cole Pierce. All rights reserved.)

Don Randi, Pat Senatore (bass), and John Clauder (drums) performing at The Baked Potato's opening night in 1970. (Photo by Jasper Dailey/Michael Ochs Archives/Getty Images)

A Baked Potato advertisement from 1977. (Author's collection)

Quest performing at The Baked Potato in the 1970s. Left to right: Pete Willcox (guitar), John Sumner (drums), Hal Gordon (percussion), Richard Maloof (bass), and Don Randi (piano). (Author's collection)

Dave Coy, Chet McCracken, Chuck Camper, John Goux, and Don Randi in Quest in the early 1980s. (Author's collection)

Don Randi, Glen Campbell, and Hal Blaine at the Wrecking Crew's induction into the RockWalk at Guitar Center in Hollywood, June 25, 2008. (Photo by Robert Knight Archive/Redferns)

A group shot of Don Randi's family in 2014. (Photo by Karen "Nish" Nishimura)

Jack Nitzsche, would stop by on nights I played there. I met Shelly Slussman at Sherry's and he not only became one of my closest friends, he later helped me manage my club, The Baked Potato.

There was a beautiful horseshoe-shaped bar in Sherry's, and the grand piano also had seating around it for a piano bar with a tiny stage where my trio played.

The piano bar was the setting for this funny story that happened there . . . A man who frequented Sherry's came in one night with his wife and sat at the piano bar with her. I greeted the couple and we continued playing. Between songs the guy said to me, "Don, play mo for my wife." I replied, "Sure," but I didn't know what he meant by *mo*. We played another song, then the guy said, "Don, mo, play mo!" I looked at John and Putter, whispering, "What's mo?" and they shrugged. So, I said, "Yes, we're going to keep playing." And we played another song. Then the guy said, "Okay, I guess I have to give you a tip to get you to play it," and put a twenty-dollar bill in the tip bowl. Then he said, "There, now will you play mo?" I asked him, "Mo?" He replied, "Don, you play it all the time! Mo from *Mondo Cane!*" I said, "Oh, this?" Then I played a few notes on the piano of "More," the theme from the film *Mondo Cane*, and he emphatically replied, "Yes, that's it!"

Pat Dinnocenti, originally from Pittsburgh, was the owner of Sherry's and shortly after I started working there we became good friends. In fact, Pat was more like a dad to me because he supported my talent, gave me good advice, was very candid with me when I needed it, and was a protective layer between me and the not-so-virtuous characters that came into Sherry's. One night he made a wish for me that came true. After a couple of years of playing there, I was forever booking different substitute piano players to take my place in my trio because I was doing recording sessions or was playing out of town. Some of my sub piano players were Leon Russell, Bruce Johnson, Mike Melvoin, Mike Rubini, and others. I often paid more to the sub I hired than I got paid from Pat, but my other gigs were bringing in good money for me by then, so it wasn't a problem paying great talent and I wanted to help out friends who loved to play live jazz. I also never wanted to give up my gig at Sherry's because I love to play live jazz and wanted to be able to play there whenever I could. This would irritate Pat, so one night he proclaimed, "Don, I want you to have a nightclub of your own someday so you can know what a pain in the ass it is to manage!" Pat's prophecy came true when I opened my club, The Baked Potato.

Sherry's was a union gig and Pat paid the health and welfare and pension fees according to union contract guidelines, which meant he filled out and submitted union contracts and payment to AFM Local 47 for every musician who played there all those years. There weren't many club owners who did that and because of this Pat will always be remembered and appreciated by me and the many musicians who played at Sherry's.

The waitress at Sherry's, Irene Clifford, was terrific and we became good friends. She was not only the best waitress, but she was also creative and wrote songs. She wrote the words and I wrote the music to "My Little Boy's Hands," which I talked about in my chapter on Jimmy Bowen. Later she helped train the waitresses when I opened my club, The Baked Potato.

Pete Willcox was the parking lot attendant and became a very close friend of mine. When I met him at Sherry's, Pete was trying to break into music as a singer-songwriter and guitar player, and soon we worked together on several projects. He also played with my band at The Baked Potato a few times.

Pat's son Gino, Greg Bach, and Louis Pampina also worked at Sherry's, as bartenders.

Alex Garafolo was the main bartender at Sherry's and is quite a complicated person. He comes off to some as a wise guy, very tough, but he is charming, very intelligent, and very handsome. Producers who came into Sherry's would tell him if he got headshots done, he could easily get cast in TV or movies. Of course, the ladies adored him and he became a close friend of mine. Alex was always a fanatic on exercise and bodybuilding before it became a craze and kept his body in top physical shape. Despite his age, he's still in great shape, lives in Las Vegas, and works at one of the popular casinos. Alex could have gone far and been successful in a legitimate business or entertainment, but something inside him was attracted to the thrill of a life on the wrong side of the law and got in trouble a time or two. Being at Sherry's made it easy for him to get involved with shady individuals, unfortunately.

Though I stayed away from any business that wasn't mine, sometimes it got dropped in my lap, literally! One night a known mobster, Jack, came into Sherry's and sat at the piano bar. Jack was out of prison on parole and was being watched by every law enforcement agency you could name. At Sherry's, I learned to become mindful and aware when things were going down and to stay cool. Right in the middle of a song, undercover detectives came up to Jack to arrest him and tried to do it quickly and as quietly as possible. As he stood up, one of the detectives pulled Jack's left hand behind his back to cuff him. Jack leaned over the piano bar, and with his right hand, very quickly flipped a gun out of the breast pocket of his jacket into my lap while I was still playing. Then he put that hand behind him to allow the detective to cuff him, but while he was being cuffed he leaned over and gave me a hard stare. No one had seen the gun fall except me and I kept as cool as I could while we continued to play the song for a few more seconds. When the song ended, there was a commotion as the detectives escorted Jack out of the club and all eyes were on him. That was the right time to let the gun drop from my lap to the floor, and then I kicked it to the back of the piano bar so no one could see it. It's a miracle that the gun didn't go off! The next morning Pat called me at home and asked me to come in before the club opened. When I got to the club I was greeted by Jack, a couple of his "associates," and Pat. The police released Jack because he didn't have the gun on him, which would have been a violation of his parole, and there was nothing else they could find to charge him with.

Pat asked where I'd stashed the gun, so I told them how I kicked the gun out of sight. Jack growled, "It's not there, so where is my gun?" I was thinking, *Where is my thank-you for saving your ass while my nuts could have been shot off?* Pat told Jack, "Take it easy; the kid didn't take your gun." I went to the piano and showed them how I kicked the gun, so they could look for it. One of Jack's associates got down on his back behind the piano bar with a flashlight and caught a glimpse of some metal up in the back of the piano bar. Apparently when I kicked it, the gun had bounced up behind the boards in the back section of the piano bar. They had to take that section apart to get it out. Thank God, the gun was found and hadn't gone off when I kicked it!

Paul Butterfield Blues Night . . .

One evening, Jack Nitzsche came into Sherry's with Paul Butterfield to hear my trio. What a fantastic honor, as Paul was a master blues harp player and I was a fan of his. I asked Paul if he would come up and play his harmonica and he accepted, to our delight. We had one of those big, chrome, old-style Shure 55 microphones and Paul took that mic and his harmonica and cupped his hands around both and proceeded to play the most phenomenal blues harp performance I have ever heard. My trio began to accompany Paul and we ended up doing a straight forty-five-minute set of nonstop blues. When we finally ended the song, I was completely drenched in sweat. I wore a black mohair suit with a white shirt and black tie every night at Sherry's, and this night, sweat soaked completely through my jacket. I looked over at Paul and he was looking at me and we acknowledged that we just played a once-in-a-lifetime performance. It was a magical set and the audience was going crazy when we finished. After that night at Sherry's, I was asked to play piano on an album with Paul Butterfield.

The Tree That Grew Back . . .

In the parking lot behind Sherry's there was a big beautiful pine tree; it had to be seventy-five feet high. Pat always complained about the tree taking up too much room, needles making a mess, or the sap getting on his car, etc., so when a city construction crew came out to do some work on the street and in the alley behind the parking lot, Pat paid those guys to cut down the tree. The crew cut the tree off very cleanly at the trunk and left about three feet of a stump that Pat would have to remove. When we got to Sherry's that evening, it was such a sad sight to see the beautiful pine tree cut down, lying next to the fence and the stump where the tree once was. Pat was so happy the tree was down and told us how he was going to get someone out right away to take the tree and pull out the stump. He left smiling later that night. After closing, we (Alex, Gino Dinnocenti, Greg Bach, Louis Pampina, and me) drank a few tequila shots toasting the fallen tree like you would at a wake for a deceased relative. After getting thoroughly plastered, we went next door to Googies coffee shop for breakfast. While we were eating, Alex suddenly had an idea and said, "Let's put the tree back up!" We replied, "What?!" We went back to Sherry's and Alex started talking and got us all involved . . . he said we had to pull the tree up and put it on the stump, so we looked around at what the construction crew had left that we could use and found some baling wire, large nails, rope, and a (skip loader) tractor.

After a discussion of how we could put the tree back up, like a team of engineers at NASA, we quickly came up with a brilliant plan. We decided to tie the rope around the tree and use the tractor to pull the tree upright, guide it back to the stump, then use the baling wire to hold the tree in place by nailing the wires to the eaves of the roof in three places and wrapping the wires around the tree. I took the job of driving the tractor since I had experience with that in the Catskills when I was a kid. But before we attached the rope, we had to figure out how we were going to get that rope high enough to lift the tree. It had to be strong enough to support the rope and weight of the tree. Alex went on the roof of Sherry's and discovered that the peak of the roof was reinforced with steel, so it was going to work perfectly. Now we were worried that the rope might not be long enough to fit around the tree and go all the way from the back, over the roof, and to the street, Crescent Heights, but it was! I attached the rope to the tractor and Gino tied the rope around the tree. Since we didn't have walkie-talkies, we opened the front door and back door of Sherry's so Gino could yell instructions from the back to Louis, who was at the front door, to relay directions for pulling the rope with the tractor. It was early in the morning, around 3:00 a.m. to 4:00 a.m., that we were doing this, so there was no traffic on the street. Amazingly, once I started pulling the rope slowly with the tractor, the tree stood up and Alex and Greg held the tree and guided it to the stump. The whole time Alex barked instructions to Gino, who repeated them to Louis, who shouted them to me, like *go forward, stop, a little more*, then finally *back up and stop*, which was when Alex and Greg had the tree perfectly over the stump and let the tree down. As the tractor with the rope kept the tree in place, we all quickly got the baling wires attached to the roof and around the tree and nailed the wires securely in place. When we thought we had it secured with the wires, we untied the rope from the tractor and the tree held. The baling wire was a silver gray color and wasn't too thick, so it had the illusion of being invisible. We were in awe as we stared at the big pine tree that stood up like it had never been cut down. By this time it was sunrise, so I drove the tractor back to where it was parked before and put the rope back, and the rest of the guys cleaned up the parking lot so no one could detect how the tree got back up. Just before we left, we all had a good laugh, speculating what Pat's reaction was going to be when he arrived later.

Later that day we were all at Sherry's waiting for Pat to arrive. Like giddy teenagers we waited outside in the parking lot for Pat. He drove up and parked like he always did, got out of his car, then greeted us with something like, "Don't you guys have better things to do than stand around in the parking lot?" We just shrugged and kept quiet, waiting for the moment of recognition. Pat walked into the club and we waited for a few seconds, thinking he didn't notice, but Pat came running back out looking frightened and shouted, "Fuck! The goddamn tree grew back!!" Yeah, that was our payoff and worth the work putting that tree back up, for the laugh we got from Pat's reaction.

Pandora's Box and Lou Rawls

Pandora's Box was a club located across the street from Sherry's and is where I met Lou Rawls. Lou was performing at Pandora's with Sid Levy's quartet when my trio was playing at Sherry's, and each of us would walk over to the other club on or breaks to hear the other perform. I was blown away by the talent Lou had.

Soon we became friends and occasionally Lou would run across the street to Sherry's to sing a couple songs with my trio, then run back to Pandora's to finish his set. That was the beginning of a close friendship that lasted for many years as we both worked together on recordings, TV and film scoring, and live performances. I miss my friend Lou Rawls, who passed away in 2006.

The Regency Room and Slim Gaillard

A couple of years after my trio started playing at Sherry's and other clubs on our off-nights, we got a gig at the Regency Room on La Cienega Boulevard, opening for the incomparable Slim Gaillard. Slim was an amazing musician, singer, composer, and performer. He was fantastic as a guitar player, but his piano playing was the stuff of legends. Slim was tall, had huge hands with very long fingers, and could play the piano perfectly with his hands turned palm up, which was one of the performance tricks he would do to awe the audience. In fact, I considered Slim a mentor because he taught me a lot about showmanship and live performance that included how to tell stories, which he did so entertainingly during his set. He had a sparkling presence during his show that naturally attracted the undivided attention of the audience. About halfway through his set he would take the tip money given to him and stick the bills on his face, which was moist from perspiration by then. It was a fun challenge that delighted the audience, for Slim to stick as many bills to his face as he could before the song ended. It was also a lucrative feature as more people tipped during that song and often the bills were fives, tens, and twenties.

When my trio (Hersh Hamel replaced Putter on bass) opened for Slim at the Regency, he really liked us and especially my drummer and bass player. Slim would have John Clauder and Hersh Hamel play during his set, too, and would also share his tips with them.

Slim was a brilliant and creative man who had many talents and abilities beyond his musical talent. He once installed a new sound system in the Regency overnight, by himself, which required him to totally rewire the electrical for the system. When we got in the next day, we were amazed at what Slim did on his own and the system sounded remarkable.

Slim Gaillard moved to London in the 1970s and performed in England for several years. The BBC did a series on Slim Gaillard. For one of the segments, the production came to Los Angeles and Slim selected my club, The Baked Potato, as where to tape that segment. We also taped a driving tour of LA, pointing out the locations of clubs that had existed back in the '60s. It was great to see Slim again and I was very glad that the BBC recognized how important Slim's influence was to American jazz music.

The Regency Room was owned by Ray Luna and Richie Morris. Ray Luna was also a good friend of Art "Golden Boy" Aragon (famous lightweight boxer) and even though he had retired from professional boxing by 1960, he was still a celebrity in Los Angeles and would often come into the Regency.

One night, before our set started, Art was there and was talking to a beautiful young woman at the bar. She wasn't responding to Art's flirtations, so he asked her if she recognized him. She said no even after Art introduced himself. Then he mock-punched himself in the jaw, fell to the floor sprawled out, eyes closed like he was knocked out, then said, "Do you recognize me now?"

A gentleman named Major Arteburn Riddle, the entertainment manager for the Dunes Hotel in Las Vegas, was a regular guest at the Regency. He was impressed with my trio and booked us at the Dunes in Vegas for two weeks, which was the first time I played in Vegas but certainly not my last.

The Melody Room

The Melody Room was located on Sunset where the Viper Room is now. It also had a very nice Steinway B in the piano bar and my trio played there on Wednesdays for close to a year, on and off. At this time we were also playing at Marianne's on Sundays, so my trio included John Clauder on drums and Ron Retchin on bass. Henri Rose and Frankie Ortega played at the Melody Room the other nights of the week. On the nights my trio played, Henri Rose often stopped by to see us and occasionally would sit in on piano with John and Ron. Ron wasn't the most experienced bass player, which was a touchy situation for me at times because what Ron lacked in musicianship, he had double in business sense. Ron was the one who got us the gig at the Melody Room, so I felt I could not replace him on bass. But anyway, one evening when Henri was sitting in, he leaned over to Ron and asked, "Is there something wrong with your bass?"

How We Lost at the Losers

The Losers, located on Sunset, became (renamed) the Winners when some guys from Chicago took it over. At the Losers, my trio was the featured band and included Gene Stone (drums) and Jack Layton (bass). One evening a guy from Phoenix, Arizona, came in with his beautiful girlfriend. He really loved our set and came over to us on our break to offer us a two-month gig at his resort in Phoenix. The money he was offering to pay us was so much more than we were making currently; it was going to be a major step up. I told him we were definitely interested and he said he was in town for a few more days and would come back to finalize the details. While he was in town, he came to our show every night with his girlfriend; that's how much he enjoyed our playing. On the last evening he was in town, he came to the Losers as usual and had the contract for the gig in Phoenix to finalize after our set. He brought his beautiful girlfriend with him again as he did every night, and this time they sat at the piano bar. The lady was sitting in the spot at the end of the piano bar that was next to the drums. One of the cymbals was close enough to her that she could touch it. Well, she did . . . we had just finished a song when she ran her fingernail across the cymbal, making it ring. Gene, obsessive about his drum kit; he didn't like anyone touching his drums. He struck the lady on her hand with his drumstick and barked, "Don't touch!" Gene scared her and hurt her hand, which made her cry. The guy from Phoenix stood up and left with the lady and our contract. I shot a look at Gene and said, "Bye-bye, Phoenix."

On our breaks, Barry McGuire (the New Christy Minstrels, "Eve of Destruction") or Trini Lopez would play for twenty minutes, then we came back to finish our set. Trini was born in Dallas, Texas, he grew up in a Latino neighborhood, and his parents were from Mexico, but I noticed he never performed Latin songs. One night I asked him why and he told me that he didn't want to be a Latin recording artist; he wanted to be a mainstream American artist. I thought he should combine both into his style because I could hear the Latin influence in his talent.

PJ's and Trini Lopez

A few years later (1963) my trio was the featured band at PJ's, located on

Santa Monica and Crescent Heights. A very popular club, PJ's was unique because there were two rooms, so guests could choose which artist they wanted to see. We played in the front room. Trini Lopez was playing in the back room of PJ's at this time. Johnny Rivers, who is well known for recording many hit songs, including "Secret Agent Man" and "Poor Side of Town," played during my trio's breaks at PJ's.

One night I arrived at PJ's and there was a remote recording truck parked in the lot. It was Wally Heider's truck, which was the premier remote recording setup that Wally was famous for developing. Wally Heider, a recording engineer, was the pioneer in remote recording and he also owned the famed Wally Heider Studios in San Francisco and Hollywood. His live recordings at the Monterey Pop Festival with Jimi Hendrix, the Who, and Ravi Shankar are among his best-known live albums. I've worked many sessions at Wally's Hollywood studio, including Neil Young's first solo album, and played piano on "Here We Are in the Years."

Incidentally, Wally Heider was the best and fastest tape editor in recording, ever. This was back when we were mixing on tape. He'd have several strands of tape hanging around the mixing booth. He knew what each piece had on it and was able to pick the right segment and splice it into the master. And when he played back the master, you could not tell the tape was edited.

Don Costa, who at the time was a top arranger and record producer working for Frank Sinatra and Reprise, was there, so I went to him and asked what was going on that night. He said they were recording a live album with Trini in the back room. That album became his debut record, *Trini at PJ's*, and his single "If I Had a Hammer" from the album went to number one. He also recorded the song "I Want to Live in America" for that album, which was released later, and Trini became very successful and mainstream, adding Latin music to his repertoire.

The Cloister

The Cloister, located on Sunset not far from where the House of Blues is now, was an upscale supper club, so the dress for my trio was black tuxedos. The time my trio played the Cloister will always be memorable for me because that is where I met Sarah Vaughan. We opened for her and I was already a little nervous, hoping the audience was going to like our set while waiting for her show. Milton Berle was also there, backstage, and I was excited to meet him, too.

One of the owners of the Cloister, Joe Miklos, came up to me before we went on and told me to introduce Sarah Vaughan after our set. I was surprised by this request, plus I had never done this before so I got nervous, but he told me I would be fine. Milton Berle was close by and heard my conversation with Joe.

So, the moment came, our set was done, and I stood up, took the mic, and introduced Sarah Vaughan. I was very nervous as I stood before a packed house of very distinguished guests that included Hollywood celebrities and top music industry executives and artists. I did it and felt good that I didn't mess up her name or stumble walking to and from the mic. When I got backstage, Milton Berle was standing there and said, "You did a good job kid, but here's some advice . . . always wear black socks." I looked down and saw I had put on some bright argyle socks that day, absentmindedly, and they didn't go well with my tuxedo. My pants were just a little short, so the socks really stood out. I was devastated.

The Party and the Actress

My trio played at The Party around 1965. Located on Sunset Boulevard, this club was a very popular hot spot for celebrities of the day, where paparazzi and social columnists would hang out to be the first to break the latest gossip story. Sidney Skolsky, a well-known Hollywood gossip columnist syndicated in many major newspapers around the country, was a regular at The Party and also at Sherry's, where I met him before. Years earlier, Sidney's column in *Photoplay* magazine, "From a Stool in Schwab's," made Schwab's Drug Store famous.

The Party was owned by a man named Speed Copp, not kidding, and he had the first karaoke setup before anyone even heard the word *karaoke*.

Speed showed the films of the *Sing Along with Mitch* series, hosted by Mitch Miller, on a screen in the club during our breaks. *Sing Along with Mitch* was a popular TV music sing-along show where the lyrics of the songs would scroll on the screen and Mitch, who conducted the band, would say, "Sing along and follow the bouncing ball."

One evening the beautiful actress Glynis Johns came into the club. Glynis Johns is a Tony Award–winning and Oscar-nominated actress who in the early '60s starred in a few television series, including her own series, *Glynis*. She has had a very distinguished and successful acting career and I had always admired her, so when it appeared she was enjoying listening to my trio and looked right at me during our set, I was really thrilled. She stayed for both sets, and at the end of the night, she asked the waiter to introduce me to her. Glynis, who is a few years older than me, was so charming and sexy with her South African accent as she told me how much she enjoyed hearing my trio and complimented my performance on piano. I was a little nervous because it seemed unreal, being a fan of hers, to have Glynis Johns flirting with me, but I couldn't help flirting back. As she said good-bye she came forward as if to hug me, but she gave me a very big passionate kiss that the paparazzi was quick to photograph. The next day that picture appeared in Sidney Skolsky's column with a short paragraph on how enamored Glynis Johns was with a young jazz pianist, Don Randi.

The Capri

The Capri (not the Villa Capri restaurant) was another popular club for the Hollywood "in-crowd." We had a gig there to open for the popular jazz artist Anita O'Day. Anita was a talented jazz singer well known for her ability to improvise vocally. She was also an attractive woman.

My trio played our set to a packed house with many celebrities in the audience and got a very positive and enthusiastic response for our performance. It was gratifying to be well received by an audience that was mostly hearing us for the first time.

When we got backstage and saw Anita's band, it was obvious they were all ripped (high and drunk), including Anita, and I wasn't sure if they were able to perform. It's a thing I've seen too much of during my life and career. Many years later, Anita O'Day spoke very candidly about her drug and alcohol addiction.

When Anita and her band finally got onstage and were about to start, Anita thought she heard someone in the audience make a comment. Anita wanted the audience to be silent before she began, so this upset her and she decided to sing with her back to the audience and never turned around for the entire set. I had not seen her or any other artist do that before or since. The audience had mixed reactions to the performance.

At the end of the evening I was standing just outside the front door of the club when Mel Brooks and his wife, Anne Bancroft, were leaving. Mel and Anne stopped when they saw me and said they really enjoyed my trio's performance. I felt honored to receive such kind compliments from them. After I thanked them, Mel Brooks, with that wit he's known for, said, "Tell Anita that her ass ain't that good to look at."

My trio was booked to play there a few more times to open for the Cal Tjader Quintet. Cal's superb Latin jazz band included Willie Bobo and Mongo Santamaria.

Johnny Magnus and the Villa Capri

The Villa Capri was an Italian restaurant on Yucca Street in Hollywood and was a favorite restaurant for many celebrities, like Frank Sinatra. The Villa Capri was where the dish Steak Sinatra was created in honor of Frank. The restaurant was also a favorite lunchtime hangout for radio disk jockeys in Los Angeles. The DJs who did the morning shows and the evening shows usually met there several times a week. Johnny Magnus, who is still a popular DJ in LA, was working at KGFJ-AM radio at the time and a friend of mine who liked my records and played them on the station. I would occasionally have lunch at Villa Capri and one time I was there, lunching and joking around with Johnny and a few other DJs, when he said teasingly, "You should be happy I play your records, Don." I told him I would return the favor someday.

It was a few months later and I was playing in Las Vegas at the Castaways, when I remembered that conversation with Johnny and my promise to him. The Borden Twins (Marilyn and Roz Borden) were performing a terrific comedy act in the Barry Ashton revue at the Castaways. They were quite famous in comedy, appearing in many television shows (*I Love Lucy, Colgate Comedy Hour*) and nightclubs in the 1950s and 1960s. They often went by the stage names of Teensy and Weensy, but they were the opposite of small. They were "big-boned" full-figured women. I got to know these very nice ladies when my trio opened for the Barry Ashton revue at the Castaways and they told me one evening that they adored Johnny Magnus. That is when I got the idea to make good on the favor I promised Johnny.

I asked Marilyn and Roz if they would be going to LA anytime soon and they said they were quite often because their agency was in Hollywood. Perfect! I told Marilyn and Roz that Johnny Magnus was a friend of mine and I could arrange for them to meet him the next time they were going to be in Hollywood. I called Johnny and told him I had met two showgirls, twins, from the Barry Ashton revue who were big fans of his and were going to be in Los Angeles soon and wanted to meet him. I told him that I would arrange for them to have lunch with him at the Villa Capri and I would pick up the tab for the whole thing as my thank-you for his friendship. Marilyn and Roz were very excited to meet Johnny.

I knew Johnny would brag to all of the other DJs about this upcoming lunch date. He told his pals that Don Randi was sending gorgeous twin Las Vegas dancers from the Castaways to have lunch with him. He and the other DJs imagined the twins would be young, tall, blond, sexy dancers, so of course the restaurant was packed the day the Borden Twins went to the Villa Capri to have lunch with Johnny Magnus.

When the Borden Twins walked into the Villa Capri, some of the people in the restaurant recognized Teensy and Weensy from seeing them on TV shows and it started a buzz in the restaurant. All the DJs and Johnny, who were waiting for the "showgirls," quickly figured out I sent the Borden Twins there to meet Johnny. Everybody, including Johnny and Marilyn and Roz, thought my joke was hilarious and I ended up paying for everyone's lunch that day.

The Castaways, Las Vegas

While I worked at Sherry's, I had a booking agent who got my trio other gigs. One was for a two-week engagement, opening for the main show at the Castaways in Las Vegas in 1963. The pay wasn't that great but we wanted the chance to play in Vegas, so we took the job. We opened for the Barry Ashton revue and that is when I met Norma Waterman, the gorgeous lead dancer in the troupe, and we fell in love. Norma and I got married just a year later.

The audience we played to each night really enjoyed the preshow we were doing, so when our two weeks came to a close, the manager, Garwood Van, came up to me after our last show and said the owner of the Castaways, Mr. Jacobs, had an idea for a lounge show with my trio. He asked if we wanted to stay a couple more weeks and play in the new lounge they were going to open. I loved the idea and asked where this lounge was going to be. He took me to over to the bar that was just off the casino floor near the blackjack tables and slot machines. He said they were going to clear out a couple things and put in some tables and chairs, but they needed a piano there for my trio. Garwood asked me what kind of piano I wanted and I told him a Steinway like the one in the theater. He said, "Okay, in the morning go to the office and Mr. Jacobs will give you a check to go to the piano store in town and pick out the one you want."

The next morning I went to Mr. Jacobs' office and got the check and was surprised to see it was a signed blank check. I thought it would have an amount on it as my budget for the piano. When he gave me the check, Mr. Jacobs said he'd called the piano store, so they knew I was coming. When I got there they were expecting me, just like I was told, and the salesman asked me what kind of piano I was looking for. I said a Steinway grand and he showed me to the room where all the grand pianos were. I played several really good pianos, then I found a beautiful-sounding Steinway B. The salesman said he could have the piano delivered and tuned at the Castaways that afternoon, but I told him I wasn't sure when the lounge was going to be ready. He said Mr. Jacobs told him the lounge would be ready that day. I was shocked . . . there were no tables there the night before when I was shown the potential lounge area.

When I got back to the Castaways, I went to the lounge area, and sure enough, a few tables and chairs were already there with more being set up, and a space big enough for a grand piano and my trio to set up and play. It was amazing how quickly they got that done and it looked good, like the lounge had always been there. That night we began a twelve-week gig in the new Castaways lounge and were getting paid much more than when we began opening in the main showroom.

Our set started at midnight and went till 6:00 a.m. with a couple of breaks. It wasn't long after we began playing there that word got out to other jazz musicians in Vegas, and they started showing up at the lounge to jam with us. Woody Herman's band took over the gig we just had in the main showroom and the guys came to the lounge after their show to hear my trio and often sat in with us. Sal Nistico (sax), Bill Chase (trumpet), and Jake Hanna (drums) were among the awesome musicians that we had the pleasure of playing with. Sammy Davis Jr. heard about the jazz jams in the Castaways lounge and came to see us a few times.

Every two weeks our contract at the Castaways was up for renewal, which gave us the opportunity to renegotiate our compensation. Each time the contract renewal came up, we got an increase in pay. By the time we left the Castaways, we were getting the top pay in Las Vegas for musicians. Three months later we had a gig in San Francisco and left the Castaways, but by that time there were no shortage of jazz musicians who wanted to play the gig we started.

Executive Suite, San Francisco

In 1964, just as our sixth consecutive contract was ending at the Castaways in Vegas, my trio was booked at the Executive Suite restaurant and club. The Young Brothers, who owned about five or six furniture stores in the Bay Area (San Francisco, Oakland), also owned the Executive Suite, which was in downtown San Francisco on California Street.

This turned out to be one of my most enjoyable and memorable short-term gigs. The Executive Suite was a very popular restaurant and the food it served was outstanding. Monday through Friday the restaurant was open for lunch and because it was located in the business district, the place was packed with the people who worked in the office buildings. It closed after 2:00 p.m. and reopened for dinner around 5:00 p.m. At 9:00 p.m. our first set would start and we would do a second set, ending at 2:00 a.m.

When John Clauder (drums) and I drove up together from Las Vegas and got to San Francisco, we had to find a place to stay that was relatively cheap and found a motel at the end of Lombard Street. On the first day, bored because we had hours to kill before our show, John and I went out for a walk around the neighborhood to see what was around us. As we walked I caught a whiff of something heavenly cooking. I said, "John, do you smell that? Let's find out where it's coming from." Following my nose, we walked up to a new Italian restaurant that had a sign "Opening Soon." When we looked in, there were some men working on finishing touches, so the place was close to being ready to open. One of the men spoke up and said, "Sorry, we aren't open yet." I told him that John and I had followed our noses there because whatever was cooking smelled absolutely delicious, and asked him when the restaurant was going to open. He said in a couple of days, but to wait right there. We were getting hungrier by the moment, smelling that food. He went to the kitchen and after a few moments came back and said, "We are going to have lunch now and you both can join us if you want." We didn't hesitate to accept the invitation and followed the man to the kitchen, where a large table was set. John and I enjoyed a fantastic meal with the man's family, his wife, mother, father, and grandmother. They were such gracious people and didn't accept any money for the feast they served us, so before John and I left, I promised the man I would try to get the word out about his restaurant when it opened.

Once we started playing the Executive Suite, word got out about my trio and many notable people came in to see us. Norman McKay, who was a local bass player, joined my trio for this gig. Wilt Chamberlain (I knew Wilt from the Catskills, when he worked at Kutsher's Resort) was playing for the Warriors then and would come in. Wilt was a big fan of jazz music and also came into Sherry's a few times when I played there, as well as The Baked Potato when he lived in Los Angeles and was playing for the Lakers.

Pulitzer Prize–winning journalist Herb Caen came in one night and just loved my trio, so he wrote about us in his daily column in the *San Francisco Chronicle*. Herb's column had such a huge readership that it drew crowds to the Executive Suite for our show and dinner. The Young Brothers were ecstatic over the great review and the boost to business. Herb came in a few times after that because he really liked my trio and he liked the dinners at the Executive Suite. This gave me a chance to make good on that promise I had made to the guy at that Italian restaurant on Lombard Street. One night, I told Herb Caen about the restaurant and he went there the next day and told the family I'd sent him. Herb wrote a wonderful review in his column and the restaurant became very popular. So popular that when John and I went back there for dinner, we had to eat in the kitchen again because all the tables were full and others were waiting to be seated.

After a few weeks we had to go back to LA for a recording session with my trio to record my composition "Mexican Pearls." Joe Young liked us so much that he booked us to come back after we were done with the record. When we went back to San Francisco, we needed a place to stay again, but this time Joe made arrangements for us to use an apartment of a friend of his who was in Europe for several weeks.

I drove up with John Clauder. We had the directions to the apartment of Joe's friend. It was night when we arrived at the address but when we did, we thought we must have made a mistake, took a wrong turn or something, but we double-checked and were at the correct address. The neighborhood looked a little dicey and the building itself looked old and neglected. John had his drum kit in the car and didn't want to leave it there for fear it would get stolen. I got out of the car and walked up to the building. The key for the apartment was in a flowerpot just as written in the instructions. The front door was open to the small lobby of the building and as I looked in, my impression of the place didn't improve. Just from the appearance of the building exterior and interior, I felt like we'd stepped into a flophouse. I wasn't sure we'd be able to bring all of the drums up to the apartment in one trip because the choice we had was a small, ancient metal cage elevator, or to carry the drums up five flights of stairs to the top floor where the apartment was. We chose the elevator and barely got the drums and ourselves in.

At the top floor we got out of the elevator with the drums and went to the apartment. I took the key and opened the door, expecting the worst. The room was dark, so I flipped on the light switch next to the door, and wow, I was stunned by what I saw. The apartment was spacious, splendidly decorated, and furnished beautifully. I recall feeling like I was stepping into a movie set from the contrasting background of the grungy building and neighborhood where this apartment was located. I called Joe Young to let him know we got in and told him about how we had our doubts about the apartment when we arrived. He laughed and said he knew the apartment was going to really surprise me. Joe also said the apartment included maid service. We had it made!

During this second booking at the Executive Suite, my trio's popularity soared in San Francisco. Herb Caen, Wilt Chamberlain, and other sports figures from the Warriors, Giants, and 49ers all came in to see my trio, which attracted many new fans to our shows. Plus my single "Mexican Pearls" had been released.

Don Graham was the promo man for the record company Palomar, on which my album and single "Mexican Pearls" was released. He was hard at work promoting my record and got it in the hands of Alma Greer, the programming director for the radio station group that owned KSFO radio in San Francisco. She liked my record and programmed it for play on KSFO and other stations around the country. But Don Graham didn't stop with Alma ... Since he knew I was playing at the Executive Suite, he contacted Al "Jazzbeaux" Collins (popular DJ at KSFO radio) and asked him to promote my trio's gig when he played my record. Jazzbeaux, who did volunteer work at prisons in northern and central California, thought this would be a great opportunity to ask for a favor. Jazzbeaux said he would happily play "Mexican Pearls" heavily with a mention of the trio's playing live at the Executive Suite, if he (Don Graham) would ask me to come to the prisons and play piano with the prisoners who were learning music. Jazzbeaux thought if I could visit these guys who never had a chance to learn from a professional musician, it would inspire them. Anyway I did agree to go to the prisons with Jazzbeaux and he played "Mexican Pearls" very heavily on his radio show.

San Francisco will always be one of my favorite cities to visit and perform in, with so many fond memories I've had there.

CHAPTER 40

"Oh Yeah" and Jukeboxes

I met record producer Nik Venet a few years before I worked with him at Capitol on the Stone Poneys album with Linda Ronstadt. When I was working at California Records Distribution as a stock boy, I had an opportunity to meet Richard Bock, the owner of Pacific Jazz and World Pacific Jazz record companies. In 1960 my trio was playing gigs in different clubs around Los Angeles, but mostly at Sherry's in Hollywood. Richard Bock used to come into Sherry's nightclub and he heard me play with my trio there. He approached me one evening about recording an album for World Pacific Jazz. Richard asked Nik Venet, one of the producers on staff at his two record companies, to produce my first album, *Feeling Like Blues*, and a single, "Oh Yeah." Nik and I were both young guys in our early twenties, starting our careers in the music business, so we connected easily and became friends while working on my album and single.

When Nik produced my first single, "Oh Yeah," he decided not to put the song on my album because he wanted to include it on my second album. I liked how Nik thought, but unfortunately I didn't get to record a second album for World Pacific Jazz. "Oh Yeah" was a great single with a different, more contemporary arrangement than the jazz style my trio usually played, and it had a very good guitar player on it, Phil Spector. "Oh Yeah" did well on the radio and sales and Pat Dinnocenti, the owner of Sherry's, let me put my single in the jukebox in the club. Sherry's opened at eleven o'clock in the morning every day, but the band didn't start until nine in the evening, so customers would play the jukebox during the day. A guy who came into the club one late afternoon played "Oh Yeah" on the jukebox and loved it so much he played it over and over. That evening, when I got to the club for my gig, Pat told the guy that it was my song, so he introduced himself to me and told me how much he liked it. I thought he might have been drunk, which was probably true, but he told me that he was from Texas, visiting Los Angeles on business, and was going back home the next day. He asked me if I had any copies of the single he could buy from me. I just happened to have a box of them in my car because I would sell a few copies of it at my gigs. The guy bought the whole box from me and he had a grin from ear to ear as I handed him the singles. I wish every person that liked my records would by them by the box!

Speaking of jukeboxes . . . I arranged and recorded many sound-alike records for the Seeburg jukebox company. In most jukeboxes, the actual 45 rpm singles of popular songs would be loaded into the machine. Nowadays, modern jukeboxes have gone digital and have CDs in them. Anyway, every time a song is played on the jukebox, that play is printed on a receipt inside the machine. When the representative from the jukebox company comes to service the box, he or she takes that receipt back to the company so the license fees can be paid to ASCAP or BMI for the songs played. Seeburg tried to avoid paying that licensing fee by putting sound-alike records in its machines. For example, there might be a single in the jukebox titled "Be My Baby" by the Bonettes. The original record is "Be My Baby" by the Ronettes.

Arnold Silverman was the representative for Seeburg who hired me to arrange and record the sound-alike songs and I was the contractor for all the sessions, so I hired all of the same musicians who worked with me recording the original songs. The singers who worked on the sound-alikes were often the background singers on the original records. Darlene Love, Edna Wright, and Jean King were among the fabulous singers that sang on these sound-alikes. You could not detect that the leads were not sung by the original singer.

I got paid a very nominal fee for my arrangements, around fifteen to twenty dollars for each song, but Seeburg did pay union scale to me and all musicians playing on the recordings. We would record up to twelve songs a day at Sunset Sound Recorders.

Some songs we recorded for Seeburg were original songs I wrote, but again I received only a nominal fee for composing and arranging. These original songs were sound-alikes for Herb Alpert and the Tijuana Brass, only the band name was changed to something like Herm Arnold and the Tujunga Band. All of the guys, including me, were the same musicians that played on the original Tijuana Brass records.

I recorded a couple hundred sound-alikes and made good money at the time for this work, but it was a one-time deal as we can't receive royalties for this work. These records only played in Seeburg jukeboxes and were never sold to the public. However, because these recording dates were union contract dates, the Seeburg Company paid health and welfare and pension fees to the union, which today I am very grateful for.

CHAPTER 41

Winro Records

F or about a minute, I was a "big-time" record company executive. In 1968, Mike Curb, Burt Rosen, and David Winters formed the record company Winro Records and they hired me as their record producer overseeing A&R (artists and repertoire). This is a dream job for anyone who wants to work for a record label. I would be able to sign and produce new artists and receive a share of the profits from sales and publishing of the records and songs produced. I had worked with Burt and David doing music on television projects for their production company, Winters/Rosen Productions, and I also worked with Mike Curb (Curb Records) on other recording projects, but knew Mike's reputation of being a very shrewd businessman. I was not apprehensive about getting involved with Winro, except the record producer position was going to limit my availability to accept other types of music production, recording, and touring opportunities that might be offered to me. I weighed the potential of the Winro Records opportunity against the loss of my freedom to work on a few projects and the income from them. I decided to take the chance and possibly succeed in a new and very lucrative direction for my career.

I was very excited to begin my job as the record producer and set out to sign artists that I knew would be successful and who deserved the chance to record and release records. It was also exciting to have much more creative control over a project that I was certain was going to be a hit.

One of the first artists we signed for Winro was a talented composer and singer from Texas, Christopher Kingsley. He wrote a charming song titled

"Long Haired Lover from Liverpool," and I produced the song as a single. The song was later recorded by Jimmy Osmond, the youngest brother of the Osmond Brothers group, and it became a huge hit in England.

David Conrad was another artist we signed for Winro Records. It was actually a group, David Conrad and Tomorrow. David sings and plays harmonica and guitar, but we never got to release any records for his group. David Conrad has remained a good friend of mine through the years and his talents go far beyond music. I would call him a true artisan who designs and builds exquisite items that no one else does. In the late 1970s he designed fine men's shirts that had a very long collar. The exaggerated collar style was "in" for the time, but David's designs were distinctive and different from the rest. He designed and handmade amazing leather goods and he made me a custom briefcase that I used for many years. David is also an excellent carpenter, building unique furniture. He built custom bunk beds for my sons, David and Justin. David built a wooden pirate ship that he had docked at Marina del Rey, which is where I had my boat. His pirate boat was named *Nightingale* and when he would take it out in the marina, everyone would come out to see it. We sometimes played jazz and blues on his boat to entertain the crowds. It was such a fun time! We also recorded a song together later on my label, Bee Pee Records, called "Nightingale" after his beautiful boat. David sang lead and my daughter Leah sang background. David also designed and installed the wood panel facade on the front of my club, The Baked Potato. David Conrad still sings and plays harmonica and guitar in live shows and he has performed with me and my band, Quest, at The Baked Potato.

David Winters went out to clubs all over LA and Orange County to scout talent for Winro Records. One evening he found a band playing at a club in Orange County and he asked me to meet him there to hear the band; they were called Bigfoot. When I did, we signed them instantly. Bigfoot was incredible and had the potential to be one of the biggest and most loved bands in rock 'n' roll. The band members were: Spencer Earnshaw (drums), Virgil Beckham (bass and vocals), Art Munson (guitar), David Garland (keyboards, sax), and Gerald Belisle (horns and vocals).

All of the tracks on the album were written by the band members and every song was outstanding. Just before the album was released, Mike Curb was able to get Bigfoot on tour with Chicago as its opening act. I was certain this would thrust the band to a number one single, album, and much more. Bigfoot made its big debut on tour with Chicago and was such a big hit with the audience that it was hard for Chicago to follow it. After a few dates the concert organizer for Chicago paid off Bigfoot for the rest of the tour because it was too good. It was replaced by another band. After that occurred, I was concerned with how this might affect the record release, so I had a meeting with Mike Curb at his office on Sunset Boulevard. In the meeting Mike told me not to worry, and in fact, that the album had been shipped to most of the country already and was getting a great response on the radio in all the major markets that received the album for airplay. He said sales were starting to climb, too. Mike was blowing my mind with all of this fantastic information and I took notes so I could tell the guys in the band, who I promised to get back to with details.

I left the meeting with Mike on cloud nine and drove out of the parking lot on to Sunset going toward Hollywood. After about a mile I saw a good friend in his car, Danny Davis, who was a top a promo man for record companies. I've known Danny since he was the promo man for Phil Spector's Philles Records after Sonny Bono left to start his recording career with Cher. We tried to talk at the light from car to car, but when the light changed Danny said, "Pull over, Don, so we can catch up." So, we did and I told Danny about Bigfoot and the exciting news about its new album. Danny asked, "Don, do you have a few minutes? Come up to my office with me and I'll make a few calls for you. Let's make sure Bigfoot is getting all the airplay it should." I asked, "Really, Danny?" Danny pointed his finger back and forth from him to me and replied, "Don, this is us, of course!" We got back in our cars and I followed Danny to his office. When we were sitting at his desk, I got out the notes I took during my meeting with Mike Curb. Danny started calling the station managers of the rock radio stations in the markets that Mike mentioned, but none of these stations knew about Bigfoot and they didn't have the album. I was embarrassed. I said, "Danny, Mike Curb told me these were the markets that had the album and were playing it." I felt so bad for wasting Danny's time and the awkward position it put him in with his contacts, but he told me not to worry about that—what a good and kind friend I had in Danny.

I was furious with Mike Curb when I left Danny's office to drive back to face him. I went up to the floor where the executive offices were and straight to Mike's office without stopping to say anything to anyone, but when I got to his office, his secretary stopped me and said Mike was in a meeting and would be tied up for the rest of the day. I know he knew I was mad, real mad, but he also knew I would never push past a woman and barge into his office, so I told his secretary in a voice loud enough for Mike and the other people nearby could hear, "Tell Mike Curb, Don Randi was here to tell him he's a PRICK!"

It was about two months after the "scene" at Mike Curb's office about Bigfoot that Winro Records folded. Burt Rosen came to me and told me the record company was closing down. I always had a good business relationship with Burt and he was straightforward with me. I'm glad it was him and not Mike giving me this news, but it still didn't make the disappointment any easier to take. I was disillusioned and angry at being betrayed, plus over the year of working for Winro I had turned down thousands of dollars of recording work that I could not do because of my job there. This business failure hit me very hard.

My record company dreams were dashed and I was in financial trouble, but I felt I had an obligation to the members of Bigfoot because they had trusted me with their recording career. I checked the Winro account I had for production and there was still ten thousand dollars in that account. Right away, I called the guys and told them to meet me at Guitar Center in Hollywood, ASAP. I got a cashier's check from the bank for the amount left in the production account. When the guys got to Guitar Center, I told them the news that the record company was folding, but I didn't want them to walk away with nothing . . . I told them to pick out gear and instruments and paid for it with the check. It wasn't nearly enough to make up for the success they should have had with Winro, but at least I could give them something and not let that money go back to the undeserved.

CHAPTER 42

"They're Gonna Put Me in the Movies"

"They're gonna make a big star outta me" . . . those lines are from Buck Owens' song "Act Naturally." I didn't play on that song for Buck, but I was a composer, music director, and musician on a few movie scores. On a couple of films I also appear on screen.

Fireball 500

Fireball 500 (1966) was a movie starring Frankie Avalon, Annette Funicello, and Fabian (Forte) about race car driving. I was hired by Guy Hemric and Jerry Styner to play on the soundtrack and they also hired some of the guys that I played regularly with at the time. I also appeared in a scene where the band played on a stage at one of the races, as you can see in the photo. It was a fun experience to be in the movie and especially with Frankie, Annette, and Fabian.

De Sade

Al Simms was the music supervisor on *Fireball 500*, but I didn't get to know him until I worked on a movie titled *De Sade* in 1969. *De Sade* was the story about the Marquis de Sade. Billy Strange was doing quite a bit of film scoring for AIP (American International Pictures) and this was one of several films he worked on. He hired me to play a music cue on *De Sade* for him. Billy was doing another session that day, so he wasn't going to be at the session, but he told me it would be fine and Al Simms knew I was coming in to do the cue. Billy gave me the music, which was for harpsichord. Looking at the music, which had Billy's direction and guidelines, I saw it was very simple, with some chords and just a little melody line. It was more for improvisation or ad-libbing on the harpsichord.

I got to the session and this cue turned out to be the hardest one I have ever done. This was a three-minute cue, but it was complicated because of a variable click track. As I mentioned in my story about the scoring session for the TV series *Judd for the Defense* with Randy Newman, when recording music for film (or TV) there is a click track that can be heard through the headphones for the musicians to keep time to while recording the music cue. I started playing and a minute into the cue, the click track sped up, then another minute went by and it slowed back down. The difficulty was knowing precisely when that change was going to occur and to match my playing to the correct tempo. Since I was improvising and trying to think about what Billy would want me to do, trying to stay in sync at the same time with the click track was insane. It drove me crazy! The harpsichord was the only instrument on this cue, so all the focus and pressure was on me to play this solo correctly and I didn't want to let Billy down by frustrating Al Simms or Ving Hershon, the music editor. I had to start and stop a few times to get it right, but eventually I got it done.

After we finished, Al Simms came over to me and asked if I would be interested in scoring a film for him. I was caught by surprise because I thought he might have been frustrated with me for taking a bit longer than we thought to complete this session, but then I replied, "Thank you, but I don't want to take work away from Billy Strange, because he helps me with jobs." Al said, "Billy already turned it down and he suggested you." I must have looked like a deer caught in headlights for a second, then I accepted the job from Al. What a kind gesture it was for Billy to recommend me to Al, especially because I could not recall ever a time Billy would turn down a job. Billy was in such demand and he was often overbooked. Thanks to Billy's recommendation, I got to work on two more films with Al Simms, *Up in the Cellar* (1970) and *Bloody Mama* (1970).

Up in the Cellar

Larry Hagman and Joan Collins starred in *Up in the Cellar*, which was a film about a young man, played by Wes Stern, who has to leave college because he loses his financial aid. He blames the college president and decides to seek revenge by seducing his wife, daughter, and mistress. I was the music director on this film and wrote the score. The theme song for this movie was "Didn't I Turn Out Nice," which Dory Previn and I wrote, and Hamilton Camp sang.

Bloody Mama

Bloody Mama was a big film-scoring project for me. I was the music director on *Bloody Mama*, and as you see in the photos I took, I went on location to Arkansas with the crew to work with the producers and the cast. The film, directed by Roger Corman, was based on Ma Barker (played by Shelley Winters), who was the matriarch of her notorious gangster clan called the Barker Gang, set in the Depression era (1930s). Ma Barker was known to carry a machine gun, and near the end of the movie there is a very complex shootout scene where Ma Barker is killed by the FBI.

I was asked to go on location to Arkansas with the production because Shelley Winters had many ideas for the music for the film, and she wanted to help me find music by local artists from that time period to inspire me and include in the film. Shelley Winters was wonderful to work with because she was so enthusiastic about this project and loves music, so she was very open about discussing the score with me. Robert De Niro and Bobby Walden played Fred and Lloyd Barker, two of Ma Barker's sons. Don Stroud played Herman Barker, and Bruce Dern and Diane Varsi were also in the cast.

I was in a scene in *Bloody Mama* that takes place at a fair in the country near a small town. My part was as an acoustic bass player who tries to prevent Herman Barker from stealing the money that is being donated for the town's volunteer fire department. On the stage I am playing the bass and there is a bowl near me that people are putting their donations into and it is getting full of money. I see Herman Barker grab the bowl, so I try to stab him with the point of the bass stand. Herman shoots a gun at me and the bass breaks apart. The bass I was using was scored in various places so when the gun was fired and I thrusted the bass, it broke apart easily. And there were four basses there, all scored the same way, in case we had to do the scene that many times to get it right.

Before filming the scene we rehearsed it a few times and Don Stroud, who had become a friend of mine during the production, started joking around with me, trying to make me forget what I was supposed to do, but it was all in fun. During rehearsal Don did not fire the gun (which had blanks); he just said, "BANG," at the moment when he would fire the gun at me. After rehearsing a couple of times, we tried shooting the scene and something went wrong, so we did it again and something else happened, or didn't happen. Now we were going a third time and when Don shot, he fired every shot in the pistol at me. It scared the crap outta me and my reaction was real, like he was killing me, and that was the take Roger Corman edited and used in the movie.

My friends Bob Silver and Guy Hemric wrote the *Bloody Mama* theme song, and Bigfoot, the group I was producing for Winro Records, also played music on the soundtrack. My son David was six years old then and sang a version of the *Bloody Mama* theme. I was amazed at how it turned out because it gave the theme a very eerie quality with a child's voice singing. I suggested that version as the song to play while the end credits rolled, but Roger Corman didn't use it. However, that version is on the soundtrack album.

Greg Dinallo

Besides being an author, scriptwriter, producer, director, and photographer, Greg Dinallo is my friend. The film projects Greg hired me to compose and direct the music for were always interesting and challenging.

My favorite project was *Circus Time*, a featured exhibit, sponsored by Sears, at the Chicago Museum of Science and Industry. The music I wrote for the *Circus Time* exhibit was very intricate and I conducted a full orchestra and chorus when we recorded it in quadraphonic sound. The unique feature of this exhibit was that the screen for the film was huge and curved so it went over the audience sitting in the middle of the room. This made the room feel and look like you were in a circus tent. *Circus Time*, shot in 70mm, was an interactive film experience where physical objects would become animated as the film ran. Technically it was brilliant, but the simplest way for me to describe how it worked is, there were notches placed in certain spots on the film so when it ran, these notches would trigger objects to animate at the correct time. For example, there is one point when the object was a tightrope artist triggered to ride a bike on a wire suspended over the audience. And the music flowed and changed seamlessly to go with each scene and event that happened in the experience. It was a really remarkable exhibit that I am so proud of doing with Greg. I wish that the exhibit was still there for you to see, but it was removed several years ago.

While editing *Circus Time* at Todd Martin's studio, we were playing back the music soundtrack in quad sound and a gentleman editing in another room came by and commented on how much he liked the music. The next day he contacted me; his name was Tim Penland. He was the director and producer for the Radio Shack television and radio commercials. I worked on (composed and recorded) at least seventy-five commercial spots with award-winning writer Greg Cash and Tim Penland. Fortunes of the business, or fate?

Greg Dinallo and I did many other projects together over the years and though he and his wife, Gloria, moved back to New York City, we stay in contact with each other. He and his wife have remained friends with my family and me for many years.

CHAPTER 43

1984 Olympics—A Gold Medal Experience

I n 1984 my band, Don Randi and Quest, were booked to perform at the athlete villages for the Summer Olympics (the XXIII Olympiad) in Los Angeles. Bill Liebowitz, village entertainment director of the Olympic Committee, hired me and we were contracted at first for four concerts: one in each village at USC, UCLA, and UC Santa Barbara, and the Press Center.

Bill Liebowitz was a friend of mine from years earlier when Phil Spector introduced me to him. Bill would visit my club, The Baked Potato, to hear me play. I am not sure what led him to work for the Olympic Committee, but Bill Liebowitz was well known for the Golden Apple comic book store in Hollywood. Bill and his store were very popular with celebrities and comic book fans alike. After Bill passed away, his sons continued managing the store and it is still a pop culture destination where comic book fans from all over the world come to visit.

At the Olympics, the villages were where the athletes from all of the participating countries were housed during the Games, and there was a great deal of security involved to keep these Olympic athletes safe. Every member of my band—Bobby Torres (percussion), David Hunt (drums), Pops (Robert Lee) Popwell (bass), Chuck Camper (reeds), Chris Winters (guitar), and I—had to undergo a strict security check before we could enter the facilities and perform. We went through a basic background check by the Olympic committee, and also through a very detailed security clearance by the FBI, because of the access we had to the villages where the athletes stayed and other areas of the Olympic facilities that we needed to enter.

When we began our concerts during the first few days of the Olympic Games, a certain seriousness and fierce competitive spirit could be felt among the athletes. They were so focused on winning medals in their events for their countries that they weren't very social outside their own teams. After a few days, once medals were being awarded, the pressure eased for the athletes and you could see them come together as friends and they started to enjoy themselves. I saw many were forming friendships with people that they would not have imagined meeting in their lives. So much diversity, yet there was an equality among them that was beautiful. Barriers like language and cultural customs were bridged and the villages became home and family. I can't begin to express how wonderful it was to see and experience this, but when I reminisce about playing these concerts I feel hopeful that it's possible one day we'll see a world in peace.

In each venue, everything that the athletes could possibly need was provided for them. There was an abundance of food and other treats for them and us wherever we performed. I recall there was a table that had a mountain of oranges on it and I saw a young athlete staring at it in awe. He had never seen or eaten a fresh California orange before. I guessed that he thought it was just there for display, but when I took one I encouraged him to take one, too, and he was so delighted. He thought he needed permission to take it and the other types of fresh fruit and other food that was all around us on tables.

We were asked to come back to do three more concerts at the village at USC from the requests and positive response from the athletes and Olympic officials at our shows. As far as I know, my band was the only band asked to add more shows and we were thrilled. Don Randi and Quest did a total of seven shows for the Olympic villages. Bill Liebowitz sent me a letter a couple of weeks after the Olympics closed, to thank and compliment me for the concerts. What a kind and professional gesture of gratitude from Bill that I will always treasure. (This letter is reproduced in Appendix C.)

Just as I do in every concert, I usually told stories and jokes between songs, gave some background on the compositions we played, and introduced each of my band members. I tried to entertain and connect directly with the audience by speaking to them and hearing their response. At the last concert we did for the Olympics I asked the athletes, who by now had toured the Los Angeles area and absorbed some of our culture, "If you could stay in Los Angeles, where would you live?" One athlete stood up and introduced himself being from the Nigerian team and said in his charming accent, "Mah-lah-booo, mon." He was very passionate about the beauty of Malibu and why he wanted to live there that his response inspired me to write and record a song titled "Malibu Nights."

I actually wrote, produced, and recorded an entire album titled *Malibu Nights*. The band members on the album included Rick Braun on trumpet, Steve Marston on bass, Rob Whitsitt on guitar, Chuck Camper on sax, Bobby Economou on drums, and Tom Rhode on percussion. It was recorded at Gold Star Studios in Hollywood and was originally released on my record label, Bee Pee Records. If you are curious, "Bee Pee" stands for Baked Potato.

There are nine songs on my *Malibu Nights* album, but the title song is the best. When we recorded "Malibu Nights," we did that song in one take. In the studio, as we played the song we immediately fell into a groove that felt really good, and when we finished, we just sat there and looked at one another. After a minute or two I said, "I think that was it." We listened to the playback and all agreed, that was it, "Malibu Nights." The song was a hit for me by being popular among fans; it was chosen several times for television and a DJ on the East Coast used the song as a musical background for his poetry readings. A copywriter for KNBC-TV News in Los Angeles just loved "Malibu Nights" and he would often come see me play at The Baked Potato. I wish I could remember his name, but he was a sweet guy and he would tell the news staff at KNBC to visit The Baked Potato for my show and be sure to request "Malibu Nights." When he passed away, KNBC News did a beautiful tribute to him in a video montage of the many stories he wrote and the station played "Malibu Nights" as the musical background of the tribute.

I still play "Malibu Nights" when I perform at The Baked Potato and other venues where I play live, and I usually tell a short version of my 1984 Olympics experience and the inspiration for the song, because it is still so meaningful to me.

CHAPTER 44

The Baked Potato—A Club of My Own

In 1970 I went to London to work on a TV special *Raquel!* with Raquel Welch (details in the Raquel chapter) and while I was there, I would see vendors with carts selling little baked potatoes with awful toppings and thought, *Who would eat that?* But people were eating them, so when I got back to LA, the thought came back to me. I thought that with the size of potatoes that we can get in the USA, we could make a good meal out of a baked potato. And the idea of a club was also fueled by Pat Dinnocenti, who owned Sherry's, the club I played at for fourteen years; I had to keep hiring sub piano players to do my gig there because I was constantly on other projects. Pat told me I needed to open my own club to find out what a headache it is to run a club. But I also wanted to open a club to have a place for my friends and me to come to, to play the music we love after working all day playing music for other people.

I started looking for a location and found this little building on Cahuenga Boulevard in Studio City. It was owned by John Harlan, a successful TV game show announcer. Two of the many shows he worked were *Queen for a Day* and *Name That Tune.* I leased this building from him with an option to buy, then I had to get busy renovating the place from an office building to a club. I did most of the work myself because I didn't have a lot of money to hire contractors. I built the two restrooms, which entailed me having to dig trenches to connect the plumbing. When I started this project it was in late February and one of the coldest winters in Los Angeles, which sounds funny but once you move to the West Coast from the East Coast, you get ultra-sensitive to cold.

The kitchen, which I built, was situated right next to the stage at first. Five years later we expanded and moved the kitchen to where it is now, enlarged the bar, and added more seating next to the stage. If you have been to my club, you know that it's a pretty small place, so imagine it even smaller when it opened.

I did have some help from good friends John Maglieri (brother of Mario Maglieri, a partner in the famous Rainbow Bar and Grill on the Sunset Strip) and David Conrad (musician, carpenter, and entrepreneur). John helped me with some of the interior work, and David created the front of the club with beautiful woodwork and plants.

I lived only ten minutes from the club when it opened, so it was convenient for me to be there every day, but I knew I couldn't handle everything and still do the session work that I kept getting, thankfully, so I partnered with a good friend of mine, Sheldon Slussman. Shelly was a top salesman for the famous Sy Devore men's store in Hollywood. He also worked at a more hip men's store in Hollywood called Beau Gentry. I met Shelly when I was playing at Sherry's with my trio years before The Baked Potato opened and we became friends. Shelly loved jazz and was a regular at Sherry's and he was a fan of my trio. One night after a show he came up to us and said we were great jazz musicians but dressed horribly. Shelly told us to come into Beau Gentry and he'd give us suits at a reduced cost. We went and were fitted with the best suits and other clothing and often Shelly would not take our money. If he did take cash, he'd give us a hundred-dollar suit for ten dollars. He was incredibly kind and we were the best-dressed band in town. I knew Shelly had a good head for business and he loved music, so we became partners in The Baked Potato and he helped me manage the club.

The Baked Potato didn't have a full liquor license when we opened, so we only served beer and wine and the baked potatoes. Back then we had twelve different types of potatoes on the menu, compared to now, when we have twenty-one. My wife, Norma, and I came up with the original menu and Norma did all the cooking when we first started. I would get the extra-large potatoes from Idaho for the club and they sold so well that we were able to get our full liquor license in about a year and a half. I laugh when the chefs at The Baked Potato these days boast and complain about making up to 60 potatoes in one night. Norma would make 100 to 120 in one night and it wouldn't be such a big deal for her. And speaking of Norma, it is incredible to picture her, a beautiful top-paid professional Las Vegas dancer, in the kitchen cooking stuffed baked potatoes and doing it better than any chef in LA.

The Baked Potato opened November 17, 1970, and critics said the club wasn't going to last. They gave us six months, but here we are forty-five years later. The only person who said positive things about the club when we opened and said it was going to be a success was Carmen Miceli, whom I have known for years. Miceli's Italian Restaurants have been a success and favorite in Los Angeles since the '50s and there is a Miceli's just up the street from my club.

In the beginning I played six nights a week with my band, and on Sundays Mike Melvoin (who passed in 2012) played with different band members all the time. In fact, for a whole year he played there with a different bass player and drummer for each show and they were all terrific players. Mike was a dear friend and a fellow jazz pianist, composer, and arranger who worked with all of the same producers I did back in the '60s and '70s. Mike served as the chairman and president of the Recording Academy for several years.

Before I opened this club I had to find a piano for it. There was a piano store on Beverly near La Brea; I think it was called Finnegan's. Anyway, it was having a big sale and had the discounted pianos lined up in one row. I was playing these pianos one by one and some were pretty good, when I got almost to the end of the row and played a piano that was very exceptional. I saw it was a Steinway B. I looked at the price tag and it said $2,680, which was a steal for this piano. I didn't hesitate for one second and called over the salesman and told him I wanted to buy this piano. He wrote up the sales contract, had the manager sign it, and I signed it and got my carbon copy so I could go the Musicians Union and get money out of my account. I made sure that the sale was confirmed so I would not lose the piano to someone else while I was out. It took me about thirty to forty minutes to go to the union and come back with a check. When I got back, the manager of the store was waiting for me and said he couldn't sell the piano for that price, that it was a mistake. Well, I told him I had a signed sales contract for that piano and had just come back from the Musicians Union. I was insistent and said, "If you don't honor this sale, you can bet I will go back to the union and report this to all of the members. Trust me that not one union member will ever come to this store." So, the guy relented and I got the piano for the club.

There is a story behind why I jumped at the opportunity to buy that Steinway B . . . Years earlier when I was playing in Chicago, one night I went to see Oscar Peterson playing at the London House. He was playing a Steinway B, and of course, his performance was dazzling. I dreamed from that night I would someday get a Steinway B of my own. So, now I had the piano in the club and everyone who played it just loved it, including me, of course. In a couple of years we started getting great talent in here, like Harry "Sweets" Edison, who was in Count Basie's band. Sweets played here often on Sunday nights, and this one Sunday I was standing by the front door when Oscar Peterson walked in! I was in shock and awe and surprised I got the words out; I introduced myself to him. We sat together in the front and Sweets saw Oscar and asked him to come up and play. Oscar said no; he was there to see him. Sweets kept asking him and Oscar kept saying no, and I was really hoping he would say yes, too!

At the break Sweets came over and talked to Oscar for a few minutes and then went out back for a smoke (even though back then you could smoke in the club, the band usually went out back during the breaks). So, I had an opportunity to talk to Oscar and I told him that it was because of him that I had the Steinway B. I told him the story of how I heard him play at the London House and since then always wanted to have one. He told me that he also had one. I pleaded with him to play just one song on the piano. It would mean so much to me. Oscar said he would, just for me. I was thrilled.

Oscar got up and sat at the piano. By this time Sweets was back in the club and saw him, so he rushed the band over to get ready to play. But Oscar said he was just going to do a one-song solo, so Sweets and the band could just relax. Oscar played and the audience was silent. You could hear a pin drop in the club; everybody was spellbound. His performance was amazing and we went wild when he finished!

If that wasn't extraordinary enough, another incredible thing occurred. Sarah Vaughan was at the bar and we didn't even realize it. Where she was sitting, my view of that part of the bar was actually blocked by the piano so I didn't see her. She came up to greet Oscar and he asked her to stay and they sang together while he played and I felt I must have been dreaming! They performed together for about forty-five minutes, and I'll tell you, that was one of the most exciting evenings at The Baked Potato that I can remember. It's too bad that back then we didn't have portable recording devices like cell phones, because that was a night I would love to share, but for the lucky audience that was there with us, we were treated to a night we'll never forget.

The Steinway B was in the club for over thirty years and so many great pianists played it. Keith Albright was the piano tuner that worked all of the studios and he tuned our piano at least once a week, twice if a lot of bands were playing it that week. If a band came in to play but didn't have a piano player, we pushed the piano as far as we could to one side to give the band a little more room onstage. Eventually we had to sell the piano because we just needed the room onstage, electronic keyboards started becoming more popular, and I was the only one playing it. I now play different electronic keyboards but I wish that I had kept the Steinway and moved it to my house.

As The Spud (the nickname for the club) gained popularity and was filling up with fans, young musicians started asking if they could play there. And in the early days we didn't have a door charge, so the bands got paid union scale, which was hardly anything, but we did pay the pension and health and welfare per union contract if you were in the union.

Soon musicians who became very famous, like Lee Ritenour, asked if they could play on Tuesday nights. Then Larry Carlton asked us if he could play on Tuesdays. And one of the greatest scat singers who was unknown then, Al Jarreau, asked if he could sing there. Joe Sample and Patrice Rushen started playing there, and many other talented musicians started playing at The Spud before they became well known. Soon word of mouth spread and The Spud became THE place for all of the musicians to hang out. It was a melting pot for talent to form bands and share their music talent with one another. The fans just loved it, too, because it was their place to come to hear the best new music talent in town.

Here's a recent story about how those Tuesday nights were more than a magnet for talent onstage and in the audience . . . In 2007 I was being inducted into the Musicians Hall of Fame and Museum in Nashville with my fellow musicians of the Wrecking Crew. We were setting up to play when Vince Gill came up to me and was so nice and congratulated me. Then he grinned. He had his guitar and started playing, not country, but some bebop jazz riffs. Vince saw that I was surprised and he laughed and said he was in the band Pure Prairie League, which was booked out of Los Angeles, and spent a lot of Tuesday nights at The Spud listening Lee Ritenour and Larry Carlton! So, I asked him to play with me a bit and we jammed jazz for about ten minutes, which drew quite a few people to watch us. It was a lot of fun! His wife, Amy Grant, sang "These Boots Are Made for Walkin'" in the awards show as a tribute to us.

The club received great PR from *Cosmopolitan* magazine when it published an article for businesswomen who traveled to different cities. The article said that if you were in Los Angeles and looking for evening entertainment, The Baked Potato was a great place to visit for good food and music and it was a safe place for a woman alone to go to in the evening. I think that article came out in the early '80s and it was a boost that attracted more business into the club. I didn't know this article was being written until it came out. The Baked Potato is still a very welcoming and safe environment for a woman to enjoy an evening of jazz entertainment.

There are a lot of reasons The Spud has been a success over all these years, but I can tell you that this room has the best sound quality by far, over just about any club in town. Over ninety live albums of various artists have been recorded there. I think that the low ceiling in the room helps and it is just dense enough so the sound is not dead and has the live feeling; the room is easy to record in because of that. Also the musicians love to play there, as do I, because it's an open and comfortable atmosphere, yet there is a vibe in The Spud that lifts you musically. The artists are welcome to experiment and try new music, styles, and techniques. Sometimes it works astoundingly well and sometimes it doesn't, but that never discourages any of the talent to keep trying new things, or to debut their latest compositions at The Spud before they go elsewhere to perform or record. I am always playing my new material there and love to hear the reactions and feedback from the fans and other musicians who come to my shows.

I get a big kick out of seeing the young talent who started there become a great success in music. Here's a story about this very thing . . . I was working on an album project with Cannonball Adderley and he was not feeling too good, so he decided to vacation in Hawaii for a few days to rest. While he was over there I got an excited phone call from him. "Don, you have to hear this band called Ox. The alto player is so incredible! Don, you have to bring them over!" Cannonball was so excited and I was sure he was right, but I couldn't afford to bring them over. After Cannonball got back, we finished the album, which was for Letta Mbulu, the great singer from South Africa. She is terrific and very interesting because she could do all the African rhythm sounds with her voice and this was on a jazz album, so it was really a unique recording. Cannonball was the producer along with David Axelrod.

But to get back to the story, a couple of years later these scraggly kids came into the club through the back door and asked for me. To Shelly and me they looked like some homeless teenagers. The singer of the group, Pauline Wilson, said, "We're a band from Hawaii and we used to be called Ox, but now we call ourselves Seawind." Then I remembered Cannonball talked about Ox when he was in Hawaii and how good they were. Pauline said, "We have no place to play our music; can we play here?" I said, "Sure, I'll give you one night a week; which night would you like?" And I think they played on Mondays. When they started, no one came to see them for the first couple of weeks; only a few regulars came in and heard them. They hung out there every night even though they only played one night a week, and Shelly and I fed them potatoes every night. As a thank-you, Ken Wild, the bass player, would get mango bread sent to him from Hawaii and would bring me some. That mango bread from Hawaii is simply delicious and he knew I loved it!

After the third week Seawind started there, the word of mouth got out how good it was and people started coming in for the band and soon there was a line outside. You had to get there early or you would not get in if you wanted to see Seawind. The band went on to release its own albums in the '70s and early '80s. Pauline Wilson did vocals, Jerry Hey played trumpet, Kim Hutchcroft played flute and sax, Ken Wild was on bass, and Bob Wilson was the drummer and wrote most of Seawind's songs. All of the members of Seawind went on to very successful careers in music, performing with top acts, like B.B. King, Rod Stewart, Michael Jackson, Gloria Estefan, and Barbra Streisand.

It wasn't just the new talent that was a hit with fans. We've been very fortunate to have famous talent play and appear there, like Lou Rawls and Redd Foxx.

I had known Lou Rawls for many years before I opened The Baked Potato. I met him in the early '60s when he was performing at a club called Pandora's Box. Sherry's, the club I was working at, was right across the street, and Lou would sometimes sing a tune with my band and would walk across the street to Sherry's, then go back to Pandora's to do his set. Years later we were working on various recording dates together, whether it was sessions for film or TV projects or his records. After these sessions that occurred during the day, Lou would stop by The Baked Potato in the evening when I would be playing and sing with my band. It was a big treat for the fans and for me to have him there.

One night when I was playing and it was a pretty packed night, I looked up to see Lou Rawls seating people coming into the club. I started laughing and said, "Lou, what are you doing?" He replied, "Well, it was hard for me to find a seat and I was just standing here, so I thought I would help these people find seats." The people coming in didn't realize they were being seated by Lou Rawls! As usual, I asked him to come up and sing a few tunes with us.

Redd Foxx was a friend of mine who I met in Las Vegas when he was doing his stand-up act at the Castaways. He was one of the first black comedians to get a headline show on the Las Vegas strip. He came in to The Spud frequently and would often get up and do thirty to forty-five minutes of his routine here. He just loved the club and he was also a good friend of Shelly's. There are a couple of funny stories about Redd Foxx and this club . . .

One night I was performing and the deans of music for both USC and LA City College came in with their wives and teenage kids. They were good friends and I knew them both. Redd Foxx came in as he did quite often, and at the break he got up and started doing his shtick. I was panicking because Redd did some very adult material and both deans were in the front row with their families. Inside I was praying that this was the night Redd did some milder material. I hoped he was aware of the two deans in the audience, because I had mentioned them during the first set. But Redd went into his "blue" comedy and I thought that was going to be it for the club's reputation. Fortunately, *Sanford and Son* was already on TV and popular, so the teens were excited that they were getting to see Fred Sanford and I was spared a big embarrassment.

On another occasion, Flip Wilson came into the club and it just happened that Redd Foxx was there, too. Flip had just come in to relax and hear my band, but Redd went up and introduced Flip Wilson and coaxed him to get up and do some stand-up. Flip didn't want to do it, but Redd was unrelenting. At first Flip was bombing and didn't want to continue. *The Flip Wilson Show* has been off the air for a while and he hadn't done stand-up for a long time and wasn't really prepared, but Redd would not let him stop. He kept telling Flip to keep going and if the next joke flopped, he'd yell out, "KEEP GOING!" Soon, though, Flip found his groove and we were in stitches. Everyone was laughing and just about rolling on the floor!

Many more famous, talented artists have played and sung here either on a regular basis, or for a night because they showed up. And as this club became LA's music house to enjoy the best new music and talent, a new generation of talent is starting to play here. The grown-up kids of Lee Ritenour, Brian Auger, Joe Sample, Steve Lukather, Larry Carlton, Abraham Laboriel, Larry Coryell, and many more are now playing here. Of course, this also makes me feel old (ha ha).

Besides being a launch pad for other musicians' professional careers, The Baked Potato was a key that opened new doors for me and boosted my career during the '70s and '80s. I met TV producer and director Andy Sidaris, whom you read about in previous chapters in this book, at the Baked Potato. He came into The Spud and was a regular there because he loved jazz. We became friends and one night he asked me if I composed and arranged music and offered me a job to provide the music for his TV and film projects. One of the projects was *ABC's Wide World of Sports*, which Andy directed. I wrote all of the themes and music cues for the series. Even when Roone Arledge took over *ABC's Wide World of Sports*, I continued to provide the music for the shows.

I also got a big break when SQuire Rushnell, a programming executive for ABC-TV, came into the club. He is a jazz fan and was in town from New York for business. A friend brought him to The Spud, knowing he would enjoy it. It just happened to be a night when I was playing with my band. He loved the music and the club, so he came up to me at the break to give his compliments on the set and we started talking about music. I told him if he was still in town over the weekend, he would enjoy going to the Laguna Jazz Festival, where my band would be opening for the singer Ruth Brown. I didn't expect him to show up at the Laguna Jazz Festival, but there he was! After our set he came up to me and asked if I would be interested in composing and arranging music for a new series of children's programs for ABC. SQuire Rushnell had just become the VP of family programming for ABC, after being the successful executive in charge of *Good Morning America*. That is how I got the gig to write and arrange the music for *ABC Afterschool Special*, *Schoolhouse Rock*, and the intros and bumpers for the ABC Saturday morning kids' programs block called All-Star Saturday on ABC. SQuire Rushnell is now a successful author who writes the best-selling *When God Winks* series of books.

For years my band has headlined here and played several times a week, but now we play one night a month. When we opened the club, I called my band the Baked Potato Band, but soon we were Don Randi and Quest.

There have been many members of Quest through the years. These are some of the regular members from the past and present. Guitar: Takeshi Akimoto, Roland Batiste, John DePatie, Chris Fields, John Goux, Jamie Kime, Jimmy Mahlis, Mike Miller, Rob Whitsitt, and Chris Winters. Reeds: Chuck Camper, Steve Douglas, and Larry Klimas. Trumpet: Rick Braun, Clay Jenkins, and Ralf Rickert. Drums: Dave Anderson, Mike Barsamento, Hal Blaine, Tom Brechtlein, John Clauder, Vinnie Colaiuto, Mark Converse, Bernie Dresel, Jonathan Dresel, Bobby Economou, Doug Gore, Jason Harnel, Paul Humphrey, David Hunt, Jim Keltner, Ricky Lawson, David Libman, Chet McCracken, Toss Panos, Miles Robinson, Steve Samuels, Andy Senise, Gene Stone, John Sumner, Joel Taylor, Steve Turner, Walter Valdez, Carlos Vega, and Todd Wolf. Bass: Ed Alton, Rico Belled, Lou Castro, Dave Coy, Al Criado, David Edelstein, Frank Fabio, Ric Fierabracci, Leon Gaer, J.K. Kleutgens, David LeVray, Tom Lilly, Richard Maloof (acoustic bass), Steve Marston, Ray Neapolitan, Harvey Newmark, Taras Prodaniuk, Dan Pierson, Pops Popwell, David Randi, H Chris Roy, Pat Senatore, Pat "Putter" Smith, Chad Watson, and Jerry Watts. Percussion: Lenny Castro, Luis Conte, Joakim Ekberg, Mike Faue, Gary Gardner, Hal Gordon, Lee Ann Harris, Billy Hulting, Pete Korpela, Tom Rhode, Jerry Steinholtz, and Bobby Torres.

Out of all of those musicians, Chuck Camper has remained in my band the longest. Chuck has been a consistent member of Quest for over forty years and is a loyal friend of The Baked Potato and mine. Chuck Camper is a brilliant musician who plays sax, flute, and some percussion in my shows. When fans come into The Baked Potato for Don Randi and Quest, they may see a different drummer or bass player, etc., but they always expect to see Chuck Camper and hear his terrific sax solos.

The Baked Potato could not be run smoothly without the help of some fantastic guys and friends who were doormen. Bob Silver, who was one of my best friends, was our first doorman, but he was also a very talented singer and songwriter. Bob composed several songs with me. His son Jamie Silver became a doorman for The Baked Potato years later. Jamie is also a drummer and was in a group named Lost Breed.

Larry Duran was also one of our doormen in the early years at The Baked Potato and became a good friend. Larry was also a stuntman and a bit part actor who was a friend of Marlon Brando.

Danny Jones was another doorman. I met him at Heritage Studios when I worked with producer Ray Ruff. Danny is the only black person I know who is fluent in Japanese. This ability came in very handy when tour buses of Japanese tourists would come to the club, because The Baked Potato is famous with the jazz lovers in Japan. It was hilarious to see the looks on the Japanese tourists' faces as Danny spoke to them in fluent Japanese.

Speaking of Japanese . . . Daisuke "Richard" Nakano was another doorman at the Spud, but Richard was not fluent in English when I met him. Danny Jones helped Richard learn English and trained him as a doorman. We also helped Richard get a green card so he could stay and work at the club without the fear of being deported. Daisuke Nakano went back to Japan after living in the USA for several years. He is also a very talented photographer and visits Los Angeles almost every year; he stops in The Baked Potato when he does.

Greg Cash, the writer I worked with on Radio Shack commercials, moved to Los Angeles from Texas several years ago, and while he was getting settled here, he also worked as a doorman at The Baked Potato.

Sadly, Shelly passed away after a battle with cancer in 1998. Everyone who knew him—fans of the club, the musicians, my family and me—were very upset at his passing. He was more than a friend, partner, and manager of The Baked Potato; he was a part of our lives and the success of the club. Al Jarreau was an especially close friend to Shelly, and during the last days he would visit him in the hospice every day and sing to him.

The Baked Potato became a family-run club with my kids helping me manage it after that. David, who also played bass in my band, helped manage the club and worked the door many nights, while he also had a day job and a family. My younger son, Justin, started bartending and managing the club for me and he does all of the talent bookings now. Justin also has his own band (Nothing Personal) and plays at The Spud once a month; he occasionally sings with my band when we perform. Justin owned The Baked Potato in

Hollywood and he designed the interior of that club as well as The Baked Potato in Pasadena. We now just have the original Baked Potato in Studio City.

For the past nine years "Monday Night Jammmz" has been a regular feature at The Baked Potato. Following the tradition and heart of what The Baked Potato is to fans, friends, and many top and aspiring musicians, the Jam Band on Monday nights at The Baked Potato encourages people to come in and get a chance to play or sing onstage with professional musicians. Guitarists Jamie Kime and John Ziegler and bassist Chris Roy host this jam night and play with everyone that gets to sit in. It's a fun night because you never know who you'll get to hear. Many times Danny Carey from the band Tool would sit in as the drummer. Recently John Mayer sat in on vocals. Thanks, guys, for keeping this tradition going for everyone in music.

There are so many more stories to tell about The Baked Potato that I really have to devote a separate book just to The Baked Potato to include it all.

CHAPTER 45

The Day I Stopped

In my youth, like most musicians and artists, I drank alcohol and smoked cigarettes like there was no tomorrow. When I played in various clubs in Los Angeles, it was common for guests to send over drinks and I would happily and gratefully toast and drink up the shots of tequila or vodka or whiskey they sent my way. It was a party every night and I never thought about the consequences of my actions.

One evening when my trio was playing at Marianne's Surf Club, the guys and I were drinking tequila shot after tequila shot after our set. We had a bottle of tequila on the bar and kept refilling our glasses. Well, I thought, *Why not skip the part of pouring the booze into the shot glass and just pour directly into my mouth?* Brilliant! As I tipped the bottle back, I went with it and fell over on my back and passed out. Hilarious and stupid!

Smoking was allowed everywhere in those days and it seemed like everyone smoked. If you didn't, you did anyway, just breathing in a smoke-filled club. My club, The Baked Potato, is a small room with a low ceiling, so it looked like it was on fire at times when over half of the guests were smoking at once. We tried to keep the front and back doors open to help clear the smoke, but it wasn't very effective.

I stopped smoking and drinking in the mid-'60s when it wasn't "cool" to stop, but this wasn't a decision I made out of a concern about lung cancer or liver disease. I was a partier and drank and smoked during my set and while socializing with my band and friends after work. That is what I did, as usual, one evening in 1965.

I was coming down with the flu, but like a maniac I kept on working because I never wanted to miss an opportunity to play in recording sessions and clubs. I felt progressively worse as the day went into the evening when my trio had a gig at Sherry's nightclub. I played the gig and had several drinks that guests bought me during the show. My head was pounding even then, but I kept on performing, and after the last set I had a nightcap with my band and friends who worked at Sherry's. I don't remember getting into my car or driving home, but in the still-dark early morning I found myself waking up in my car, in my garage at home. The engine was off but my radio was on, and I didn't know how long I had been passed out. The flu was now full blown and my head was hurting so bad, like a vise was tightening on it. I was dizzy and felt really nauseous. I threw up on myself, and as I was heaving, I heard the radio. It was a news broadcast and the announcer was reporting on a fatal, hit-and-run car crash that had occurred at the intersection of Fairfax and Sunset about an hour earlier. There were two cars involved and one driver was dead at the scene, but the other car had driven off, so the police was looking for that driver. I threw up on myself after hearing this report. I was not only sick with the flu, but a fear rose inside me as I realized the intersection where the accident occurred was one that I usually drove through on my way home from Sherry's. A minute or two after that broadcast, my wife found me in the garage and helped me get cleaned up and into bed. I was so sick and so shocked that I didn't say a word to her.

After spending the day in bed, I felt a little better physically, but panic and a very deep dread was filling my gut about the accident I heard on the radio. I still had not spoken to Norma about it because I was so afraid I was involved in that accident. I lay there in bed knowing I had to get up and go look at my car to see if it was damaged. I would have to turn myself into the police if it was I who had caused the accident that killed the other driver. It felt like I was in hell, with all the emotions and dark thoughts that were going through my head along with the high fever and aches, pains, and nausea that come with the flu. After a while I summoned the courage and went downstairs to look at my car. To my relief there was no damage. The weight lifted and I even felt much better physically at that moment, but going through those feelings of dread, fear, and immense guilt was a wake-up call. I decided to stop drinking. That experience shook me to the core, but for my own good.

I stopped smoking, too, because the flu caused me to come down with bronchitis and when I tried to smoke, it was extremely painful. Besides being painful, smoking only made my condition worse. I couldn't smoke while I had bronchitis and I never smoked again after I recovered.

CHAPTER 46

I Keep Going

Geir Ólafsson

I've known Geir Ólafsson, who is a very well-known singer in Iceland, for almost five years and I have recorded and played concerts with him in his home country of Iceland. He has also performed in Los Angeles with me at The Baked Potato. He is not only a very talented singer and entertainer, he is my friend.

While I was working on my book, Geir phoned to ask me to plan on recording a new album with him and assembling a band of top musicians from Los Angeles to come with me to Iceland to record. That will be later this year.

More . . .

My life in music does not stop and I would never want it to. I am planning to record another solo album in 2015 as well as tour many cities and perform my latest compositions and fan favorites. I really love performing and seeing the audience enjoy my music. That is still a thrill for me.

I'm also looking forward to meeting many readers when this book releases and tell you more of my stories, in person.

CHAPTER 47

My Family

I have told stories about my career for years, but my family life has not been included in my stories, except to a few of my closest friends, and most of them are so close they were like an extended family. Though I wasn't the traditional dad, my feelings about being protective of my family are traditional. For that reason, this is a challenging chapter to write because I want to respect them and protect them, but I have to include this very personal chapter about my family because they mean the world to me. We didn't have a typical family life, but it's been an extraordinary life . . . so far.

Norma was the lead dancer in the Barry Ashton revue in Las Vegas, Nevada. My trio was opening for that show in the main showroom till they built a lounge in another part of the Castaways hotel. We started in September 1963 and left the end of January 1964. What was supposed to be a two-week engagement turned into five months. It was at this time we were dating and fell in love. Norma's show moved to Reno, Nevada, and I went to San Francisco with my trio to play a gig at the Executive Suite. We worked Tuesday to Saturday, so to see Norma I would fly to Reno on Sunday morning and return Tuesday to play my gig.

Despite our schedules and locations, we managed to get to know and see each other without the communication devices that are available today. It wasn't easy to maintain a long-distance relationship. In some ways it was like that for many years in our marriage, while our kids were growing up and I was working all the time.

I was married twice before I met Norma. The third time was definitely the charm and the best thing to happen to me. My daughters Tani and Lori are from my second marriage and were with us every weekend while growing up.

Norma and I have two sons and two daughters: David, Justin, Leah, and Treesa. Treesa was a sweet baby whose smile could melt your heart. She came to us as a foster baby, but from the moment she arrived, Norma said the angels brought Treesa to us. We couldn't think of Treesa's not being a Randi, and adopted her. We have also been foster parents to fourteen incredible children.

David and Leah share the same birthday, September 11, only six years apart. We had no idea how unforgettable the date 9/11 would someday become.

Tani and Lori were very young when my second marriage fell apart, but I always wanted to be part of their lives and see them as often as I could. Tani Schwartz, my eldest daughter, is a very successful hairstylist and has long list of loyal of clients, including me. She is a wonderfully kind and exceptionally hardworking woman and a talented stylist.

Lori is a successful and hardworking manager at a well-known retail store. Lori has a heart of gold and is a real people person who is great with the public, which is why she is so successful in her career. Lori and her partner, Lisa, got married earlier this year in a beautiful ceremony that celebrated their commitment. They are one of the happiest couples you could ever know.

Lori told me one of her fondest memories growing up was getting to go to sessions with me and on tour, especially one of the times in Las Vegas doing a Nancy Sinatra show, where she got to meet the Osmonds. She also loved being at the "Drummer Man" recording session with Nancy Sinatra. Lori said she had no idea how famous the songs I played on would become, and neither did I.

When Tani and Lori were very young, six and seven years old, I took them to a recording session with me. It was a Phil Spector date for the Ronettes and I was a young, clueless dad who thought the girls would behave and enjoy being in a studio watching their daddy at work, but they soon got restless and were starting to drive me crazy. I was afraid any minute they were going to drive Phil crazy. Fortunately, Ronnie Spector and her sister, Estelle, saved me when they saw the girls acting up. Ronnie said to Tani and Lori, "Girls, come with me and we'll find something fun for you to do." While I was working, Ronnie and Estelle kept them entertained and I was so grateful to them for helping me out. After that I knew little kids and recording sessions are a bad mix.

Tani's son Donnie is a creative executive at one of the top entertainment, marketing, and advertising firms in Hollywood. I am very close to my grandson, as we share a lot of common interests, like Dodgers baseball. Donnie is a very talented artist and when he was attending college, a major animation studio kept trying to recruit him to work for them, but it would mean he would have to leave school. I told him to stay in school and get his degree, which he did and now he's the creative director on the production of promotions for major motion picture releases. He also designed the cover to my latest CD release, *Acoustimania*.

I also share my birth name with my grandson. I was Donald Schwartz until I changed it legally to Don Randi. I have used the last name "Randi" for my professional career in clubs and in recording sessions since I first used it on the marquee at Marianne's Surf Club. When my trio was hired to play at Marianne's I had to help put our band's name up on the marquee but I could not find a *w* or a *z* in the box of letters. After thinking it over for a few minutes and looking at the letters that were available in the box, "Randi" luckily fell in order and it's been that way ever since. Since I never liked my full first name, Donald, it was easy to decide on "Don Randi Trio" for the name of my band, and there were enough letters for the marquee. When I made Don Randi my legal name, Norma and our kids, David, Justin, and Leah, all got their last names changed from Schwartz to Randi, as well.

When the kids were young, I was rarely home because I was in the studio all day recording and all night in clubs performing, or performing out of town. Despite the limited time I had with my kids and Norma at home, we managed to have great times together as a family and shared those good times with our close friends from the music, entertainment, and dance circles. As the kids got older, they often came with me to work, either to my club or sometimes a recording session with Nancy Sinatra after she had her daughters.

My younger son, Justin, works closely with me at my club, The Baked Potato. He manages the club, handles bookings, and bartends several nights a week. Justin is a talented guitarist, singer, and composer and he not only has his own band, Nothing Personal, but he also often sings with my band, Quest, when I perform at The Baked Potato. Justin is married to Pamela Gray, whom he met at the club a few years ago. Pamela is a very talented actress who has performed in many plays on Broadway and off Broadway, movies, and TV shows—most recently she had a recurring role on the FX series *Sons of Anarchy.*

As a child, Justin was a busy actor and appeared in many TV commercials for Campbell's soup, Kellogg's cereals, and others. He also was in a TV movie, *A Sensitive, Passionate Man*, as the young son of the main character that was played by Angie Dickinson. Angie Dickinson liked Justin and thought he was such a talented and adorable kid. She sometimes requested the casting directors call him in to audition with her on projects just because she wanted to see him and read with him.

One time Justin was called to audition for a part in a TV show that described the character as a quick-witted boy. Justin, at age seven, was very quick to learn lines and improvise, but he didn't have any experience with stand-up comedy. Shelly Slussman, my good friend who also managed my club, had a friend, Leonard Barr. Leonard was Dean Martin's uncle and a famous comedian who often visited Shelly at The Baked Potato. I thought of him to coach Justin with one-liners. I brought Justin to the club the day before his audition, to meet with Leonard, and before I knew it Justin was working with Leonard in the parking lot, learning one-liners from him, like "I can't get over a girl like you so answer the phone yourself." It was so hilarious watching Leonard, a comedian in his seventies, coaching seven-year-old Justin deliver these classic jokes with such skill.

Justin is dad to my granddaughter Savanna, who also has musical talent and plays the cello. She has played cello in the acclaimed Los Angeles Youth Symphony and in Justin's band. Savannah is now off to college, which reminds me how quickly time has flown by.

David is also very talented musically. David plays bass and was in the group Damn the Machine in the early 1990s with Chris Poland, Mark Poland, and Dave Clemmons. David also played bass in my group, Quest, and worked at The Baked Potato with Justin and me. David became a successful marketing executive for Playboy Entertainment and relocated to New York with his wife, Margo, and their two daughters, A.J. and Avalon. After several years on the East Coast, David and his family are returning to live in Los Angeles.

Leah showed interest in music at a very young age, playing flute and singing in the Los Angeles Children's Chorus and Choir. Leah picked up the bass in her late teens and is self-taught. She began playing in punk and alternative rock bands around LA. Leah now plays professionally, recording and touring worldwide with top artists and groups like Pink, Conjure One, Delirium, and Abandoned Pools, to name a few. She has also played bass and sung on many other records and performed live on several popular television and radio shows around the globe. Leah collaborates with her husband, Rhys Fulber, on many creative music projects, writing and recording.

As well as playing music, Leah has an affinity to coaching recovering substance abusers. She travels extensively as an addiction specialist, reaching people who are in desperate need of change.

Leah and Rhys have a son, Rex, who is the light of our lives. We enjoy all the interesting ideas and magnificent energy he has at seven years old. Rex amazes Norma and me every time we spend time with him. Rex is showing an interest in music and loves to spend time with his dad at their studio.

Our youngest daughter, Treesa, is a beautiful and intelligent young woman who has the biggest heart. Norma and I are very proud of Treesa. Though she is only in her early twenties, Treesa is incredibly mature, yet so fun and full of life. She loves animals and has a job caring for them, but she is also very sharp in business. Treesa is also my sidekick when we feel like checking out a new restaurant or have a craving for good sushi!

I tried to spend as much time as I could with my sons when they were young and we shared memorable father and sons' time together. When we were living in the Hollywood Hills, I bought them both moped bikes that they rode up and down the hill. What they were doing was actually dangerous, so I made them a deal . . . I upgraded their mopeds to motorcycles that we could take to designated motocross courses if they promised me they would not ride them on the streets.

The boys loved those dirt bikes and I got one for myself as well to ride with them. We would go to Indian Dunes Park in Valencia (North Los Angeles County), a large area that had trails created for motocross (dirt bike riding). I was not as good a rider as David and Justin, but I rode well enough to keep track of them on the course. One day I was riding with the boys and having fun, but going along the course very carefully, or so I thought. A guy rode up next to me and motioned for me to pull off to the side, so I did. The guy told me he would show me how to ride so I wouldn't kill myself. I laughed because I didn't think I was doing that badly, but when the guy took off his helmet, I recognized him . . . it was the actor Gene Hackman!

That wasn't the only time we ran into a celebrity at Indian Dunes. One late afternoon the three of us were riding in an open area that was deserted at the time and we saw a small private plane descending toward the flat area of the park and landed. We rode over to see if they needed help and a guy hopped out of the plane . . . it was Steve McQueen. He told us that he was scouting this location for a movie and wanted to know if we could give him a ride around so he could get a feel for the terrain. Justin volunteered. As Steve got on the back of Justin's bike he said to him, "Just take it easy. You don't have to do any stunts." Well, this was Justin's cue to pop a wheelie as he took off with Steve.

Both David and Justin loved going dirt bike riding and they took care of their motorcycles. David, even as a young kid, had natural mechanical skills and he kept our bikes in good shape. He also helped his friends with their bikes. One afternoon David was working on his dirt bike in our yard and I looked outside to see who he was talking to because I heard a man's voice. It was Jay Leno . . . he was visiting Budd Friedman, owner of the Improv Comedy Club, who lived across the street, and when he saw young David working on his bike, he had to see what he was doing. Jay, being a car and motorcycle enthusiast and collector, couldn't resist talking about motorcycles with young David.

Born in England, Norma was one of eight children in the Waterman family and her family did not lack talent. Norma's brothers Ken, Peter, and Dennis were introduced to boxing because her father, Harry, loved the sport and had been an amateur boxer in his youth. Peter Waterman excelled in boxing and was the European welterweight champion in 1957. Dennis Waterman found his talent in acting and began his acclaimed career from the age of ten on the stage with the Royal Shakespeare Company, followed by many featured and starring roles in theater, films, and TV series. Norma also had another brother, Allen, but he passed away when he was a young child.

Norma and her sisters, Myrna, Joy, Stella, and Vera, sang and danced together in their home with their mother, Rose, playing piano. Dance became Norma's dream and she focused her talent and training on becoming a dancer. When she was sixteen, Norma's professional dance career took off.

Norma has danced on British and American television shows, such as *Benny Hill* and *The Dinah Shore Show*. She performed in a spectacular dance number in concert shows with the remarkable Shirley Bassey. Norma was part of the famed Bluebell Girls revue dancers and performed many times at the renowned Lido in Paris. In 1962 she appeared in Barry Ashton's production of *A Night in Paradise* at the 1962 World's Fair in Seattle, Washington, and remained with that show when it was brought to Las Vegas by Barry Ashton. Norma was in Barry Ashton's revue at the Dunes in Las Vegas when my trio played there before getting our gig at the Castaways, but we never met at the Dunes. Norma became the lead dancer for Barry Ashton and was his assistant, coordinating the choreography and training the other dancers learning and refining their routines.

When I met Norma, she was a dance star and rising higher in her field. I almost feel guilty for persuading Norma to change her career direction. I say "almost" guilty because Norma has really been a star in my life and our family.

It is very challenging to have a stable marriage and family life while working in any part of the entertainment business, but Norma and I have made it work for over fifty years. We are very lucky that we were able to work together when Norma was one of the featured background singers with Nancy Sinatra opening for Frank Sinatra.

When we opened the club in 1970, Norma helped put the Baked Potato menu and recipes together and was the cook, on and off, for a year while we got the club off the ground.

Later, after our kids were older and starting to go off on their own, my wife decided to become a foster parent and open our home and hearts to children, mostly newborn and in need. She went through all the training and approvals that the State of California required and because of Norma's and my commitment, we are lucky to have had a chance to foster babies that needed love and a safe, stable environment.

I am so grateful for having such a big, wonderful, loving, and supportive family, and Norma is the heart of our family. Certainly we have had our ups and downs, but Norma has been a constant champion of the Randis through and through.

Friends, I've Had a Few . . .

Dr. Louis Lemberger and I grew up in Woodridge, New York. Some people in Woodridge said Louie would not amount to much but he proved everyone wrong and became one of the world's most renowned pharmacologists. We have been friends for seventy years.

Jim Ruisi, who I met through Greg Dinallo, is an artist, designer, and Italian chef, as well as my horse racing buddy, and he is very close to my family and me.

Jeffrey Tambor (an award-winning actor) is a good friend of mine and has been for many years. He frequently comes to see me play with my band at The Baked Potato. Some years ago, Jeff directed a play titled *Burn This*, written by Lanford Wilson, that ran in LA, and he chose "Too Many Broken Dreams," a song I wrote, as the background music for many scenes in the play. One thing many people do not know about Jeffrey Tambor is that he is a hell of a softball player and played on The Baked Potato softball team.

In the last few years of writing my life's stories, I've made a new friend in Karen "Nish" Nishimura; she has been there for me helping me tell my stories. Thanks, Nish.

Russ Wapensky is not only a very good friend of mine, he is also a friend to just about every musician who is an AFM union member. Over many years and including the present, Russ has tirelessly researched and accurately archived thousands upon thousands of union contracts that would have been lost forever and with them millions of dollars of royalties owed to musicians, composers, arrangers, and music directors. He was also very important to Nish and me while we worked on this book by verifying a lot of the details and facts on recording sessions I did many years ago. Russ is a great guy and knows nearly every story in my life, and he is probably the best historian of the "Wrecking Crew" era of recording there is.

CHAPTER 48

From Mono to Digital

Amazingly, through the technical advances in recording from mono to two-, four-, six-, eight-, sixteen-, twenty-four-, and forty-eight-track analog recording and now practically infinity with digital recording, I have managed to see and work in it all.

Having the opportunity to play and record some of the greatest music ever written and recorded with some of the greatest artists of all time is really unbelievable. I enjoyed every minute of it from the early '60s to the present, and producers still hire me to work for their artists today.

As much as I love recording, I equally enjoy playing live before an audience, whether it's fifty people in a nightclub or ten thousand in an arena. Being able to play almost any kind of music that I've been asked to play, I always enjoy playing jazz the best.

To be a professional musician you have to really love what musicians do, as it is truly a twenty-four-hour gig, and it's a privilege for me to be part of that. As I say . . . the rhythm section rules!

Thank you, especially to the pianists.

Appendixes

APPENDIX A: DON RANDI CAREER STATS

Don has worked with (among others). . .

Musical Duos and Groups

ABBA

The Animals

The Association

The Baja Marimba Band

The Beach Boys

Bigfoot

The Blossoms

Bob B. Soxx and the Blue Jeans

Buffalo Springfield

The Checkmates

The Commodores

The Crystals

Dino, Desi and Billy

The Electric Prunes

The Everly Brothers

The 5th Dimension

The Four Tops

Gary Lewis and the Playboys

Gary Puckett and the Union Gap

The Honeys

Ike and Tina Turner

The Jackson 5

The Lovin' Spoonful

The Mike Curb Congregation

The Monkees

The Osmonds

Paul Revere and the Raiders

Redbone

The Righteous Brothers

The Ronettes

Simon and Garfunkel

Sonny and Cher

The Spiral Starecase

Sweet Inspirations

The Teddy Bears

The Tubes

The Watts 103rd Street Rhythm Band

Female Solo Artists

Susie Allanson

Joan Baez

Debby Boone

Lynda Carter

Marilyn Chambers

Petula Clark

Rosemary Clooney

Randy Crawford

Doris Day

Sheena Easton

Cass Elliot

Dale Evans

Lola Falana

Donna Fargo

Annette Funicello

Bobbie Gentry

Lesley Gore

Goldie Hawn

Judy Henske

Suzi Jane Hokom

Wanda Jackson

Carole King

Peggy Lee

Darlene Love

Tricia Lynn

Deana Martin

Gail Martin

Tina Mason

Letta Mbulu

Bette Midler

Mrs. Miller

Laura Nyro

Michelle Phillips

Dory Previn

Linda Ronstadt

Diana Ross

Nancy Sinatra

Joanie Sommers

Dusty Springfield

Sarah Vaughan

Dionne Warwick

Raquel Welch

Stephanie Winslow

Tammy Wynette

Male Solo Artists

Cannonball Adderley

Pat Boone

Tony Brantley

James Brown

Roy Brown

Delaney Bramlett

Tim Buckley

Dorsey Burnette

Glen Campbell

David Cassidy

Sanford Clark

Leonard Cohen

Jerry Cole

Bobby Darin

James Darren

Mac Davis

Sammy Davis Jr.

Neil Diamond

Donovan

Duane Eddy

Marvin Gaye

Buddy Greco

Bob Hope

Rick Jarrett

Davey Jones

Tom Jones

Christopher Kingsley

Frankie Lane

Don "Dirt" Lanier

Arthur Lee

Bob Lind

Mark Lindsay

Trini Lopez

Dean Martin

Wink Martindale

Roger Miller

Chris Montez

Rick Nelson

Mickey Newberry

Harry Nilsson

Buck Owens

Elvis Presley

Eddie Rabbitt

Lou Rawls

Marty Robbins

Tommy Roe

Neil Sedaka

Del Shannon

T.G. Sheppard

Bobby Sherman

Bob Silver

Frank Sinatra

O.C. Smith

Joe South

Frank Stallone

Hank Thompson

Tiny Tim

Townes Van Zandt

Gene Vincent

Virgil Warner

Jimmy Webb

Pete Willcox

Hank Williams Jr.

Gerald Wilson

Stevie Wonder

Neil Young

Frank Zappa

Background Singers

Billie Barnum

Phyllis Battle

The Baylor Brothers

Al Capps

Anita Cortez

Ron Hicklin

Fanita James

Barbara Kessel

Jeanie King

Cody Lambert

Darlene Love

Melissa Makai

Gracia Nitzsche

Janice Pendarvis

Norma Randi

Thurl Ravenscroft

Edna Wright

Producers

Herb Alpert

David Axelrod

Jimmy Bowen

John Boylan

Tutti Camarata

Mike Curb

Jerry Fuller

Dick Glasser and Ted Glasser

Kelly Gordon

Dave Hassinger

Lee Hazlewood

Quincy Jones

Marshall Leib

Jackie Mills

Dave Pell

Richard Perry

Ray Ruff

Wayne Schuller

Lester Sill

Phil Spector

Buck Stapleton

Nik Venet

Steve Venet

Brian Wilson

Arrangers

David Axelrod

H.B. Barnum

Harold Battiste

Jimmy Bond

Perry Bunny Botkin

Tutti Camarata

Ry Cooder

Don Costa

Ernie Freeman

Benny Golson

Jimmy Haskell

Bill Justis

Anita Kerr

Michel Legrand

Peter Matts

Billy May

Jack Nitzsche

Gene Page

Don Peake

Ray Pohlman

Don Ralke

Nelson Riddle

Shorty Rogers

Billy Strange

John Tartaglia

Albums by Don Randi

Feelin' Like Blues (1960)

Where Do We Go from Here? (1962)

Last Night with the Don Randi Trio (1963)

Don Randi (1965)

Live at the Sunset Strip (1966)

Jungle Adventure in Music and Sound (with Curtis Amy) (1966)

Revolver Jazz (1966)

Rubber Soul Jazz (1966)

Mexican Pearls (1964)

Don Randi Plays the Theme from Romeo and Juliet (1969)

Live at The Baked Potato (1972)

New Baby (1979)

California 84 (1984)

Don't Look Back (1989)

Wind and Sea (1990)

Malibu Nights (1990)

If It's All Night It's Alright (1990)

Bermuda Triangle (2012 rerelease)

Acoustimania (2013)

Notable Songs and Albums

(includes credits as musician, composer, or arranger)

And Then . . . Along Comes the Association (The Association)

Songs of Experience (David Axelrod)

Songs of Innocence (David Axelrod)

"God Only Knows" (The Beach Boys)

"Good Vibrations" (The Beach Boys)

"Help Me Rhonda" (The Beach Boys)

Pet Sounds (The Beach Boys)

The Smile Sessions (The Beach Boys)

"Wouldn't It Be Nice" (The Beach Boys)

Funk City Express (Harold Betters)

Big Foot (Big Foot)

Texas Woman (Pat Boone)

"Get on the Good Foot" (James Brown)

Hard Times (Roy Brown)

"Broken Arrow" (Buffalo Springfield, Neil Young)

Buffalo Springfield Again (Buffalo Springfield)

Goodbye and Hello (Tim Buckley)

"I'm Not Gonna Miss You" (Glen Campbell)

Death of a Ladies' Man (Leonard Cohen)

"And Then He Kissed Me" (The Crystals)

"Da Doo Ron Ron" (The Crystals)

"He's a Rebel" (The Crystals)

"The Candy Man" (Sammy Davis Jr.)

"Cracklin' Rosie" (Neil Diamond)

Tap Root Manuscript (Neil Diamond)

Mass in F Minor (The Electric Prunes)

The Road Is No Place for a Lady (Cass Elliot)

"It's My Party" (Lesley Gore)

Love and Other Crimes (Lee Hazlewood)

"Ode to Billie Joe" (Lee Hazlewood)

I Remember Elvis (Wanda Jackson)

ABC (The Jackson 5)

"ABC" (The Jackson 5)

"Popsicle" (Jan and Dean)

"Spanish Harlem" (Ben E. King)

The Best of Love (Love)

"Do You Believe in Magic?" (The Lovin' Spoonful)

"Everybody Loves Somebody Sometime" (Dean Martin)

"Empty Bed Blues" (Bette Midler)

The Birds, the Bees and the Monkees (The Monkees)

More of the Monkees (The Monkees)

Perspective (Rick Nelson)

The Wichita Train Whistle Sings (Michael Nesmith)

An American Trilogy (Mickey Newbury)

The Point! (Harry Nilsson)

The Lonely Surfer (Jack Nitzsche)

"Save the Country" (Laura Nyro)

"I Love How You Love Me" (The Paris Sisters)

"Corinna, Corinna" (Ray Peterson)

Victim of Romance (Michelle Phillips)

"A Little Less Conversation" (Elvis Presley)

The Capitol Jazz and Blues Sessions (Lou Rawls)

Contemporary Sound of Nelson Riddle (Nelson Riddle)

Back to Back (The Righteous Brothers)

"Ebb Tide" (The Righteous Brothers)

"Unchained Melody" (The Righteous Brothers)

"You've Lost That Lovin' Feelin'" (The Righteous Brothers)

Beginnings (Tommy Roe)

Presenting the Fabulous Ronettes (The Ronettes)

"Different Drum" (Linda Ronstadt and the Stone Poneys)

Linda Ronstadt Greatest Hits (Linda Ronstadt)

"Touch Me in the Morning" (Diana Ross)

"Something Stupid" (Frank Sinatra and Nancy Sinatra)

Boots (Nancy Sinatra)

"Burnin' Down the Spark" (Nancy Sinatra)

Country, My Way (Nancy Sinatra)

How Does That Grab You? (Nancy Sinatra)

Nancy (Nancy Sinatra)

"Jackson" (Nancy Sinatra and Lee Hazlewood)

Nancy and Lee (Nancy Sinatra and Lee Hazlewood)

One More Time (Nancy Sinatra)

Sugar (Nancy Sinatra)

"These Boots Are Made for Walkin'" (Nancy Sinatra)

"The Son of Hickory Holler's Tramp" (O.C. Smith)

"I Got You Babe" (Sonny & Cher)

Look at Us (Sonny and Cher)

A Look Inside (Joe South)

Back to Mono (Phil Spector)

"I Love You More Today Than Yesterday" (The Spiral Starecase)

Evergreen Vol. 2 (The Stone Poneys)

Young and Rich (The Tubes)

High, Low and in Between (Townes Van Zandt)

Our Mother the Mountain (Townes Van Zandt)

"The House Song" (Virgil Warner and Suzi Jane Hokom)

Family Tradition (Hank Williams Jr.)

A Christmas Gift for You from Philles Records (various)

Films

Bloody Mama (Shelley Winters, Robert De Niro, A.I.P.)

Circus Time (Chicago Museum of Science and Industry, producer Lou
Girolami, writer and director Gregory Dinallo)

Dragon Wagon (Industrial film, Lockheed, producer and editor Todd Martin,
writer and director Gregory Dinallo)

Fireball 500 (Frankie Avalon, Annette Funicello, A.I.P.)

IBM (Industrial film, IBM Corp., producer, writer and director Gregory
Dinallo)

J.W. Coop (Cliff Robertson, Columbia)

Racing Scene (James Garner, Cherokee Prod.)

Salvatore (Documentary of an Italian immigrant craftsman who made
carousel horses, producer C.B. Wismar, writer and director Gregory Dinallo)

Santee (Glenn Ford, Vagabond Prod.)

Stacey (Anne Randall, Sidaris Prod.)

Three in the Cellar (Larry Hagman, Joan Collins, A.I.P.)

William Penn (Philadelphia exhibit, producers, writers and directors
Gregory Dinallo and Marvin Rubin)

Television

All-Star Saturdays (ABC-TV)

The Bunjee Venture (ABC-TV)

Bunny Awards 1977 (Playboy Prod.)

Craig Breedlove Story (Craig Breedlove, Sidaris Prod.)

Elvis' '68 Comeback Special (NBC-TV)

Kids Are People Too (ABC-TV)

The New Mike Hammer—Season 3 (Stacy Keach, Greg Dinallo, Columbia
Pictures TV)

1968 Summer Olympics (ABC-TV)

Nitty Gritty Hour (Sonny & Cher, Winters/Rosen Prod.)

Once Upon a Wheel (Paul Newman, Winters/Rosen Prod.)

Playmate of the Year 1976 and 1977 (Playboy Prod.)

Raquel! (Raquel Welch, Tom Jones, Bob Hope, Winters/Rosen Prod.)

Spring Thing (Bobbie Gentry, Noel Harrison, Winters/Rosen Prod.)

Travelling Sunshine Show (5th Dimension, Dionne Warwick, Winters/Rosen Prod.)

Weekend Specials (ABC-TV)

Wide World of Sports (ABC-TV)

Commercials

DermaTan

Iron Weave

Jantzen

Mattel

Mazda

Mitsubishi

Radio Shack (over 100 commercials)

Sunkist

Suzuki

Zacky Farms

APPENDIX B: NANCY SINATRA TOUR DOCUMENTS

Nancy Sinatra's concert tours were managed very professionally. Here are examples of a detailed tour schedule and show itinerary prepared by tour manager John Dubuque.

Page 1 of the schedule shows gigs all over the Northeast—eight venues in nine days. One day involved travel from Washington up to Massachusetts and back down to New York City.

NANCY SINATRA TOUR
VENUE/HOTEL ITINERARY

DATE/VENUE	HOTEL
MON MAY 1 DAY OFF	SHARON MOTOR LODGE ROUTE 41-SHARON, CT 01069 TEL# 203 364 0036 FAX# 203 364 0462
TUE MAY 2 TICKETS ROUTE 343-AMENIA, NY TEL# 914 373 8888	SAME AS ABOVE
WED MAY 3 THE STING 677 W. MAIN, NEW BRITIAN CT. 203 229 0990	HOWARD JOHNSON LODGE 400 NEW BRITIAN AVE. PLAINVILLE, CT. 06062 TEL: 203 747 6876, FAX 9747
THURS. MAY 4 MA MA KIN 33 LANDSDOWN ST. BOSTON, MA. 617.351.2581	NO HOTEL TODAY/ NOON DRIVE TO BOSTON AFTERSHOW DRIVE TO PHILLY
FRI. MAY 5 TROCADERO 1003 ARCH ST. PHILLADELPHIA PA. 215.722.7776	SHERATON UNIVERSITY 36 & CHESTNUT, PHILLY, PA. 19104 215.387.8000 FAX: 367.7920 (POSSIBLE EARLY CHECK-IN!)
SAT. MAY 6 TRUMP CASTLE 1 CASTLE BLVD. ATLANTIC CITY, NJ. 08401 609.441.2000 FAX: 441.8541	TRUMP CASTLE 1 CASTLE BLVD. ATLANTIC CITY, NJ. 08401 609.441.2000 FAX: 441.8541
SUN. MAY 7 DAY OFF/ATLANTIC CITY	TRUMP/SAME AS ABOVE
MON. MAY 8 THE BAYOU 3135 K. ST. N.W. WASHINGTON, DC. 703.683.1900	SAVOY SUITES 2505 WISCONSON AVE. NW- WASHINGTON, DC. 2007 202.337.9700 FAX: 337.3644
TUES. MAY 9 RAZZLS 77 WEST ST. SPRINGFIELD, MA. 413.732.8181	(DAY ROOMS ONLY!) TBA AFTERSHOW DRIVE TO NYC CHECK INTO BELOW HOTEL
WED. MAY 10 LIMELIGHT 47 W. 20 ST., NYC. 212.807.7850	B.W. PRESIDENT HOTEL 234 W. 48 ST., NY. NY. 10036 212.246.8800 FAX: 974.3922

The tour continued with seven more venues in eight days, from Pennsylvania and New York State up to Canada and then back to points in the Midwest.

<u>NANCY SINATRA</u>
<u>VENUE/HOTEL ITINERARY</u>

THURS. MAY 11 CHAMELEON CLUB 223 N. WATER ST- LANCASTER, PA. 717.393.7133	DAYS INN 30 KELLER AVE- LANCASTER, PA. 17601 717.299.5700 FAX: 295.1907
FRI. MAY 12 ROXY MUSIC HALL 279 NEW YORK AVE-HUNTINGTON, NY. 516.424.7703	COMFORT INN 333 S. SERVICE RD PLAINVIEW, NY 516.694.6500 FAX: 696.4718
SAT. MAY 13 GRAFFITI 4615 BAUM BLVD. PITTSBURGH, PA. 412.682.4212	BW PARKWAY CENTER INN 875 GREENTREE PITTSBURGH, PA. 152220 412.922.7070 FAX: 922.4949
SUN. MAY 14 R.P.M. 132 QUEENS QUAY TORONTO, CANADA 416.869.0045	HOTEL VICTORIA 56 YONGE ST. TORONTO, CANADA M5E1G5 416.363.1666 FAX: 363.7327
MON. MAY 15 DAY OFF! TORONTO	SAME AS ABOVE
TUES. MAY 16 THE ODEON 1295 OLD RIVER ROAD CLEVELAND, OHIO 216.574.2525	HOLIDAY INN LAKESIDE & 12TH. CLEVELAND, OHIO 44114 216.241.5100 FAX: 241.7437
WED. MAY 17 INDUSTRY 15 S. SAGINAW PONTIAC, MICHIGAN 313.963.7237	HOLIDAY INN 1500 OPDYKE RD AUBURN HILLS, MI. 48326 810.373.4550 FAX: 373.8220
THURS. MAY 18 PARK WEST 322 WEST ARMITAGE CHICAGO, IL 312.929.1322	COMFORT INN 601 W. DIVERSEY PKWY CHICAGO, ILL. 60614 312.348.2810 FAX: 348.1912
FRI. MAY 19 END	TRAVEL DAY HOME FROM: CHICAGO HAVE A GOOD TRIP!

This is an itinerary for a single day on the schedule: two shows at Trump Castle in Atlantic City. It has all essential information—where to go, what to do and when, the names of contacts, the eating arrangements, and whether or not people could smoke. There was a page like this for each separate venue.

Artist: NANCY SINATRA

Daily Itinerary PERFORMANCE DAY! 2 SHOWS!
Date: Saturday May 6
City: Atlantic City, NJ   **Time Zone: ESDT**
How: by bus. Bus Call: 12noon
Travel: Philly to Atlantic City 68 miles = 1-1/2 hours
Band Hotel:
Trump Castle
1 Castle Blvd-Atlantic City, NJ 08401
Phone# 609 441 2000
Fax# 609 441 8541
Contact: Bobbie
Conf#
Meal badge entitles you to complimentary, 24 hour cafeteria. 24 hour room service (not included as meal badge priviledge)!
Dist. to venue: adjacent.
Bus Parking: In Marina area. Fenced in!

Promoter: **Promoter Rep**
Trump Castle   Steve Geitka
                                                 Bobbie Taylor
Phone# 609 441 8306 (Entertainment Dept)
Fax# 609 441 8656

Venue (NON SMOKING!!!)   Pro Con: Bill (Backline & PA)
Crystal Ballroom   Res: (in hotel) 609 441 2000
Phone# 609 441 8306   LD: Karen Johnson
Fax#   Res: 609 697 4073
BK/Stg# 609 441 2000 x2677 & x2676
Rider reqs: OK   CAP: 1000   DR: several

Load In	Snd Chk	Doors	Shows(2)	Nancy
300P	400-500P	700P	800&1100	1st: 800-930 & 2nd: 1100-1230A

Aftershow Travel:
Stay in hotel. Tomorrow is day off! Will stay over here Sunday night!

Notes: THIS IS A NON SMOKING VENUE!
Margo, Faith, & Robert,rom TCI, will be staying at hotel on Saturday night.

APPENDIX C: OLYMPICS LETTER TO DON RANDI AND QUEST

Bill Liebowitz of the Los Angeles Olympic Organizing Committee penned this warm letter of gratitude to Don Randi and Quest for entertaining the athletes in the Olympic Villages in 1984.

Los Angeles Olympic Organizing Committee

Los Angeles, California 90084 USA
Telex: 6831420
Telephone (213) 305-1984

August 30, 1984

DON RANDI and QUEST
    Nichols Canyon
Los Angeles, California 90046

Dear DON RANDI and QUEST:

On behalf of myself, the Los Angeles Olympic Organizing Committee, the athletes, and staff of the 1984 Olympic Villages, we wish to thank you for your performance during the 1984 Games.

As you know, the Villages were set up to provide a pleasurable and interesting experience for the athletes during their stay. The entertainment program has been an integral part of Village life and has been well received and appreciated by the athletes. Your contribution to the program provided the athletes with a much needed and deserved relief from their competition schedule and afforded them with a view of America which they will most certainly take back with them and share with their friends and family.

As far as I am concerned Don, your attitude and energy are matched only by your talent. Aside form playing all three 1984 Olympic Villages and the Press Center, yours was the only group asked to play three times at the USC 1984 Olympic Village. It is certainly a testimony to your talent and the warmth you exude on stage that you were indeed brought back by "popular demand." Despite language differences, the warm reception you received was a proof of to the universality of your music and excellence of your musicianship.

Again, thank you for your cooperation and contribution to the success of the 1984 Olympic Villages.

Very truly yours,

Bill Liebowitz
Director, Village Entertainment

bnk

INDEX

ABOUT THE AUTHORS

Don Randi

Don Randi is best known in music circles as the busy studio keyboard musician during the prolific period of the early 1960s through the 1970s when the Wall of Sound session players (a.k.a. the Wrecking Crew) were turning out every top ten hit. Don's incredible music talents and career cover performance, composing, arranging, and producing, as well as directing many of the most popular artists and their songs that are fan favorites and have sold millions worldwide.

In 1970 Don opened The Baked Potato jazz club in Studio City, California, where his band, Don Randi and Quest, still plays each month. The Baked Potato is known worldwide as one of the best jazz clubs in the United States and it has been named the best jazz club in Los Angeles for several years in a row.

Over the years, while working on just about everyone else's recordings, Don managed to release twenty jazz albums of his own, including *New Baby*, which was nominated for a Grammy Award in 1980. The jazz album *Acoustimania* is Don Randi's most recent album release.

Karen "Nish" Nishimura

Nish, as she prefers to be called by her nickname, is a Los Angeles native who grew up in the heart of the city. Her career background is primarily in television and online promotion, including the production of branded digital entertainment.

A trained recording engineer, Nish's passion has always been music. She grew up listening to hit songs that Don Randi has played, composed, arranged, and produced, only she never knew it until she met Don a few years ago at his club, The Baked Potato.

When she began working with Don on his biography, a story about his harpsichord solo on the hit song "Different Drum," by Linda Ronstadt and the Stone Poneys, inspired her to suggest the title of this book, *You've Heard These Hands*. It was at that moment Nish realized she has been a fan of Don Randi for as long as she has loved music, but didn't realize it . . . till now.